ART IDEAS HISTORY

DIMENSIONS OF
THE 20th CENTURY

1900-1945

ROBERT L. DELEVOY

TRANSLATED FROM THE FRENCH BY STUART GILBERT

★

Distributed in the United States by
THE WORLD PUBLISHING COMPANY
2231 West 110th Street, Cleveland 2, Ohio

★

CONTENTS

I
THE PREDICAMENT OF RATIONALISM

Modern or Contemporary? 9
An Historical Myth: The "Belle Epoque" 13
A New Aesthetic Venture 24
    1. The World of the Poster 27
Creation and Technology 35
From the Rationalist Attitude to Functionalism 41
    2. "Ornament and Crime" 45
    Notes on the Plates 18, 37

II
SIGNS OF THE TIMES

Anguish and Revolt 55
    3. A Time of Violence 63
Dismemberment of the Image 71
An Aesthetic of Discontinuity 82
Dynamism and Duration 94
The Space-Time Dimension 97
    4. Vision in Motion 107
Signs, Signals, Symbols 115
    Notes on the Plates 58, 77, 87, 101, 119, 123

III
THE PRINCIPLE OF INDETERMINACY

Chance and Indeterminacy 131
Mechanized Realities 134
Promotion of the Imaginary 145
    5. The Challenge to Painting 159
    Notes on the Plates 138, 151

IV
THE REJECTION OF PERSPECTIVAL VISION

From Surface to Space 169
The Aperspectival Vision 182
    6. Towards an Architecture 189
From the Invisible to the Visible 205
    Notes on the Plates 172, 185, 197, 199, 207, 212

BIBLIOGRAPHY 215
INDEX OF NAMES 217
LIST OF ILLUSTRATIONS 221

I

THE PREDICAMENT
OF RATIONALISM

MODERN OR CONTEMPORARY?

Since the end of the Second World War we have been living through a vast mutation, aftermath of the metamorphoses that took place in the first half of the century. Already the world of 1900-1945 is coming to seem curiously remote and alien, so greatly has the tempo of our lives been speeded up since then, and, as a result, conventions adumbrated only yesterday, attitudes, needs and customs that had barely taken root, art movements that had only just come to fruition are now acquiring the air of vestiges of a remote epoch. In less than fifty years mankind has undergone more drastic changes than the world had known in two millennia. During this brief period new discoveries, scientific, political, economic, social, literary and artistic developments have succeeded each other at such a pace that all the previously accepted structures of thought and conduct have been shattered and we have lost touch with many of the *points d'appui* which had served for many generations to orient man's outlook on the world and to determine his ways of thinking and behaving.

We shall not attempt to discuss in detail the various cross-currents that led to these changes; this would necessitate a survey of the entire history of an age still too near to be assessed with confidence, and too complex, too crowded, to be dealt with in the compass of this volume. The reader must not expect to find in these pages, devoid as they are of encyclopedic information, a panoramic view, or even a summary, of the kaleidoscopic manifestations of the period: the rise of the philosophies of intuition and existentialism, the scornful laughter of the bourgeoisie and the exultant clamor of the working class, the development of the musical arabesque and the break-up of tonality, the applications of positivism and the triumphs of chance, the emergence of Art Nouveau with its lush, free-flowing line and the ostracism of the story-telling image, the premonitory salvoes of the Boer war and the ultimate apocalypse of Hiroshima.

In all these seemingly disparate events and trends can we trace common points of reference indicating a basic solidarity? Or should a period so full of contrasts be interpreted, rather, in terms of a conflict of opposites? Perhaps it had, after all, a "still center" in which a latent unity can be detected. Maybe the confusion of the spectacle presented by vociferous antagonisms, clashes of dogmatic opinions, negations and cleavages, is more apparent than real, and, in the last analysis, they will turn out to be but different facets of one and the same mode of seeing and of an equal sagacity (in the strict sense of the word). It is this none-too-easy program of detecting affinities, associating phenomena which at first sight appear wholly incompatible, of relating isolated developments to a wider over-all conjuncture which we have set before us in our survey of the seeming chaos and confusion of this eventful half-century. Basing ourselves on its works of art, ideas and history (supplemented by our personal experience), we shall attempt to strike beneath casual correspondences and to disclose the underlying relations, vital links and simultaneous activities of the period. And in approaching the heart of our problem we shall try to bring to light certain dimensions furnishing data for a synthesis that still awaits formulation.

Given the complexity of the subject, this work is bound to appear hazardous, partial (in both senses), often rash. Raising more problems than it solves, it teems with question marks. It selects, eliminates, speculates on the future. It is based on *partis pris* —personal prejudices leading to a choice of themes tending to bring out an implicit, surmised unity. An historian such as Merleau-Ponty might say in this context that "he is necessarily led to make a choice in a given historical situation, in a given set of problems, which rules out certain solutions, though without imposing any—that frame of reference to which Gide, Proust and Valéry, despite their differences, owe their common character as spokesmen of their age." Endless explanations and glosses would obviously be needed to prove an objective affinity between Husserl's philosophy and Faulkner's novels. Yet somehow we feel they speak with the same voice. From the viewpoint of a third party even those who, like Ingres and Delacroix, think they are opponents, meet on common ground, since they are conditioned by the selfsame cultural complex. We are the same men, men who have confronted, as a problem shared by all, the rise of communism and a world war; who have read Gide and Valéry, Proust and Husserl, Heidegger and Freud. Whatever our reactions, we surely have means of defining certain zones of our sensibility to experience, and formulating, if not the ideas of man common to all of us, a new awareness of our present-day predicament.

As with biochemistry, astral physics and the social sciences, art history and its corollary, art criticism, if they are to reach these "sensitive zones," must renovate their methods of interpretation with due regard to the fundamental unity of all the sciences, though without making arbitrary conjectures and over-hasty simplifications which falsify our scale of values and tend to obscure the true import of phenomena. For all these reasons the work of art will be treated in this essay—for this study is in fact an essay in the strict sense Lukacs gave the term: a form midway between philosophy and literature —as involved in a network of relations which both give it form and authenticate its "message." It will be assigned a place at the heart of the struggle that has always been (and still is) taking place between man and his environment, man and technics, technics and matter. For inevitably the work of art forms an integral part of our mental equipment and has its place among the chain reactions which determine the ever-accelerating course of history today. If our work can lay claim to any originality, this consists in its attempts to restore to the work of art, apart from its aesthetic dimensions, its full value as a poetic (i.e. creative) entity and its basic function as an instrument of social and inter-individual communication. In this volume we have set ourselves a program which seems indispensable in the present state of our knowledge: that of seeing and thinking in terms of the twentieth century, and with this in mind we shall begin by considering a problem of a semantic order which is certainly of prime importance. This is the exact connotation of the two words "modern" and "contemporary."

It is common knowledge that a truly living language both expresses and endorses current trends of thought. Hence the need to begin by clarifying the ideas and words we employ, so as to avoid being handicapped by an outworn terminology. If when using certain words today we give them the same meanings as Pascal, Diderot or Baudelaire gave them, how can we hope to convey our ideas to any good effect? "Modern" is one of the words that frequently recur both in scientific language and in ordinary conversation. But it has several different applications and for this reason lends itself to ambiguities and misunderstandings. In evidence of this we need only mention the titles and subject matter of some well-known and authoritative works. *The Formation of the Modern Genius in Western Art* by Schneider and Cohen (Paris, 1936), now regarded as a classic of its kind, deals with the fourteenth and fifteenth centuries. The period covered by Robert Mandrou's admirable *Introduction to Modern France* (Paris, 1961) runs from 1500 to 1640, whereas Maurice Raynal's great *History of Modern Painting* (Geneva, 1953) begins at the close of the nineteenth century and ends in the 1940s. It is the same period that Bernard Dorival describes in an essay which he names more accurately *Stages in Contemporary French Painting* (Paris, 1946). And the most recent survey of international painting between 1940 and 1960, by Nello Ponente, bears the title *Modern Painting, Contemporary Trends* (Geneva, 1960). In another domain, a "Center of Researches in the History of Modern Architecture" was founded in France in 1959, and its field of inquiry stretches from the sixteenth century to the present day. In 1899 Auguste Choisy dated the beginnings of "modern architecture" to the early seventeenth century, in other words to the period following the end of the wars of religion. These examples show that the term "modern" can be applied indiscriminately to works produced in 1960 and to events and modes of thought current in the sixteenth century. And it is with the same confidence that we describe indifferently as "modern" or "contemporary" Seurat's *Grande Jatte* (1886), Picasso's *Guernica* (1937) or a painting by Matta made in 1964. In common parlance the words have become synonymous, interchangeable. Nevertheless there seem to be good grounds for establishing a clear-cut dichotomy between these terms, based on the historical frame of reference and recognizing the importance of the temporal factor in the creation of any given work of art. Viewed from this angle, "modern" and "contemporary" cease to overlap. The two epithets would come to indicate, not concomitant but *successive* episodes, events, phenomena. In other words "modern" and "contemporary" would relate to sequences, to structures having their own place in history. And to articulate them correctly it would only be needed definitely to fix their location in time.

What limits, then, should be assigned to the "modern" period? The first thing to do is to discard the traditional answer to this question, which compels us to describe as modern all the cultural activities of the western world subsequent to the fifteenth century. Unaffected by the evolutionary viewpoint adopted by subsequent European historians and their notion of "universal progress" (a notion introduced by Descartes, that came to fruition in the eighteenth century and, later, in the age of Positivism, developed into a popular ideology), the men of the Renaissance thought it had now become possible to formulate *definitive* values appropriate to an age of supreme perfection and a climactic point of history. This age whose general outlines they sketched out was, according to Ruano, "to last indefinitely, but its basic characteristics, they believed, had already been established once for all." It inaugurated Modern Times, third and final volet of the triptych of History, its predecessors being Antiquity and the Middle Ages. But the triptych in question is incomplete and fails to meet the requirements of present-day historians, determined to break with long-established mental habits and to explore wider, extra-European horizons. The term "modern" is no longer confined to manifestations of human genius based on values deriving from the western Renaissance, and can no longer be linked up with a specific period. Thus liberated, it will serve to designate a mental, non-temporal zone, including every form of living sensibility incarnated in a given moment of history, every mode of acting, thinking and creating which, at that moment, contributed to installing a new way of life. (The word "recent" as opposed to "ancient" will cover its previous usage.) Thus, each in his own time, Ictinos, Donatello, Eiffel and Lautréamont were no less "modern" than Cézanne, Kafka and Nervi. But Claudel is as foreign as Renoir to the spirit of the twentieth century. For archaisms always manage to survive in a period that has its own modernity and the fact that men are contemporaries need not mean

that their minds are open to the ideologies of their day. Monet belonged to a different age from that of Picasso; the water-lilies he was painting at the close of his life came long after the cubist guitars. Men and objects that chance has grouped together in a given span of time may be passively contemporary without being actively modern. In short, there has never been a conflict between contemporaries and the "ancients"; that between "ancients" and "moderns" has persisted through the ages.

Contemporaneousness is a state, whereas modernity is a force that establishes itself within the Zeitgeist and plays an active part. If, leaving aside the permanent, we turn to segmented periods of history, we find it necessary, once again, to look beneath the outer husk of the contemporary world to determine its relation vis-à-vis Modern Times (an awkward vocable which might be discarded with advantage in favor of some less absolute equivalent). The notion of contemporaneousness implies that the events and persons covered by it belong, in effect, not only to the same generation but also to the same historical time, the same field of human activity.

It is clear that we are no longer living in an age qualitatively assimilable to that of Francis I, Louis XIV or Robespierre. Are we, then, nearer, more "contemporary" with, Tolstoy, Delacroix or Shelley? Or, *per contra*, can Frank Lloyd Wright be introduced, without clashing, into the same category as Ledoux? Where are we, then, to place the beginning of Modern Times which some of our school histories date back to the capture of Constantinople by the Turks in 1453, others to the discovery of America in 1492?

Nineteenth-century historians believed that the 1789 Revolution was an event decisive enough to mark the beginning of a new age. They then invented a new period styled "the contemporary epoch," and a first *terminus a quo* was assigned to Modern Times. An over-hasty step; for it was soon to become clear that the French Revolution and its aftermath had no more challenged the traditional western ways of thought than had the world view sponsored by the Renaissance. During the second quarter of the twentieth century the beginning of the "modern" phase was post-dated to 1815. And finally, for the last ten years, a view has prevailed that the contemporary epoch began in 1848.

Thus today the epoch in question is generally held to span a little over a hundred years—actually, we believe, too long a period. For the second half of the nineteenth century witnessed a succession of events that transformed the whole world structure at an unprecedented speed, with the result that it is growing harder and harder to assimilate the period of Baudelaire to ours. Where then locate the still active "yesterday" which (we are told) linked up with a "today" pregnant with the future, thus creating a single "moment of the mind" in which a cultural homogeneity can be perceived, a coherence strong enough to justify our application of the term contemporary to this phase of history?

When I try to elicit the dominant values of the age in which I live, of the moment of time to which I belong, and when I seek out its sources, roots and origins, my gaze is led beyond the year 1900 and halts somewhere in the 1880s. It was then—not in 1815, 1848 or 1789—that our so-called Modern Times, it seems, came into being; there that we find a past opening on "a wide horizon of the future." For that was when the ancient edifice of humanist tradition and conceptions stemming from Greco-Roman antiquity came under fire; when new social realities joined issue and the age-old system of agricultural life began to be affected by the coming of mechanization. We can trace back to the 1880s the institutions, forms of organization and production and modes of plastic expression which marked the dawn of a new civilization, the civilization of "waves" we have today.

Needless to say the year 1880 is not to be regarded in any exact sense as the year of cleavage inaugurating the contemporary era. For us it matters little that 1880 witnessed the invention of the bicycle, the publication of Taine's *Philosophy of Art* and Dostoevsky's *The Brothers Karamazov*; was the year of Rodin's *Thinker* and Renoir's *Box at the Theater*, the year in which Renan "cut the figure of the sage of the régime," and Zola and Alphonse Daudet, both aged forty, were regarded as the "high priests" of the attic where Edmond de Goncourt sat in state. No, it is not the year 1880 alone, but the whole

decade which points to the fact that this was the time when a group of events conspired to herald the ending of one world and the birth of another.

Mankind no longer lives in slices of time (e.g. decades) or in terms of generations, but in terms of "secular upheavals" as Focillon aptly puts it. To apprehend the unity of the present-day conjuncture, we need to grasp it as a whole, in depth. And the only way to do this is to employ the synchronic dimension, for only thus can we avoid the traditional, linear, horizontal synopsis, and effect simultaneous soundings in time and space, along the axis of "long duration." Taine was right when he said that a chronology of years is not necessarily the same as a chronology of ideas.

If the contemporary epoch, from 1880 to the present day, can be envisaged as a whole involving a new vision of the world, it may also be interpreted as an integration of substructures based on certain salient, preponderant historical realities. Thus a working program for the study of the epoch might concentrate on three distinct phases, throwing light both on its structural components and on its evolution. The three distinct (and decisive) phases in question would be: (1) the phase of the apotheosis of thermal energy, of the proliferation of railroads and the systematic use of steel (1880-1920); (2) the phase of worldwide diffusion of electric power, of the motor car as a means of private transport, the prevalence of ferro-concrete as the building material *par excellence* (1920-1945); (3) the phase of nuclear energy, the universal use of the airplane as a means of collective transport, great forward strides in the techniques of communication, the diffusion of automation, a rapid increase in the demand for and production of consumers' goods (1945-?). But there can be no question here of any such comprehensive program. In this volume we shall deal with the contemporary epoch whose first phase—a favored period of relative stability—began at the turn of the century and take as our terminal point the year 1945 or thereabouts, a moment of violent transition to a new evolutionary cycle, a cycle still in active progress.

AN HISTORICAL MYTH: THE "BELLE ÉPOQUE"

Our notion of a "Belle Epoque" centering on the year 1900, carries something of the fragrance of a lost paradise. This amiable illusion took form after the First World War, when a middle class, weakened and disheartened by the turn of events, looked back with wistful adulation to a past which, though recent, now seemed romantically remote. That golden age of 1890-1914, when Europe seemed to prosper under the aegis of "liberal capitalism," seemed the ideal setting for an easy-going, carefree way of life. The wealthy French bourgeoisie conjured up a roseate picture of the world at large and, shutting its eyes to the Revolution of 1789, sought to recapture the specious glamour and gay insouciance of the age of Louis XV. Wealth became self-assertive, generosity hypocritical, dignity an affectation, kindliness mere make-believe. Behind the monocle of the successful businessman lurked the uneasy conscience of a spurious paternalism. The rallying points of these defunct ideas were the salons where the new-rich forgathered with a titled élite. The myth of intellectual endowment camouflaged the crudities of wealth and the common front of idlers refused to face up to the vital problems of the hour, flaunted its elegance, affected a romantic "dandyism," reveled in spectacular *affaires*. At the close of a notorious love life a much-admired lady declared complacently: "I've been a frivolous woman and I've lived in a frivolous age. Frivolous people are happy people." In the wake of the Impressionists, Ensor, Bonnard, Vuillard and their friends depicted family life and opened up vistas of fêtes galore. The myth they celebrated was implemented by a flood of facile, reassuring literature, and it sealed the ears of a privileged class against the disquieting note which, struck at Oslo, traversed holiday-making Europe. It was the same myth that had blurred the message of Van Gogh's anguished warnings and Lautrec's sardonic wit. When, leaving her boudoir, the lady of fashion deigned to attend a lecture by Bergson she shut her ears to the attack that he was launching on the traditional bases of human knowledge. In the front rows of the auditorium of the Collège de France, the wisdom of our great philosopher fell on the barren soil of a colorful array of lorgnettes, silks and satins, enormous picture hats. None of these people knew that, at the selfsame moment, Cézanne was stating in visual form the problems to which Bergson was giving similar answers—problems on which a no less bold advance of science was casting a new light. They had no notion that Munch and Kierkegaard were joining forces in a fraternal challenge to the *status quo*, as Rembrandt and Spinoza had done in an earlier age. Impervious to all that lay outside its narrow field of vision, the "high society" of the day saw in Jarry's *Ubu Roi* no more than a tasteless, crudely provocative farce—despite the warranty of the stage sets by Pierre Bonnard and Paul Sérusier. True, Jarry's revolt discountenanced any sort of trickery and sponsored a sort of super-reality, "a reality composed of signs." Alarming signs. Especially so for a social order that aspired to a comfortable lethargy, a slowing-down of the march of progress, and clung to the illusion of a static, socially exclusive world. But did it realize the fragility and transience of that world or perceive that it was threatened on all sides, politically enfeebled, decadent, incapable of generating new ideas? The Dreyfus Case (which was to supply Méliès with the theme of one of the earliest masterpieces of the new art of the motion picture) had come in the nick of time as a means of shoring up the tottering ramparts of conservatism. As one of its commentators observed, "for a staunch conservative it was self-evident that this famous case imperiled the Catholic religion." It was evident, too, that an occasion of this kind was also what was needed to stimulate the ardor of a revolutionary intelligentsia at issue with the forces of reaction. And this conflict between the champions of tradition and those of a new order, between faith and reason, individualism and collectivism, nationalism and internationalism, was in full swing at the turn of the century.

For this was a many-sided age, torn by cross-purposes, and the term "La Belle Epoque" applies only to one of its aspects and extols what was but a fragment of a crumbling social structure precariously shored-up by the grotesque puppets wearing death-masks that we see in Ensor's pictures. The term holds good exclusively for that class of society in which the *Songs of Maldoror* were still anathema and Gide's *Nourritures terrestres* ignored; that class in which the least viable appearances were zealously safeguarded, the "bankruptcy of science" was glee-fully proclaimed, clerical pragmatism the order of the day and symbolism vulgarized by a streak of morbid sensuality. This designation, "Belle Epoque," conjures up a world reserved to a favored few in which under their finery princes were always "charming," young girls well-behaved, officers "irresistible," manservants models of decorum. To this social group belong the patrons of the Opera and cabarets, of the great picture-dealers, of the vendors of cycles with pneumatic tires and the earliest automobiles. For a long while these people regarded the cinema as a form of entertainment suitable for fairs and café basements, and the circus as a spectacle for children and the rabble. It was on the support of this privileged class, or anyhow of a handful of financiers and businessmen with an eye to personal prestige or the speculative possibilities of investment in works of art, that such famous picture-dealers as Durand-Ruel, Vollard and Kahnweiler in Paris, Cassirer and Walden in Berlin, Thannhauser and Gaspari at Munich, Flechtheim at Düsseldorf and Seligman in New York relied when they launched a campaign for what was then styled—borrowing a term from the military vocabulary—the *avant-garde*, that is to say the vanguard of a free, forward-looking art. Disregarding the regular Salons (which had originated in the eighteenth century) and heir at a far remove of the humanist merchants of the sixteenth century, the new picture-dealer sought out truly original artists whose work seemed both to body forth contemporary trends and to open portals on the future. He "revealed," he proposed to connoisseurs the novel, the difficult and unexpect-ed, and displayed to them new, promising fields of art. Like the wizard of primitive communities he initiated the collector into the arcana of worlds that at first sight seemed inaccessible, often incompre-hensible, and, encouraging him to gamble on the prospects of the new art, used the money staked to ensure the livelihood of the pioneers and encour-age them to pursue their ventures in uncharted fields. The artist now began to cut the figure of an enemy of the bourgeoisie from which he stemmed or anyhow of the drab conventions which it spon-sored. Thus, as Roland Barthes has aptly said, the artist's revolt took the form of a violent attack limited for the time being to an indictment of the old aesthetic, and this revolt contained the ferment of a new creative urge, an urge to shatter all restraints and win his independence.

On all fronts—aesthetic, ethical, political—the artist vigorously took part in the fray and broke decisively with the encroaching past. This is appa-rent in the various activities of Lugné-Poe, Appia and Craig, Stravinsky and Schönberg, Matisse and Kandinsky. For the vanguard artist this was a wonderful adventure, like the discovery of a new language or a passionate crusade against an odious established order. Everywhere, from London to Vienna, from Paris to Moscow, Brussels to Munich, Rome to Berlin, official art—stigmatized as academic, hidebound, retrograde—came under fire. "Institutes, grants, diplomas only serve the turn of half-wits, humbugs, playboys"—thus Cézanne in 1904. It was not the French Institute but La Goulue who gave Lautrec the chance of painting a large picture for that famous dancer's booth at the Foire du Trône. "At the turn of the century," Jacques Villon tells us, "the younger painters and sculptors turned their backs on official commissions and were all for a total rupture between the fine arts and the State."

The avant-garde movements which developed in the Belle Epoque—Fauvism and Cubism in Paris, Expressionism in Munich, Rayonism and Suprem-atism in Moscow, Futurism in Milan—led to the formation of coteries (located in Paris at the Bateau-Lavoir and in Vollard's basement) and numerous art groups: the Blue Rose at Moscow, Die Brücke at Munich, Les Vingt at Brussels, the Golden Section in Paris. They also promoted the launching of combative, if esoteric, periodicals such as *Pan* and *Der Sturm* in Berlin, *Die Fackel* in Vienna, *Arte Joven* in Madrid, the *Golden Fleece* in Moscow, the *Revue Blanche* in Paris, and a militant art criticism that shaped the taste of a minority and fired their enthusiasm for "revolutionary" works in which they found the makings of a new *gnosis* reserved to adepts and particularly welcome at a time when the cultural center of gravity was being shifted from the religious to the social plane. "A new world," Mircea Eliade tells us, "was in process of being built out of the ruins of the past and chaos of the present: a private, jealously secluded world. The incomprehensibility of the works of art, the obsession with the enigmatic that now prevailed, reflected a desire to discover a new, esoteric significance in the Universe and in human life. Young men sought to be 'initiated,' to learn the occult significance of all these drastic changes in the artists' repertoire of forms and of all those 'original' departures which at first sight seemed to have nothing in common with art."

One of the first steps was gradually to dispel the romantic myth of the outcast artist and to replace it with a conception of the artist dedicated to a subversion of accepted forms and that permanent revolution in which Camus saw one of the essential activities of man. The "revolutionary" artist boldly discarded all the stock-in-trade of illusionism, *trompe-l'œil*, cheap effects, and, plunging heart and soul into an art of "action," championed the cause of a new human order. When, in the same period, a spirit of revolt made its appearance on the stage of history, it was inspired by the negations of Kropotkin and Jean Grave. Taking the form of an anarchism based on Nietzschean nihilism, it incited men to break free from the thrall of God and their human masters, and to translate into action their loathing of the old order, its outworn creeds and codes. In the year 1892 alone there were over a thousand dynamite outrages in Europe and nearly five hundred in America. In 1894 President Carnot was murdered at Lyons and in 1897 Canovas del Castillo was shot by an anarchist in Spain. A similar fate befell the Austrian Empress Elizabeth in 1898, King Humbert of Italy in 1900, President McKinley in 1901, Grand Duke Sergius in 1905, the year of the "bloody Sunday" at St Petersburg and of the mutiny on the cruiser Potemkin at Odessa (which in 1925 provided Eisenstein with the theme of one of the finest films of all time).

But terrorism does not necessarily lead to armed revolution. In all the great cities of the industrialized countries the uneasy co-existence of an ever-increasing working class and the forces of capitalism led to a state of constant agitation palliated in some cases by purely specious concessions. But these effects were transitory and behind the optimism which ostensibly prevailed in an utopia of *laisser-faire* and easy money, combined with a policy of thorough-paced nationalism and protectionism, lurked a vast dissatisfaction and disillusionment. The lack of any ideal and the prevailing mental lethargy account, no less than the frantic quest of self-regarding pleasure, for the epidemic of suicides that marked the year 1900 both in Europe and in the United States. The period which drove Gauguin into exile and Strindberg to the brink of insanity was the heyday of cabarets and cafés-concerts, where the city-dweller sought an escape from solitude in an atmosphere of meretricious gaiety. Like Toulouse-Lautrec, Picasso was keenly conscious of the misery underlying the bright façade of the Belle Epoque. Both of these great artists stripped the veils from the "gracious" family life of middle-class homes, and sensed what lay behind the antics of the cake-walk and the raucous glee of the chansonniers. The spareness of the colors and pathetic figurations of Picasso's Blue Period reflect a poignant awareness of the moral débâcle of the rich and the material hardships of the poor. But not artists only were alive to the dark forces stirring beneath the glittering surface. In literature, too, Romain Rolland's Jean-Christophe and Martin du Gard's Jean Barois were not the dupes of a fools' paradise.

The vogue for night-life in the cities gave rise to a new art form, the publicity poster: a large lithograph executed in flat, vivid colors depicting in close-up popular dancers or singers. The palings on the slopes of Montmartre were plastered with likenesses of May Milton, Yvette Guilbert and Aristide Bruant, rendered with a masterly draftsmanship—equaled only in the art of Beardsley—by Lautrec and Steinlen. Allying (to borrow Charles Morris's terminology) the aesthetic dimension with the pragmatic, this new type of poster heralded the emergence of one of the great cultic myths of the twentieth century, that of the "star," idol of the crowd. In commissioning her own poster Sarah Bernhardt contributed to this cult, but she made a mistake when she picked on Mucha as her artist; his floral, linear, mannered style sacrificed the semantic value and mural function of the poster to the taste of the moment. The motion picture did the same thing, on still more popular lines, for its early protagonists, Max Linder and Rigadin. As a result of the publicity given to screen and stage stars and cabaret performers there arose a new mythology which henceforth was to pervade the modern world and to replace the consecrated values of the past with an ephemeral cult of the idols of the moment.

Deriving from these mythopoetic incunabula, the frankly utilitarian poster proliferated in all the great urban centers around the year 1900. Bonnard, Jacques Villon, Capiello and Chéret in France, Dudovich in Italy, Penfield in the United States and Van Rysselberghe in Belgium gave its patent of nobility to a form of publicity which, along with the sky-sign, was to dominate the city streets and provide a constant visual "alert" in the heart of a social system where competition was the order of the day. Henceforth the poster exercised an ever stronger pressure on the mentality of the man in the street. It functioned as an intermediary between commerce and the aesthetic sign, bringing into being what Max Bense names the *Plakatwelt*, a makeshift reflection of the language invented at the creative level where works expressing a valid conception of man and the world of men originate.

This period also witnessed the "prehistory" of telecommunications. Outcome of the researches of Hertz and Maxwell, the telephone and wireless now facilitated the transmission of messages to distances so great that mankind—more accurately a favored segment of humanity—could pride itself on the breakthrough into a new space-time dimension. Aside from its political, social and economic consequences, this tended to reduce or even obliterate the elements of provincialism in our western cultures, and, seconded by the development of other means of communication, to transmit to Europe artefacts of African or Oceanian origin collected in the lands where France, Germany, Belgium and Italy had founded colonies (in pursuance of the policy of "colonial expansion").

Though literature and poetry could draw inspiration from exotic sources without compromising the integrity of the language, it was otherwise with the plastic arts. After the assimilation of Japanese exoticism which had suggested to the Impressionists and was still suggesting to Bonnard, Vuillard and Ensor procedures of the utmost subtlety and elegance, there developed around 1905 a tendency to look for guidance to the African and Melanesian works of art which were beginning to flood the European market. This was especially true of Germany, where ethnological museums now were founded with a view to revealing the value of a hitherto neglected range of forms. Then, in 1907, came *Les Demoiselles d'Avignon*, a lightning flash in the clear sky of the Belle Epoque. This epoch-making work disrupted all the accepted methods of execution—methods which even Gauguin had failed to modify. Picasso's art opened up new horizons, a world in which the pasts of ancient Egypt and medieval Europe linked up with the present of remote cultures and recent advances in the field of science. For the *Demoiselles* signified more than a mere shift of sensibility or a challenge to conservative procedures. In it the integration of plastic formulas of foreign origin with classical humanism was governed by a will to *universalize* the language of art: a premonitory riposte to the denials of unity that were, later, to be voiced by Toynbee and Spengler. Here Picasso's dislocations of forms and abrupt transitions reflect the urgency of a dynamic vision coupled with a tragic sense of life. If all his work was closely bound up with the *Weltanschauung* of the period, this was because, despite its seeming uniqueness and highly personal approach, Picasso was affected by the changes coming over the intellectual climate. For he realized that the dogmatic rationalism of the turn of the century was losing ground to the discoveries of Bergson, Dilthey and Freud, who saw in the obscure forces of the mental hinterland—intuition, instinct, the unconscious—a justification for "reversing the customary direction of the processes of thought" (Bergson) and assigning its due function to the irrational. Thus, as against the Cartesian method with its insistence on the rational mind, attention was directed to the non-determinist substructure of consciousness. Life, it now seemed, could not be explained in terms of logic. "All that is vital is antirational" (Unamuno). The inmost core of our being is inaccessible to the analytical mind and in Bergsonian intuition we have a synthetic mode of comprehension, at once intellectual and affective, enabling us to get down to the heart of a phenomenon and "come into direct contact with all that is unique and inexpressible in it." At the same time, by the application of statistical methods, Gibbs and Boltzmann discovered in "chance" an irrational *sine qua non* of the mathematician's equipment. The quantum theory, formulated in 1900, dealt another blow to the conception of the phenomenal world as a continuum, an harmoniously ordered whole. Both science and philosophy ceased, for the time being, focusing attention on the visible. True, this change of approach had begun in the nineteenth century, when the measurable perspectives of Euclidian geometry had been discarded—those same perspectives that Cézanne, too, had tacitly ignored. And Van Gogh had devoted his tempestuous genius to sublimating the dark magic of the fields of force latent in the seeming equilibrium of appearances. Einstein threw new light on the nature of reality when he proved that the natural world is governed by forces acting not *within* but *between* bodies. When, starting from the premises of Riemann and Planck, he set forth (in 1905) his famous Theory of Relativity, he demonstrated that the geometric structure of our world is a complex of masses and their speeds, with the result that, envisaged purely as a form of energy, matter withdrew itself from our observation. It became shapeless, unamenable to direct apprehension, and describable only in abstract formulas and by mathematical symbols. It is the impact of these ideas that accounts for the new direction given to all the activities of the thinking mind, including those of creative art. These were now applied to discovering what was taking place beneath the surface of the phenomenal world, at a level inaccessible to the eye.

This new orientation had far-reaching effects. It necessitated the suppression or abeyance of every habit, idea or convention which barred the way to the reality behind appearances. By the same token the phenomenological research which had begun in the first years of the century was now directed to ascertaining the conditions of appearances, the "laws" of the phenomenal world. Thus the researcher now applied himself to developing a method, starting out from factual experience, of grasping by a sort of virginal intuition the underlying structure or essence of each phenomenon as it presents itself *directly* to consciousness, before the mind has got to work on it. This notion of "a return to *things*" (Husserl's leitmotiv) called for a vision free from preconceptions and for naïve, spontaneous, forthright contacts with reality. In short, a drastic revision of the epistemology of the past was clearly needed to get down to the basic stuff of things.

Was it not a similar idea, the same need to break with appearances, that prompted Rilke to turn to the *Weltinnenraum* (the world's inner space), Max Jacob to "the man who no longer has a past," Alain Fournier towards "the marvelous, low-pitched voice of childhood," Bartok towards folklore, Enesco towards the East and Klee towards primitive Christian art? Was it not a similar "aversion" that led Matisse to turn away from the outer husk of things, the Douanier Rousseau to plunge into non-culture, Odilon Redon into a dream-world, and the finest spirits of the day to immerse themselves in the ciphers of Coptic art and Byzantine symbolism? And when Maurice Denis and Wilhelm Worringer set to loosening the links which, from Giotto to Cézanne, had attached the language of painting to what might be called a physical image of man and his world, were they not inviting line and color, their combinations and relations, to give place to a new semantic order and an aesthetic in keeping with the climate of a new era? This much anyhow is clear: on the threshold of the twentieth century an implicit fellowship developed between the intellectual and the creative activities of the new generation. A movement was on foot to restate the premises and purport of art, to change its meaning and its function.

The "*1900 period*" *might be represented, pictographically, by the image of a whip-lash, launched into space by the last Parisian cabdrivers. It has all the gay bravado of that once-familiar gesture—and also something of its menace. But though it produced an illusion of driving force, it had no staying power. This curious phenomenon affected all the arts of the West in the first decade of the century and, fostered by a sort of collective obsession, rapidly developed into a "tic" characteristic of the period. The fashionable ladies of the day were not the last to succumb to it. At the Palais de Glace it guided the evolutions of the skaters who under Bonnard's watchful eye wove patterns, no less illusive and equally ephemeral, on the shining smoothness. But behind the hectic gaiety one sensed an unstable equilibrium, a febrile Angst. In Picasso's* Tumblers, *is it only the elegance of the line defining the drooping figures that so deeply moves us?*

True there was a "1900 vogue." But there was, even more, a "1900 vague," a wave that swept down from north to south, while another flowed in the opposite direction. The meeting of the waters was in Paris, capital of luxury and pleasure, City of Light, and rendezvous of lonely souls with something to say and to communicate. All alike, wherever they hailed from and whatever their personal background, had this in common: an urge to give the expression of emotion priority over purely aesthetic research. Their favorite theme was sensual pleasure, pleasure sold in the market-place, commercially exploited. "Stars" and clowns, prostitutes and nummers provided models of an infinite variety. But each conveyed, after his or her fashion, the solitude of a public, publicized life. For when the show was over, each became an anonymous figure, stripped of the tinsel, just another shade among the shadows on the screen of a shadow theater. The milieu of Parisian night-life was a closed circle, bathed in a harsh, artificial light. For some years now the electric lamp had been the pivot of the bourgeois home, lodestar of a tranquil domesticity. But boredom soon set in and the bourgeois, discontented with his lot, despite its amenities, went out in search of entertainment, danced, drank and skated. But these were the merest palliatives; no matter where he went, the same atmosphere prevailed, of a "solitude in common." Munch's great picture The Cry, *a portent and a sign without an adjective, without the least concession, voices dramatically the anguish of this rankling unrest. This expression of so radical an absolute was in the Nordic tradition; even Lautrec never went so far in his renderings of the appalling truth. The French painter's superb technique, charged with a beauty of its own, whatever the subject depicted, always modulates his violence. And the art of this aristocrat born is pervaded with a sense of humor, a genial wit, that transmutes a bitter smile into a smiling bitterness.*

EDVARD MUNCH (1863-1944). THE CRY, 1893. NATIONAL GALLERY, OSLO.

PIERRE BONNARD (1867-1947). THE ICE-RINK, 1898. PROFESSOR HANS R. HAHNLOSER COLLECTION, BERN.

PABLO PICASSO (1881). DINERS, 1901. MUSEUM OF ART, RHODE ISLAND SCHOOL OF DESIGN, PROVIDENCE, R.I.

HENRI DE TOULOUSE-LAUTREC (1864-1901). MESSALINE, 1900. E.G. BÜHRLE FOUNDATION COLLECTION, ZURICH.

PABLO PICASSO (1881). TUMBLERS, 1905. STAATSGALERIE, STUTTGART.

A NEW AESTHETIC VENTURE

Time, as Merleau-Ponty has pointed out, is no less an order of co-existences than one of sequences. Not all those living in the same segment of time live in the same moment. This is why an historical mutation can quite well function at different levels, without detriment to the organic unity of a given society. And it accounts for the ambiguity which often envelops the contrasts and antagonisms of periods when all is thrown into the melting-pot.

Like the Renaissance, the Belle Epoque was marked by a singular dichotomy. There existed simultaneously, deriving from the same economic and technical situation, a program opening vistas on the future and what was paradoxically styled Art Nouveau, a movement based on traditional arts and crafts and providing the still powerful middle class with a means of clothing everyday life in luxurious garments. That even the enlightened spirits of the time failed to perceive the real nature of the movement is proved by the fact that—probably at the instance of Remy de Gourmont—they gave the name Art Nouveau to what was in reality an intervention of the "old guard," tricked out with specious novelties and glittering with the tinsel of defunctive symbolism.

Between the frontiers of the Belle Epoque (1890 and 1914) Art Nouveau provided the so-called privileged classes with the simulacrum of a vanguard art, cutting the figure of an easily comprehensible embodiment of "modernism." It owed its success, its vogue and its solid place in history, to the fact that the bourgeoisie saw in it a living symbol of their bygone splendor, and in fact it had all the air of a reprieve accorded to the universal prestige and power of which the middle class had thought itself, not without reason, irremediably deprived. Its rapid diffusion from Moscow to Chicago, in all the centers of "tertiary" activities (to employ the term applied by Fourastié and Colin Clark to the sphere of action of the liberal professions), was also

due to the fact that it pandered to the perverse tastes, the desire for sensual titillation and the moral decadence of a social order that had been thrown off balance by a too rapid economic evolution. Though Art Nouveau hoped, it seems, to devise a code of signs equating the *praxis* of the period, all it actually produced was a pompous rhetoric charged with erotic stimulants and teeming with fluent curves, whiplash lines, asymmetrical convolutions, broken gleams of iridescent light.

That the social order in question was so quick to recognize in this rhetoric the makings of a style adapted to its glorification was natural enough; viewed from this angle the "modern style" was no more than a tissue of allusions. Its serpentine imagery and writhing forms constantly related back to the data of everyday life, and they left their imprint on contemporary furniture, bibelots, ornamental panels, jewelry, textiles, books, posters and the exteriors of buildings. In this flux of meaningless agitation Bachelard would surely have discerned, starting out from his "per contra" phenomenology, a challenge by the creative *cogito* to the Cartesian *cogito*, an appeal to the forces of nature confronted by a mechanical geometry. Kneaded, manipulated, molded, the potter's clay called on solidifying fire to transform the clock into a crowing cock, a woman's form into a toilet-tidy, a night bird into a flower-stand. Under the sculptor's knife, the ironworker's cold-chisel, the ornamenter's gouge, natural forms underwent a curious metamorphosis, while in the bronze-founder's oven the sewing machine took on the semblance of a nenuphar, the phonograph of a convolvulus, the street lamp of an acanthus, the entrance to a Metro station of a botanical garden. When Art Nouveau called on the craftsman's hand to counteract the frigid logic of the machine, it ransacked living Nature for its models, so as to combat what it regarded as the "denaturalizing" menace of the rising might of industrialism and this is why we find it also, paradoxically enough, giving a new impetus to the decorative arts at the very time when art itself was coming under fire. It was no accident that the country which gave birth to Art Nouveau was England, then the most industrialized country of the world.

This may well have been the first time in the history of urban culture that a style succeeded in establishing itself without having been beforehand matured, maintained, sponsored by architecture. For it seems evident (allowing for the experimental, precursory role of painting, a problem dealt with at a later page) that great styles have always struck root in the soil of architecture. And to this is due the adventitious character, historically speaking, of what was termed in Paris "modern style," which took form originally in two dimensions (Mackmurdo's textiles, William Morris's wallpapers). It employed all three dimensions only on the level of the *object* (Gallé's *poèmes vitrifiés*, Tiffany's "Favril glass"), and it proliferated in the arts of decoration before affecting architecture (Guimard, Horta). In this latter field Horta, Gaudi and Van de Velde created unified, self-contained architectural complexes whose lavish decoration and spectacular effects usually overshadowed the structural elements and the disposition of space. (Horta was the only Art Nouveau architect to show a real gift for planning.) And it is here that the undulating line—unifying factor of the Modern Style—can be seen at its most significant. Thickening or fined down, flexible as a liana, it winds its way up staircases, branches out into the arms of chandeliers, creeps into the leads of stained-glass windows, sustains the dripstone of cornices, weaves along façades and embrasures. Examining it closely, we glimpse perhaps a symbol of that "individual *serpentement*" which Bergson was to describe as "the key to everything."

It is noteworthy that Van de Velde took his stand on the neo-romantic theory of "empathy" (basic to certain psychologies of art) when he described line as "primarily representing movements emanating from our inner life." Better than any other element, line reveals this intervention of the inner self, tracing the drift of the artist's moods and responses so faithfully at times that it tends to reproduce them in the beholder: thus the broad curve of a Van de Velde writing desk is conducive to reflection and work; the incurved arms of his chairs appeal to us to lean on them, and the diagonal

cross-braces of their legs induce a "psychological sympathy with the movement of rising from the seat." Here, then, is an intimate combination of contradictory factors, rational and irrational—an interflow of plastic cadences and basic functions which together control and determine a form, the first being an antithetical complement of the second. The result is a singular morphology, which we may interpret in terms of the antagonistic dualism taken by Lupasco, in the 1930s, as the basis of a new mode of thought; or which we may see, more simply, as deriving entirely from the passage in Leonardo's treatise on painting where he remarks that the artist "should seek out in each object the exact way in which a certain flexuous line, acting as its generative axis, transverses it."

Thus while, theoretically, from the political and ethical viewpoint, Art Nouveau may be interpreted as an attempt to integrate art into the life of society, it played in practice, from the cultural viewpoint, a very different part. Today we can see that it had a bourgeois, indeed reactionary side, despite the fact that in its earliest phase it sponsored socialist ideas and the tenets of the Saint-Simonians. When it claimed to be rehabilitating handicrafts threatened by the machine, and bade the practising artist shut his eyes to the advance of technics, one of the vital forces of the period, it destroyed (anyhow in part) "the relation of the plant to the soil" and, depriving art activities of their contacts with the living present, plunged them into an artificial time-dimension irrelevant to contemporary needs and, so to say, short-circuited them. By identifying a meretricious synthesis of the arts with a truly communal art; by building up piecemeal a "style" conforming to the precepts of aesthetes such as Ruskin, Morris, Wilde and J.K. Huysmans; by its practice of converting the useless into the ornamental and tricking out the useful in a sort of fancy dress; and by making decoration its paramount concern, Art Nouveau has come to cut the figure, in art history, of an interlude consecrated to aestheticism. In the years which witnessed the prodigious mastery of industrial technique displayed by Eiffel, and the fructuous co-operation of an engineer (Contamin) and an architect (Dutert)—a collaboration that gave rise to a new, dynamic, logically composed structure, the Galerie des Machines at the Paris World's Fair of 1889 (it was dismantled in 1910) and also to the remarkable buildings planned by Gropius for the Fagus Works at Alfeld—Art Nouveau bade painters, sculptors and architects keep a respectful distance from the technological domain and incited them to show more interest in conscientious craftsmanship than in machinery and machine-made products. Thus, despite the incursion of speed into French life (in 1900 the fastest train made 110 kilometers an hour between Paris and Dax), Modern Style did much to safeguard the small, unhurried world pictured in such glowing colors by Tolstoy, Ruskin, Renan and how many others! At the same time, by encouraging the use of so-called artistic accessories (stained glass, tapestry, pottery and the like) Art Nouveau staked its claim on the decorative function of the arts—a program whose anachronism was glaring, given the cultural and historical conditions. All it actually did was to camouflage with a veil of illusions the dearth of creations truly attuned to the spirit of the age, to substitute the life of a style for a style of life,

and to rivet attention on decoration *qua* decoration. And a form of art that gives priority to decoration is bound to lapse into pure aestheticism and to run the risk, in the event, of dying of inanition.

In one sense, and one sense only, Art Nouveau remains an impressive venture: here was a movement which, for the first time in the history of western culture, set out to "formulate an aesthetic valid for all forms of art and for all countries" (G. C. Argan). But it was doomed from the start by a fundamental flaw. A day came when even Van de Velde saw himself torn between two irreconcilable orders of values. He hoped to find a way out of the dilemma by keeping resolutely to the path of "rational beauty." In the end he had to confess that for him "the rebirth of the idea of style and its triumph had been a tragic experience" (unpublished MS of 1930).

1

THE WORLD OF THE POSTER

For the poster to win a place in the domain of art several conditions were primordial. Industry had to develop to such a point that aggressive salesmanship was needed to find outlets for the goods produced. There had also to be a sufficiency of large distributing agencies to ensure keen competition between firms. And, last but not least, the printing presses had to enlarge and modernize their equipment so that color lithographs, instead of being a speciality of the small craftsman, could be mass-produced in the form of the large mural poster. A teleological instrument *par excellence*, the poster acted as the asterisk of commerce, the folklore of the people, modern equivalent of medieval illumination. It replaced, in the street, the fresco in the religious edifice at the very time when the elimination of the sacred in art was in full swing. Thus the image now came out into the open, for all to see, and publicity exploited the glamour of the sign.

Whether intended to attract the public to theaters, music halls or the Lumière cinema or to promote the sales of the "Little Queen" three-speed cycle; to publicize a "safety" kerosene lamp or a new corset combining "oriental languor with French elegance"; or to stimulate the circulation of a newspaper or a magazine, the turn-of-the-century poster aimed, in both its form and its content, at a provocative, eye-arresting—and remunerative—association of word

PIERRE BONNARD (1867-1947).
LA REVUE BLANCHE, 1894. FOUR-COLOR LITHOGRAPH.
KUNSTGEWERBEMUSEUM, ZURICH.

THEO VAN RYSSELBERGHE (1862-1926).
THE FOURTH ANNUAL SALON DE LA LIBRE ESTHÉTIQUE, BRUSSELS, 1897.
COLOR LITHOGRAPH. WITTAMER COLLECTION, BRUSSELS.

HENRI MEUNIER (1873-1922).
DESIGN FOR THE POSTER
"CARTES POSTALES ARTISTIQUES," 1898.
OIL PAINTING ON CARDBOARD.
WITTAMER COLLECTION, BRUSSELS.

ALPHONSE MUCHA (1860-1939).
JOB CIGARETTE-PAPER, 1898. LITHOGRAPH.
SCHWEIZERISCHE LANDESBIBLIOTHEK, BERN.

30

JACQUES VILLON (1875-1963). BAR SCENE, 1899. LITHOGRAPH (PROOF BEFORE ALL LETTERS).
BIBLIOTHÈQUE DES ARTS DÉCORATIFS, PARIS.

and image, of clear-cut figuration and suggestive distortion. Hence a feeling that all the classical techniques of persuasion needed a thorough over-haul, and in the result an aesthetic dimension was added to a form of communication which now occupies a prominent place among the systems of symbols distinctive of a culture. Chéret and Capiello were the first great specialists of poster art, but to Toulouse-Lautrec goes the credit of having invented "the vocabulary of fascination." Each of the works he made for publicity purposes is full of terse, informative allusions, flashes of sparkling wit. Of the posters with which he made the walls of London "speak," one of the most brilliant is the *May Milton.* Here the message is boldly conveyed by the juxta-position—which promptly holds the eye—of the image and the crescent of letters fanning out upon the ground: May Mi(l)ton. On the level of percep-tion the overall effect is instantaneous; yet it is the verbal sign, insignificant in itself, that begins by holding our attention. The letters are rendered in pointillist touches whose color lies midway between the chromatic intensity of the night-blue ground and that of the significant image (light yellow). To avoid redundancy the artist employs two different types for the only sign—the capital M—that is repeated, instead of utilizing this repetition as a means of setting up a graphic rhythm. Also, the letter "l" is bisected, half of it being hidden under the peak-point of the brightly illuminated area. These devices incite the observer to linger over spelling out the name and to hold it firmly in his memory and his mind's eye. This insistence on the name serves a dual purpose; it gives a fillip to the memory of those who have previous knowledge, either by hearsay of May Milton's reputation or, directly, of the attractive presence of the dancer. And at the same time it makes known her name to those who have never heard of her. For one type of beholder the visual symbol is complementary to the verbal sign; for the other, the text implements the image. It goes without saying that for Lautrec (as for us today, who have no special interest in May Milton's career) these factors are indissociable and have an equal graphic value. Thus reduced to essentials, the message strikes home so promptly and so clearly that even the least informed spectator grasps its purport and understands at once that it relates to a famous dancer. The very absence of any commentary presupposes that her reputation is well-established. Here we have a temporal ambivalence: this reputation is at once in the making and a *fait accompli*. And the lack of any explanatory text creates, also, a spatial puzzle. There she is—but where exactly? Since when and for how long? Is "May Milton" the young dancer's name or that of the show in which she is performing? All these "omissions" help to stress the idea that everybody knows of her (the cultural value of the message) and, subtly, incite the neophyte to find out more about her—a first step towards going to see her do her turn. But in what way is the image of May Milton "seductive," that is to say appealing to the man in the street? As Lautrec shows her, she is neither gay nor pretty and one wonders where the attraction lies. But this very lack of obvious charm suggests that only her artistry can account for her high favor with the public. And though for us this poster has lost its element of surprise and its publicity value, it has lost nothing of the permanent value of all those works of art which range beyond the context that gave rise to them. It is, above all, the image of a period in which woman (though her active role in society was more limited than ever) was an object of adulation, lodestar of every gaze. The fact that publicity found in the eternal feminine its most potent ally bears this out. Whether it was a matter of advertising a brand of cigarette-paper, a literary magazine or an exhibition, woman was always given a prominent place. This obsession was of a stylistic rather than of an erotic or psychological order. Even Bonnard, for whom the feminine form had long ceased to have any secrets, thought fit to muffle his Beardsleyish young woman up to the nose, revealing only a forehead and shrewd eyes, hinting perhaps at the serene clairvoyance of the *Revue Blanche*. A small figure accompanies her, a figure suggestive of a newsboy lightly tripping along the sidewalk. If it serves as the "backcloth" of the composition, this is to bring out still more clearly the "linguistic" content of the message. A message in which yet again the arabesque invites and holds the gaze of the passer-by. Before long Cassandre was to include symbols of speed in the rhetoric of the image—after Cubism had formulated the signs of a space-time aesthetic.

HENRI DE TOULOUSE-LAUTREC (1864-1901). MAY MILTON, 1895.
FOUR-COLOR LITHOGRAPH. MUSÉE TOULOUSE-LAUTREC, ALBI.

JULES CHÉRET (1836-1932).
THE ICE-RINK, CHAMPS-ÉLYSÉES, PARIS, 1894.
COLOR LITHOGRAPH. KUNSTGEWERBEMUSEUM, ZURICH.

THÉOPHILE STEINLEN (1859-1923).
MOTHU ET DORIA: SCÈNES IMPRESSIONNISTES, ABOUT 1894.
COLOR LITHOGRAPH. KUNSTGEWERBEMUSEUM, ZURICH.

LEONARDO BISTOLFI (1859-1933).
FIRST INTERNATIONAL EXHIBITION OF MODERN DECORATIVE ART, TURIN, 1902.
COLOR LITHOGRAPH. WITTAMER COLLECTION, BRUSSELS.

CREATION AND TECHNOLOGY

Reacting against the growth of mechanization, Art Nouveau sponsored handicrafts and the return to an economy based on agriculture. But soon, as was indeed inevitable, there was no evading the problem of the relations between art and industry, between a "privileged" activity—the artist's—and the competitive methods of an industrial régime.

As early as 1902 Hermann Muthesius, a German architect and theorist, had declared that only machine-made objects could match up to the economic needs of the new age. After studying conditions in England he commented severely on the "economic anachronism" of the country and the "absurdly old-fashioned" productions of the Arts and Crafts movement. Thereafter he devoted his abounding energy to laying the foundations of an institution which aimed both at superseding the aesthetic attitude and its disdain of the machine, and at furthering "a close association between artists and industrialists with a view to integrating their activities and orienting German workmanship towards a combination of technical efficiency and good taste." In October 1907 he arranged for a meeting at Munich between twelve artists (including Van de Velde, Behrens, Hoffmann, Olbrich, Riemerschmid and Schumacher) and twelve manufacturers which eventually led to the founding of the Deutscher Werkbund. A preliminary manifesto set forth the ideology and aims of the movement: "to select the best representatives of the arts, handicrafts, industry and trade; to co-ordinate their efforts towards a high standard of quality in machine products; to provide a rallying point for all who have the wish and the ability to turn out high-grade objects... There is no hard-and-fast dividing line," the manifesto continues, "between the craftsman's tool and the machine. Works of good quality can be produced alike by hand and by machinery, once man has mastered the machine and made of it a tool." The idea of *quality* is central to this program. "It applies not only to a work that is perfectly adapted to the materials employed, but also to one that has an affective value and artistic significance." The Werkbund aimed at bridging the gap that had developed between art and the public, at giving the artisan a new directive, and at encouraging painters, sculptors and architects to think in terms of the new technology. It sought to canalize the artist's creative activity into industrial production and thus to modify both the appearance of the goods produced and the taste of those who purchased them. The artist was to be invested with a social function replacing the romantic conception of him as a natural free-lance and an incorrigible individualist—a "lone wolf" at odds with his surroundings. There was, in short, a crying need for a revision of the status of the handicrafts. Denouncing the inadequacy of the "Kunstgewerbeschulen" (art training schools), the Werkbund called for a new discipline, the curriculum which, transmitted by the Bauhaus (1919-1928), was to make good in America round about 1930, under the name Industrial Design.

True, Van de Velde, one of the most ardent champions of Art Nouveau, had as early as 1898 painted a poster and made designs for packing-paper and other publicity material for a large firm (Tropon-Werke) dealing in food stuffs at Cologne. This is remarkable as being the only instance of a completely successful adaptation of Modern Style to the requirements of commerce and industry. Today these works, besides their high artistic quality and semantic value, are of much historical interest. It is regrettable that this, the earliest experiment in Industrial Design, had no sequel for many years to come; engrossed in his activities as architect and interior decorator, Van de Velde failed to exploit the possibilities of this branch of art, which now was opening up new horizons in a field beyond the two dimensions. It was left to the founder of the Werkbund to follow up the lead given by Van de Velde. In 1907 Muthesius put a young, already flourishing firm of electrical engineers in touch with a progressive-minded modern architect, Peter Behrens. He was commissioned to design machines, apparatus, catalogues, posters, pamphlets and thereafter factories and workshops for the A.E.G. (Allgemeine Elektrizitäts-Gesellschaft). This, a new departure of much consequence, not only gave practical expression to the aspirations of the Werkbund but also showed that German businessmen were prepared to "humanize" the technics of mass production. By launching a new form of activity and opening up new fields of research, it prepared the way for a wide extension of methods that were to be given full development in Industrial Design. By enlisting the services of a specialist whose task it was to see to the aesthetic value of its products, the A.E.G. provided the general public with articles of daily use, not only utilitarian, but graceful, harmonious, marked by the style of an original creative artist and at the same time appropriate to the way of living, thinking and behaving of an industrial age.

Van de Velde could not give unqualified support to the program Muthesius was seeking to enforce; this would have meant playing false to his personal convictions. His view of industry did not tally with that of the Werkbund, all for standardized machine production. It was bound up with the notion of handicraft and he pinned his faith to work carried out by groups of craftsmen amply equipped with tools of all descriptions rather than to the chain-production enabled by machinery. Thus when he lamented that "the movement towards a new style can boast of having a flag, but not of having a clear-cut plan," he was indirectly voicing a real uneasiness. Determined to maintain the tradition of German handicraft, he founded in 1908 at Weimar a "Kunstgewerbeschule" providing training in the arts and crafts. Its teaching methods were novel, thoroughly up to date. The new school of art was planned "to spare the pupil the unpleasant sensation of being an underling, to stimulate his innate joy in life and to make him proud of belonging to a creative generation." In 1911 Van de Velde made the acquaintance of a twenty-three-year-old architect who had been deputed by the School of Art at La Chaux-de-Fonds to make a survey of the state of art in Germany on the lines of the one Muthesius had made in England some years previously (1896-1903) on behalf of the Prussian Chamber of Commerce. Thus C. E. Jeanneret (now known as Le Corbusier) came in contact with Van de Velde, studied the methods of the Werkbund and participated as a student-collaborator of Behrens in the work that was being done for the A.E.G., "a gigantic concern which employed sixty thousand workers in its factories, built electric power-houses, made arc lamps, commutators, blast furnaces and a host of implements of every description, all in a pure and sober style." This was Le Corbusier's first contact with the problems set by the growth of industrialization.

Determined to swim against the current, Van de Velde did his utmost to combat the inroads of mechanization on the creative freedom of the artist. The Werkbund, however, advised its members to quit their ivory towers and to meet the growing demand for rationalized and standardized machine production. The result was a violent clash between Van de Velde and Muthesius at the annual conference of the Werkbund at Cologne in 1914. "So long as there are artists in the Werkbund," Van de Velde said, "they will refuse to countenance any idea of standardization and its servitudes. By his very nature the artist is a whole-hearted individualist, a free, spontaneous creator. He will never willingly surrender to a discipline obliging him to keep to set forms, cast-iron rules." These views, which would certainly have been heartily endorsed by Ruskin and Tolstoy, betrayed a total unawareness of the climate of contemporary culture and Muthesius riposted energetically. "Architecture and with it all the activities of the Werkbund are tending towards standardization. It is only by standardization that the artist can regain the universal prestige that was his in periods of a well-integrated civilization. It is only by means of standardization, acting as a salutary concentration of all the life forces of the age, that it will be possible to establish reliable criteria agreeable to the taste of the time." Extreme opinions, soon to be submerged in the chaos of the First World War.

It seems clear that in the heat of the debate Van de Velde had let his feelings run away with him and overstated his case. For in 1907-1908, following Behrens and Riemerschmid, he, too, had countenanced a close collaboration between art and industry by accepting a commission from a factory near Jena for a coffee service, and had not taken exception to its being mass-produced, to working in a thankless medium and conforming to the dimensions prescribed by the manufacturers.

In his brilliantly original architecture Gaudi achieved the dual feat of transposing into three dimensions that interplay of lines of force which energizes Van Gogh's dramatic interrogations of the universe, and pointing the way to a plenary realization of the aspirations of twentieth-century man. A pure creator, unique of his kind, yet steeped in Catalan tradition, Gaudi discovered in the extravagances of Spanish Baroque, indigenous folklore and North African structural design the makings of an aesthetic which treated architecture as a phenomenon subject to the laws and rhythms of organic growth, and a poetic, non-rational, fully plastic manifestation of the creative will. Of a house he makes a sculpture; of a sculpture, a palace. The traditional boundaries of modes of expression had been tending to overlap or lose precision quite early in the century, and in this metamorphosis color played a leading part. Thus the symbiosis of painting and sculpture was implemented by a process of collage *without the least detriment to the concordance between structure and plastic expression. All the dreamlike aspects of his architecture, its strange vagaries and semantic opulence have echoes in the works of Boccioni, Arp, Moore, Wright, Mendelsohn, Le Corbusier, Picasso and Aalto. Nor is it surprising that it strongly appealed to the Surrealists. But where above all Gaudi cuts the figure of a pioneer is where he gives free rein to his fertile imagination and subjects a traditional material, stone, to stresses tending to annul its natural inertia and to give it a plastic function generating forms that the building techniques of the mid-century were, later, to achieve with ferro-concrete. But this predilection for imaginary, fluid, spiral forms and contrived distortions was vigorously opposed by Hoffmann. With a view to restoring a static equilibrium, symmetrical design centered on a fixed point and the austerity of pure volumes, he opted for the "frozen eloquence" of the flat wall conceived in terms of horizontals and verticals and the clear-cut elegance of right angles. In short, so as to counteract the romantic brio of his brilliant contemporary and the current eclecticism, Hoffmann advocated a return to the disciplines of reason and the replacement of multicolored, chimerical space by measured, homogeneous space, demarcated by the axial lines of classical perspective. In other words the free play of the imagination was to be regulated by conceptions deriving from the sense of order implicit in Seurat's painting. Here we have an anticipation of Loos's Purism, of Dutch Neo-Plasticism and the drastic functionalism of* L'Esprit Nouveau *put into practice by Le Corbusier. In point of fact these tendencies stemmed from a common source, the architecture of Mackintosh; as far back as 1898 the Glasgow School of Art had given the straight line precedence over the curve and sponsored an economic, strictly rational handling of space.*

ANTONI GAUDI (1852-1926). ENTRANCE OF GÜELL PARK, BARCELONA, 1900-1914.

JOSEF HOFFMANN (1870-1956). THE PALAIS STOCLET, BRUSSELS, 1906-1911.

CHARLES RENNIE MACKINTOSH (1868-1928). MAIN ENTRANCE OF THE GLASGOW SCHOOL OF ART, 1898-1909.

FROM THE RATIONALIST ATTITUDE TO FUNCTIONALISM

In one of those widely read works which left their mark on the pessimistic mentality that prevailed in Europe in the 1930s, Berdyaev rightly pointed out that the second half of the nineteenth century and the beginning of the next had witnessed the definitive extinction of the Western Renaissance. This might have led him to an investigation of the new values that were then in process of formation. But, for the author of *The New Middle Ages*, man had exhausted all his driving force in the attainment of the highest possible culture and nothing now remained to him but to relapse into a state of anarchy and chaos. Actually, however, we can see today that the man of the new age was activated by a creative urge no less vigorous and economic forces no less potent than those of the early Renaissance. Had Berdyaev studied more closely and with less distaste the theories of Nietzsche and Karl Marx—the former's concept of the Superman and the latter's collectivism (replacing the God of earlier days)—he would have noticed that, in point of fact, twentieth-century man had much in common with Renaissance man.

True, as Berdyaev clearly saw, the Quattrocento was an age of divided purposes. "It was then," he tells us, "that a violent clash took place between Christian and pagan ways of thought, a clash that made its effects felt in all creative activities. In Quattrocento works we never find complete achievement; there is more vitality in the intention than in the end-product. Yet this very imperfection, this very shortcoming, has a charm peculiar to itself." Do not the works of the first half of our century owe their value largely to a similar inachievement, almost one might say a deliberate inachievement? And, above all, does not this period likewise owe its singular dynamism to a conflict of seemingly irreconcilable forces in which, however, we can discern not so much a clash of opposites as the operation of polarities, in the form of a constant give and take—unless we prefer to interpret it, more simply, as due to an interplay of complementaries?

Just as in the Renaissance classicism and mannerism were two complementary sides of one phenomenon, so the encounter of the Cartesian *cogito* and the irrational *cogito* determined the two poles which simultaneously attracted, from its start, the creative activity of the twentieth century and assured its basic unity, within—or despite—the multiplicity, diversity and seeming contradictions of its art forms. This is why we find a steadily increasing output both of fully thought-out works, inspired by a will to rigorous precision, ratiocination, and ordered structure, and also, alongside these, works that have the air of being essentially instinctual and intuitive, products of emotion, imagination, promptings of the subliminal self, the non-cogitative *homo faber*. And yet perhaps, in the last analysis, there is no fundamental cleavage and each type of work is but the obverse of the other.

These two art trends developed simultaneously under the aegis of what was termed in France Modern Style (suggesting its English associations). One of them aimed at lavish ornament, *décor* for *décor's* sake, sensual appeal and a slightly affected elegance; the other at spareness, austerity, functional rigor. Thus the term Modern Style is used to cover two phenomena diametrically opposed, if sometimes intermingling. Hence a regrettable confusion arises, which could be avoided if art historians agreed to apply the name Modern Style exclusively to the *formal* eccentricities of fin-de-siècle baroque. This would solve many of our difficulties, for it would then be possible to differentiate more clearly the essentially architectural movement which (by an historical convention and for critical convenience) has far too long been linked up with the Modern Style. Art Nouveau could then be envisaged and defined in terms of a dichotomy which would also be applicable to many aspects of the culture of today. And, once this was done, the highly complex problem of the origins of contemporary culture could be stated with greater clarity and confidence.

Why, then, was it that in the first decade of this century buildings of a startlingly novel type began to appear in Europe and the United States? Why, too, also in the heart of the Belle Epoque, did architecture enter on a metamorphosis synchronizing with the changes that then were coming over the arts of poetry, music and painting, but deriving from an inspiration radically different from theirs? In other words why is it that the "new architecture" had recourse to an uncompromisingly *rational* conception of its function?

Representative of this movement were Louis Sullivan and Frank Lloyd Wright in the United States, C. R. Mackintosh in Scotland, Charles Voysey in England, Otto Wagner, Adolf Loos and Josef Hoffmann in Austria, and Auguste Perret and Tony Garnier in France. Sir Herbert Read holds that there exists a common element (which he does not precisely specify) between the work of these architects and the paintings of Munch, Hodler, Puvis de Chavannes and Lautrec. This common element must presumably be the use of the spiral, flowing forms of Art Nouveau, whose influence can be seen, rather, in the work of Guimard, Hankar, Horta and Van de Velde. But the principles enounced by the chief protagonists of "rational" architecture expressly and emphatically rule out the ornamental flourishes of Art Nouveau—though it is easy to see how the confusion we are speaking of arose. On the other hand, Francastel declares that the works of Perret, Garnier, Wagner and Loos illustrate "the first steps towards an alignment of architecture to modern art, science and techniques." We find it equally difficult to subscribe to this opinion. For one thing because Gaudi's extraordinary creations in the Güell Park at Barcelona are the only instances of a style of architecture corresponding in any real sense to the distortions authorized by the new mathematics; also, and above all, because architecture, an art in its own right, was, chronologically speaking, lagging behind the far-reaching changes then taking place in painting; and, lastly, because several decades had yet to pass before the architects—Robert Maillart, P. L. Nervi, F. L. Wright and Le Corbusier—took full advantage of the constructive possibilities of the new techniques.

Needless to say, we have here no intention of underrating the pioneer, experimental role that painting has played, from the remote past, in shaping the course of architecture. Time and again we find painting heralding, preparing the way for, new architectural developments. It foreshadows, conjures up the disposition of space of which sooner or later men avail themselves when planning their dwellings, their places of activity or rest, of leisure or secluded meditation. In other words, painting should, it seems, be regarded as an active cultural factor, a most-favored means of bodying forth visual, spatial, linear and structural concepts that architecture subsequently takes over (making due allowance for its necessary social functions and its technical requirements). To take a concrete case, we are justified in regarding the architecture of Mies van der Rohe and Neutra as a direct heritage of the joint researches of De Stijl and the Bauhaus, and it is equally clear that the paintings of Fautrier, Sam Francis, Rothko and Rauschenberg prefigure many aspects of an architecture hitherto undreamed of. When Mondrian remarked that "so long as a wholly new architecture fails to emerge, it's up to painting to do what architecture has failed to do," he obviously had in mind the relationship between the two arts of which we have been speaking and which (though without suspecting its deeper implications) he consciously applied himself to promoting and revealing.

Asked to point to a pictorial prototype of the theories and practice of the architecture of the early twentieth century, we would indicate first and foremost the art of Seurat. It is common knowledge that his painting launched one of the two major art trends of the period. Yet its influence on Picasso, Braque and Gris is far more often mentioned than its no less evident orientation of the strictly architectonic "arrangements" of Léger, La Fresnaye, Mondrian and Schlemmer. As for the view that it also took effect, from Loos to Le Corbusier, on the "new" architecture, we believe that this throws light, simultaneously, both on the position of Seurat and on that of the "new" architecture in the history of contemporary art.

We are often told that Seurat, inventor of Divisionism, was first and foremost a technician. That is true, but he owes his eminence not so much to the making of that discovery as to the skill with which he exploited its possibilities. For, paradoxically enough, it was Divisionism that led the maker of *Sunday Afternoon on the Island of La Grande Jatte* and

Baignade à Asnières to devise, starting from the traditional perspective set-out, an organization of space conforming to a strict geometrical schema, and drastically to strip the composition of all anecdotal overtones, of every sentimental or "picturesque" figuration and all decorative superfluities. In the result the picture consists of units abstracted from reality, partially de-realized, boldly stylized and rearranged in groups, which, despite their seeming autonomy, co-operate and function like the working parts of a piece of clockwork. Well-defined areas of light implement the abstract architectonic concept and ensure the maximum efficacity of the formal structure. Here we have an art, based on exact calculation, that appeals no less to the reasoning mind than to the eye. It is also an example of a perfectly adjusted economy of means and the realization *in esse* of a scientific, logical ideal.

Many of the characteristics of Seurat's art reappear in the directives of the "new" architecture of the present century: static vision, frankly indicated planes, simplified volumes, functional values, technological referents, abstention from ornament, clear-cut outlines, suppression of all non-essential decoration. But though claiming to be "modern," this architecture kept to many of the classical procedures, to rectangular, rigid, self-contained forms and to the perspectival system stemming from the Renaissance. This was largely because Seurat, too, had retained the geometric formulas of cubic space, the very ones that Cézanne at the same moment was already undermining. This, yet again, goes to show both how difficult it is to establish any real synchronism between painting and architecture, and also how even the most "modernistic" architecture of the first decade lagged behind the militant intellectual vanguard. It is significant that in 1920 the first issue of *L'Esprit Nouveau*, the famous fighting review launched under the auspices of Le Corbusier to champion "a spirit of construction and synthesis, of order and conscious creative effort," which aimed at "featuring and clearly describing the works, discoveries and ideas of those who today are the pioneers of modern culture," contained an enthusiastic appraisal (by Bissière) of Seurat's art. In it the art of the painter whom Sir Herbert Read has called the Piero della Francesca of the modern movement is described as the most categorical rebuttal of all those who are bent on proclaiming the supremacy of instinct, incorrigible romantics who regard all that is the fruit of thought as frigid, all that is well-ordered as boring and reason as the most detestable of faculties.

Though this process of decoding the message of such a painter as Seurat with a view to relating it to architecture, and to establishing an optical and mental correlation between the two arts, assigns— rightly in our opinion—what might be described as a dialectical dimension to the origins of twentieth-century architecture, an ethical factor was also operative. The moral attitude of the promoters of a new architecture was (anyhow in Europe) due as much to a drastic change in the climate of opinion as to a violent reaction of the modern sensibility. In the words of a contemporary Parisian commentator it was a revolt against "the idiotic cult of period bric-à-brac and that obsession with the Louis XV style which nowadays plays havoc with the budgets of our millionaires." In the 1890s, eclecticism, pastiche, the degradation of styles and monotony of elevations, a feeble handling of planes and the general heaviness of public and private architecture had become an almost pathological phenomenon. Middle-class homes in France and Italy, in England, Belgium and Germany were murky, somniferous places cluttered up with useless furniture, tedious relics of the past. Things were even worse in working-class homes, where everything was on a meaner scale, dilapidated and uncared-for. Space was at once cramped and squandered, rooms were laid out on no fixed plan, obstacles set up in all directions to the entrance of light, sanitary amenities far to seek. Everything conspired to produce that "infinite ugliness" described by Van de Velde, "an ugliness corroding hearts and minds, foul as the slime of our big towns which clings to your skin like sticking-plaster." There were good reasons for Van de Velde's special devotion to Seurat. The "clean sweep" that he advocated in a pamphlet published in 1894 was of the same order as the one put in practice by the creator of Divisionism. In it he says that "we shall never see anything new emerge until all that now exists has been destroyed *in toto*." Later (in *Amo*, 1915) Van de Velde wrote: "My generation had the nightmare experience of growing up among a herd of dolts who toyed with the organic elements of architecture like children with their boxes of bricks; who assembled pillars, arches, pediments, and cornices without a trace of logic. With the fatuous obstinacy of lunatics they covered these with all the ornaments that were then in fashion: naked women and flowers galore. It was our loathing for these methods and the horror of picturing a similar future for ourselves that led us to cast around for some way of calling in Reason to deliver us."

Far from signifying a desire for liberty, this appeal to Reason voiced a very different aspiration, a will to submit to order and accept the constraints of a discipline. It also implied that a social system, now deprived of any mythological or religious background, was yielding to the pressure of the rationalism which pervaded the industrial, commercial and social world and assimilating its most obvious—and superficial—corollaries. One of these was an *a priori* belief in the ready-made conventions of "classical" geometry to which man's mind and nature were expected to conform as in duty bound. From this it followed that the so-called "little rationalism" of the 1900s encouraged architects to center attention on the *raison d'être* of each part of a building, and shape their plans accordingly. " No form whose reason is inexplicable can long lay claim to beauty," wrote Viollet-le-Duc in *Entretiens II* (1872). In point of fact the Socratic doctrine of a "rational beauty" which was to be summed up by Paul Souriau in 1904—"everything is perfect in its kind when it conforms to its end"— had been forcibly restated by Schopenhauer half a century before. The author of *Die Welt als Wille und Vorstellung* maintained that the beauty of an edifice consists, and consists exclusively, in a clear-cut manifestation of its aim, "by the shortest and most natural route," and that architecture should follow the example of nature, which spontaneously rejects all that is not indispensable. Here, most probably, we have the source, direct or indirect, of the theories of Sullivan, Wagner, Van de Velde, Loos and Perret. All these men, each in his own manner, have recourse to biological analogies in setting forth their view that the new architecture must be liberated from the thrall of ornament, and thus set free to work out the problems of its ends and means without let or hindrance. All alike relate the dictum "form derives from function" to the laws of nature. Stressing the changes that had come over the social structure and man's way of life, they devoted their attention to the new type of building these called for: general stores, industrial complexes, schools of many kinds, apartment houses, garages, large hotels, cinemas and stadiums. All agreed that structure must take precedence of decoration, function of fantasy, and concentrated on a range of essentially constructive, utilitarian materials: steel, reinforced concrete, glass.

From these beginnings there now developed an architectural repertoire based on an ideology of technics, for which the semantics so ably formulated by Auguste Choisy (in 1889) provided definitions of a methodological order. The anti-Ruskinian tendency to assimilate beauty to utility and, still more, the tendency to insist on an absolute correspondence of form and function led to an identification of the rationalist viewpoint with the most Draconian functionalism, and this was responsible for the predominant aspect of world architecture in the first half of the century: the austere and static aspect of an architectural order logical through and through, impervious to the stirrings of life and as tightly centralized as the "ideal" monarchy of the old régime.

But, as Henri Lefebvre pertinently observes, "a living organism is supple only in so far as it is vulnerable. Complete adaptation leads to torpor and stagnation as surely as non-adaptation leads to death." Art, too, can die of an excess of rigor no less than an over-dose of liberty. And a study in depth of absolute functionalism goes to show that it is merely an exaggeration of a normal functional concept which has been operative, discreetly but effectively, in the "spontaneous" architecture of all ages.

2

"ORNAMENT AND CRIME"

After London (1890), the seminal centers of "1900 Baroque" were located successively at Brussels (in 1894 under the auspices of Hankar, Horta, Van de Velde), Munich (in 1895, with Endell, Riemerschmid and Behrens) and in 1896 in Paris, where it was promoted by the dealer Samuel Bing. But, though there is general agreement that Art Nouveau originated in Great Britain, it has not yet been clearly recognized that London was also the place of origin of a diametrically opposed movement, whose beginnings can be seen as early as 1888 in the work of C.F.A. Voysey, pioneer of an architecture stripped of every superfluity, a typical example of which is the house he built in that year in Bedford Park.

Shortly after, in Vienna (in 1894), Otto Wagner, following in the footsteps of Viollet-le-Duc and in collaboration with his young disciple J.M. Olbrich, expounded the principles of a "new" architecture, adapted to the social conditions of the time, in which the building was to harmonize with the material employed, give priority to plan over elevation, to immediate needs over the canons of the past, to a fine spareness over luxurious effect. In his magisterial *Ornament in Architecture* (1892) Louis Sullivan had boldly told American architects that they would be wise to desist from every type of ornament for several years and to concentrate on buildings whose "nudity" gave pleasure to the eye. Then, two years

ADOLF LOOS (1870-1933). STEINER HOUSE, VIENNA, 1910.

TONY GARNIER (1869-1948).
PROJECT FOR AN INDUSTRIAL CITY:
FOUR VIEWS OF DWELLING-HOUSES, 1902-1904.
FROM "UNE CITÉ INDUSTRIELLE," PARIS 1917.

◄ AUGUSTE PERRET (1874-1954).
APARTMENT BUILDING AT 25 BIS, AVENUE FRANKLIN,
PARIS, 1902.

FRANK LLOYD WRIGHT (1869-1959). ►
MARTIN HOUSE, OAKPARK, BUFFALO, N.Y., 1904.
"PRAIRIE HOUSE" STYLE.

later, Wagner advocated the use of horizontal lines, flat roofs and a style based on "a sound constructive logic," pointing out that iron in particular opened up new, exciting possibilities. In his masterwork, the white hall of the Vienna Postal Savings Building, he used a glass and iron vaulting, treated on classical lines, which produces an effect of uncompromising rigidity, a static emptiness, a strangely bleak neutrality. Here transparency creates an illusive vastness, and light fills only a geometrically defined space, the result being that, admirable as is the technical achievement and great as is its historical importance, there is a curious lack of any "human appeal."

Adolf Loos, that sworn foe of the old order, whom Karl Kraus called "the architect of the clean sweep," was quick to perceive this. In *Ornament und Verbrechen* (Ornament and Crime, 1908) he expounded the subversive ideas he had been voicing from 1897 on in a series of articles bitterly denouncing the mania for ornament characteristic of Art Nouveau in general, and in particular the views of Van de Velde. In the opinion of Loos—a compatriot of Freud—the ornament has an erotic origin. It expresses "a primitive urge," and "the more a culture develops, the more the ornament tends to disappear." Thus it had now become irrelevant, since it had ceased to link up with any existing social order or any living tradition. "We are living in the dawn of a new era in which man's happiest dreams will find fulfilment. Soon the streets of our towns will be shining vistas of great white walls. The twentieth-century city will be bare and dazzling, like the New Jerusalem, capital of Heaven." We find echoes of these words in Le Corbusier's famous work, *When the Cathedrals were White* (1937). Indeed decoration came to be regarded as "immoral," from the socio-economic viewpoint, and the absence of ornament rated as a sign of mental purity, a quality ascribed by Loos to the peasant and the engineer. Here we have the origins of a new way of thinking, propagated by the De Stijl group and L'Esprit Nouveau, that was to influence the entire half century: the idea of constructing without decoration, like an engineer, and adapting architecture to the requirements of a Machine Age. It also led to a new application of the structural dialectic implicit in Seurat's art. The Steiner House (1910), one of the first private houses to be built in reinforced concrete, conforms to this rationalist, scientific ideology. Stylistically, it comprised several elements which, though seemingly of Mediterranean inspiration, have had decisive effects throughout the western world: flat roofs, horizontally elongated windows, suppression of cornices, bare walls, right angles. Thanks to a novel structuration, the rooms were distributed at different levels, unrelated to the traditional storeys. The shape of the house was frankly cubic (not "cubist"—this distinction has an historical importance). In this respect it conforms to the western tradition—perspectival, static, functional—of the treatment of space; the exterior surface is continuous, closely enveloping the volumes at every point.

As early as 1900 Frank Lloyd Wright had mastered Japanese methods so thoroughly as to effect a discreet revolution in American architecture. His famous "prairie houses" did not merely offer the middle-class American a wholly original type of country residence in which all ornamentation was merged into the organic unity of the edifice and the traditional building materials—bare stone, plain wood and bricks—regained their full significance. Designed in flexible cruciform plans (L- or T-shaped) the prairie houses inaugurated discontinuous layouts conceived in terms of an aperspectival vision and a singularly non-rational approach. The former led to a loosening-up of partitioned space, defined by walls, and an opening out of the edifice to the world at large, to boundless space. Similarly, the non-rational approach did away with the classical canons, ignored proportions and emphasized relations between the house and its environment (the natural scene). The French architect Tony Garnier worked out the plans of a "Cité Industrielle" answering to the sociological and technical requirements of the day. Less utopian than Ledoux's ideal city, and without departing from the perspectival layout and classical conventions, Garnier's projects provided the industrial age with a repertory of functional and morphological models, and it was from these that European architecture of the first three decades of the century derived its leading themes and cubic style—the protostyle of reinforced concrete.

OTTO WAGNER (1841-1918). MAIN HALL OF THE
VIENNA POSTAL SAVINGS BANK, 1904-1906.

▲
LE CORBUSIER (1887-1965).
VILLA SAVOYE AT POISSY, NEAR PARIS, 1928-1930.

LE CORBUSIER (1887-1965). ▶
VILLA SAVOYE AT POISSY, NEAR PARIS, 1928-1930.
FIRST FLOOR WITH RAMP LEADING TO UPPER TERRACES.

WALTER GROPIUS (1883) AND ADOLF MEYER (1881-1929).
FAGUS WORKS AT ALFELD AN DER LEINE, GERMANY, 1911-1914.

49

II

SIGNS OF THE TIMES

ANGUISH AND REVOLT

Paralleling the uncontrolled expansion of the great nations, the tentacular growth of the large cities of western Europe and the United States has imposed a new dimension on the civilization of our time. This phenomenon has spelt the end of tranquil meditation and, by the same token, shattered many of the ties that held people together in the past—family unity, neighborliness, shared parochial interests and frequent intercourse by word of mouth—ties that formerly had linked their lives with the settled, spiritually coherent life of the community.

Until the middle of the twentieth century the myth of the great city, Megalopolis, retained the characteristics which, from the rise of what has been described as "carboniferous capitalism," had qualified it: a disruption of the social structure, uncontrolled proliferation, makeshift expedients, and a tendency to subordinate collective to private interests. And the steady increase in the number of public buildings, coupled with a disregard for monumental significance, reveals a similar dissociation of functional and ideological values.

We are often told—it has become a commonplace in writings on the subject—that this phenomenon signifies the upsurge of industrial production and the concomitant world-wide development of commerce. But it must also be noted that at the heart of this process there lies an anomaly. For it is largely based on irrational impulses and activities, though ostensibly governed by the logic implicit in all technological planning, whether this involves a systematic use of standards and type-forms or the division of labor and administrative organization.

As is also common knowledge, this phenomenon reflects the attraction that the town exerts on dwellers in the countryside, resulting in an irreversible and continuous draining-away of the rural population. (This is nothing new; already, in 1900, the total urban population in Germany exceeded that of the rural areas.) But the enlargement of the cities would not have assumed such proportions had it not been stimulated by a demographic expansion unparalleled in history. As Lewis Mumford has pointed out, the population of Europe had risen from some two hundred millions at the beginning of the nineteenth century to six hundred millions in 1914, and this accounts for the emergence of a mass society, appropriate and adapted to the demands of the great hives of industry, whose denizens Apollinaire saw as "loveless shades dragging their weary way along the ground."

A traumatic change of proportions had converted human space into "a satanic chaos of rhythms and images" (Georg Trakl), the scene of "experiences blindly undergone without anyone's being alive to them" (Robert Musil). A prisoner of constraints that were becoming ever more oppressive and inadequately equipped for the life he was now compelled to lead, man was baffled and bewildered, torn between individualistic and collective urges—keyed up to breaking-point by the clashes, often of a spectacular order, between capital and labor. This anonymous man in the street, a joyless street crowded with nullities like himself, was the man whom Kirchner was always trying, vainly, to catch up with: the "man without qualities" whom Musil has tried to isolate in the seething confusion of a mass society, a man "whom the least shock from outside throws off his balance into a state of hysterical frenzy" (Georg Trakl). It was impossible for him to achieve within a few decades the psychic mutation which would have enabled him to overcome the *Angst* due to his failure to adapt himself, his uncertainties about his lot, his sense of frustration, and his rankling unrest. How, then, beset at every turn, could he fail to voice a cry of utter despair—that "cry" which Munch figured forth in an unforgettable picture, that "howling wave" which, in Alban Berg's *Wozzeck*, gives agonized expression to all the sorrows of the world.

For the man conscious of his tragic alienation this cry is a deliverance; it stands for the moment of lucidity in which, Heidegger tells us, "existence comes into its own." The anguish it utters liberates modern man, whose identity and integrity are threatened by the over-rapid process of ossification and collapse of the faith and the moral code which, only yesterday, assigned an intrinsic teleology to man's existence. For "these crowds of workers, weary of suffering and dying," as Albert Camus rightly says, "are crowds without a God." We find a similar diagnosis of the historical predicament in Rilke's description of the clotted misery of "our great damned cities":

Here frustrated men sweat and toil to live,
And die unknowing why they have suffered,
And none of them has seen the wry grimace
Which in the dark abyss of nameless nights
Has now replaced the happy smile
Of a people full of faith...

Thus, on the horizon of a life stripped of the sacred, ravaged by the technics of a machine age, death looms up as a *coup de grâce*, the end of all, and no longer, in the words of Mircea Eliade, "a rite of passage to a new mode of being." For most of the inhabitants of the western world, which now has severed all its links with the Judaeo-Christianity of earlier times, death is a portal opening on the void, a plunge into nonentity, foreseen and dreaded as an absolute finale. Corollary to this is a constant and cruel awareness of the precariousness and brevity of life, its servitude to time. This is the message implicit in Munch's *Dance of Life*, which stresses the transience of all things human in a world foredoomed to evanescence. Ensor's masks look clownish only at a distance; on a nearer view we here see death acclimatized in the living present. And Heidegger strikes the same note: "The finite, limited nature of human existence is more primordial than man himself."

But, Camus asks, is it possible to discover a rule of conduct if the sacred and its values are ignored? No, he says—and then this moral deprivation finds an outlet in a rage for living. "Everyone desires, cost what it may, to drain to the dregs all the pleasures the world offers. But he is never able to dispel his apprehension of the morrow, and he struggles to keep his balance as best he can on the débris of normal life." Thus, too, Lotte Eisner in her evoca-

tion of the dark side of the realities that so many of the generation born in the 1880s refused to face and recognize for what they were, though they sensed them in the form of harrowing tensions. "In Europe," according to Gottfried Benn, one of the accepted and most authoritative spokesmen of the expressionist literary movement, "only caricatures of reality were then the order of the day. Reality was regarded as a capitalist concept; it meant selected 'slices of life,' industrial products, mortgages etc. Reality was a synonym for Darwinism, international steeplechases and all that stemmed from privilege. Next, reality meant war, famine, lawlessness, abuse of power." In *Abstraktion und Einfühlung* (1907), a work which did much to stimulate the growth of Nordic Expressionism, Wilhelm Worringer formulated the program of an art answering to "the phobias of present-day man terrified by what he sees happening all around him, phenomena whose interactions and intricacies he is quite unable to unravel." Everywhere a revolt was taking place against the established social and cultural articles of faith: order, duty, respect, authority—a revolt energized by the mental stresses of an age of crisis which, fostered by the individual's sense of exile, tended to throw him back upon himself. When Kandinsky urged contemporary man "to direct his gaze towards himself," Benn "to cultivate a sort of secret intoxication," Kafka "to shun the life that stumbles along the sidewalks" and Franz Werfel to summon forth the world "that is beginning to dawn in man," all alike were addressing an appeal to the solitary Ego, an appeal to link up a troubled phase of human history with the secret places of the heart and give voice to the stirrings of the inner self.

As was to be expected, this view of life took most effect in the zone of Germanic culture, where Romanticism had long before struck root and flourished. But the pressure of ideological and social factors called for new means of expression appropriate to a sensibility frayed and exasperated by a surfeit of seeing and a glut of audible sensations. The inward-turned vision is ill-adapted to the long and patient scrutiny needed to record the objective form of the motif with the precision of the classical eye. Whether literary or plastic, mobile or immobile, the image is conditioned by mental imperatives, rather than by what is actually seen. And it has to be rapidly executed, isolated in the twinkling of an eye from the flux of time and the maelstrom of ideas.

"O divine drunkenness!" Pechstein cries. "My skull is bursting! I walk, devour, swallow, rend in pieces! My brush grates on the canvas, all but tears a hole in it! My teeth clench on my pipe-stem, my feet bore into the ground, sink down and down... Every day is a nerve-racking adventure." Here we see a technique of being, tacit, interiorized, aloof, and the act of painting fragmentated so as to produce an exteriorized image of the significance of the artist's vision in its entirety. This revolt against the "establishment" led to what might be termed an aesthetic of upheaval, and the expressionist cataclysm brought to the fore an art of passionate intensity. From Kubin to Grosz, Nolde, Kokoschka and Gutierrez Solana, from Kafka to Hermann Broch and Bertolt Brecht, from Gustav Mahler to Scriabin, Schönberg, Webern and Busoni, from Sant'Elia to Poelzig and Mendelsohn, from Max Reinhardt to Piscator, from Barlach to Zadkine, from *The Cabinet of Dr Caligari* to *Citizen Kane*, everywhere we find an art of elision and emotive tension in which man's inner freedom challenges the absurd "evidence" that he is not free —an art that gives full play to the distorting and disquieting forces of the irrational. Though unable to unravel them the artist tries to modify the relations between necessity and contingency and, in all the domains lying open to the activities of creative art, free, spontaneous uprushes of the subliminal self dethrone the values of the reasoning mind. Discourse proceeds at a feverish tempo, adjectives are dispensed with, classical methods of construction and analysis done away with. Sounds and words crackle like rifle fire, interspersed with dying falls and stridencies. In painting, acid, shrill, corrosive color eats away the object. A broken, spasmodic line, convulsive rhythms, violent syncopations play havoc with every imitative reflex and the rhetoric of illusion. A fantastic counterpoint of light and shade, clashes of images, disintegrated planes, liquescent volumes —everything conspires to present the recipient of the artist's message with open, discontinuous, agitated forms, inviting him to take an active share in the creative process. This is why in all its varied manifestations, expressionist art, always on the stretch, always aggressive, is essentially an art of provocation—and often has an air of incompleteness.

Always, whether the signs it employs are grandiose or dainty, brash or harrowing, Romanticism testifies to the sense of desolation that comes when, in the grip of History, man takes stock of his hopeless isolation. For then the limits of his personal freedom become apparent, and the feeling of "not being free to be free" proves the inability of any myth to assign a meaning and a value to existence. It is this impossibility of being free that lies at the root of the anguish of our time. Granted that this anguish, which Kierkegaard described as "a syncope of freedom," is (as Heidegger believes) a token of a true awareness of the human situation—a direct revelation of the state of being-in-the-world—and that the mental unrest peculiar to the twentieth century is largely due to the collapse of Faith, we can better understand why modern man is so poignantly aware of his "nothingness." For he has discovered that he is "not mortal in the sense of the familiar syllogism, but always in process of dying" (Eliade). This may explain why the break-up of the foundations of Christianity has been so calamitous, why the triumph of mass civilization has, paradoxically, emphasized man's solitude and why emotive painting has reverted to the means tested out by Van Gogh and Munch in order to reveal the gulf between the individual and the society in which he has to live.

Hence the frenetic, constantly aggressive character of the expressionist works which saw the light in Germany round about 1905 at the same time as French Fauvism. But whereas the Fauves had a very active feeling for color as such, the Expressionists (who did not share that feeling) charged their colors with a frenzied inner drive. Whereas Fauvism aimed at rendering by *and* in *color the intensity of balanced forms, the Expressionist aimed at a combined intensity of sign and signified, within a tense, contracted form, racked by an inner anguish. Whereas the Fauve created poems in color, compositions whose untrammelled figurations of a real* joie de vivre *gave them an over-all coherency, the Expressionist deliberately built up devastating indictments, critical and psychological, of the old order. The man whom Kirchner figures forth in* The Street *is man depersonalized, drugged by city life, and the space in which he goes his way is undefined. It is the futility of fashionable life that Nolde denounces in the feverish rhythms of his* Candle Dancers, *where, to stress his message, distortion is promoted to the rank of an aesthetic canon. We find similar distortion, systematically practised, in the art of Soutine, every one of whose pictures is a linear, chromatic, psychological cataclysm. As for Grosz, his* Homage to the Poet Oskar Panizza *shows how the illusions of a New Objectivity could be momentarily superseded by combining the vocabulary of Italian Futurism with bitter criticism of the contemporary social order.*

ERNST LUDWIG KIRCHNER (1880-1938). THE STREET, 1913. COLLECTION, THE MUSEUM OF MODERN ART, NEW YORK. PURCHASE.

EMIL NOLDE (1867-1956). CANDLE DANCERS, 1912. NOLDE MUSEUM, SEEBÜLL, NEAR NIEBÜLL (SCHLESWIG-HOLSTEIN).

CHAIM SOUTINE (1894-1943). WOMAN IN RED, 1922. DR AND MRS HARRY BAKWIN COLLECTION, NEW YORK.

GEORGE GROSZ (1893-1959). THE FUNERAL (HOMAGE TO THE POET OSKAR PANIZZA), 1917-1918. STAATSGALERIE, STUTTGART.

3

A TIME OF VIOLENCE

That mankind has, and has always had, a propensity for violence is one of the saddest lessons of history. Rare, however, are the moments when creative art surrenders to this instinct. Does this mean that forms have a life of their own unaffected by periods of political and social upheaval? In point of fact such periods have always favored the emergence of great works of art "by reason of the host of problems and new experiences they occasion, and the great affective and intellectual stresses they generate" (Lucien Goldmann). And it so happens that these periods are often closely bound up with advances in knowledge and the nature of the myths it brings into being. Thus it is obvious that art has successively found its inspiration, first, in the notion of a divine order, of an Other World, and of a universal system, putatively harmonious and perfectly balanced, regulating all the elements of life; then, in symbolic tokens of a sense of alienation, when man has a feeling of being overruled by something vaster, stronger than himself, stripped of his personality, changed into a "thing," deprived of any sort of freedom. Even humanity is no longer his, no one is accountable for anything, everyone is trapped in a predicament that urges him to take arms against it. At such times the image tends to express frustration, impatience, inhibition, a rankling unrest. Volcanic and frenetic, it no longer

OF DR CALIGARI," WITH CONRAD VEIDT, 1919.
ART, NEW YORK.

HANS POELZIG (1869-1936).
GROSSES SCHAUSPIELHAUS, BERLIN 1919 (DESTROYED).

ERNST LUDWIG KIRCHNER (1880-1938).
TITLE PAGE OF THE CATALOGNE OF THE "DIE BRÜCKE" EXHIBITION,
WOODCUT. STAATSGALERIE, STUTTGART.

ROBERT WIENE (1881-1938). SCENE FROM THE FILM "THE CABINET
COLLECTION, THE MUSEUM OF MODER

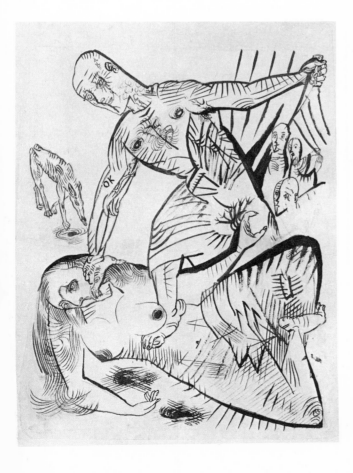

OSKAR KOKOSCHKA (1886).
MURDER, ILLUSTRATION FOR
"HOFFNUNG DER FRAUEN," ABOUT 1908.
PEN AND INK DRAWING. STAATSGALERIE, STUTTGART.

speaks in the first person (the "I," it has been said, is "a crystallized form of experience") and dramatizes life in the plural. For the image to express itself in this manner, what is needed is to subdue form to the exigencies of the sign pure and simple, to overcome the resistance of the materials employed and, abandoning the quest of perfection, to aim above all at a vindictive intensity—a dramatization of the shame man feels for his involvement in the human situation. A closer analysis might show that this aesthetic is better suited to words and sounds, imponderable entities, than to the tactile materials of the plastic arts. In these latter the artist runs the risk of lapsing into grandiloquence—but where there are no limits where does excess begin? Certainly the path is perilous and courage is needed to go to the end of it, ultima Thule of the probable and the incomplete. Yet we can proudly assert today that throughout the present century the disasters of war, crimes and punishments, and world-wide cruelty have found voices measuring up to the extreme situations with which it has confronted us. That this century witnessed the carnage of Guernica is a black mark against it. But that a work like *Guernica* should have stemmed from the hand and heart of one of us, and expressed the horror we all felt, surely gives grounds for feeling that all hope is not lost. Has there ever been so passionate, so poignant an indictment of an evil deed? In *Guernica* the artist is wholly committed, arraigns, questions and condemns. Everything—the rageful execution, the tonality of ashen grey, cast-iron, dusty brown—conspires to body forth the destruction, dissolution, disruption of all values. Here we have far more than a re-presentation of the incident itself; rather, a diagnosis of its inmost meaning. This, too, was an innovation; greatly daring, our twentieth-century art achieves plenary expression by stylistic means, and no longer feels called on to narrate. Herein lies the originality of the art which, since 1912, has been styled "expressionist." It consists in the fact that Expressionism uses elision as a means of communicating succinctly (that is to say, in synthetic and arresting terms) both a critical vision and a heightened sense of what lies behind experience. Thus the Expressionist has something in common with the Romantic artist and, again like him, is strongly individualist, though his individualism is always marked by human sympathy. And since man is *par excellence* the being who sifts out existential data and is "impressed" by them, the interest of the expressionist artist tends to center on the human figure, often ravaged by the ideological message of the picture content. The movement whose leading exponents were Kirchner, Nolde, Soutine, Grosz and Kokoschka, and with which may be associated the emotive painting, of social inspiration, practised by the Mexicans Siqueiros and Orozco, the Flemings Permeke and Servaes, the Americans Bloom and Burchfield, the Brazilian Portinari, the Englishman Sutherland, the Frenchmen Rouault and Gruber, the Chilian Matta, the Italian Vedova and the Spaniard Gutierrez Solana, might almost be described as "impressionist," were not the term reserved to another type of art. The difference between the two is revelatory. Impressionism was essentially perceptive, sensorial, contemplative and passive; the Expressionist is aggressive, fiercely critical of the established order. This violent exteriorization and proselytizing zeal reveals the so to say protestant nature of this art, "the revelation of a heart and soul appalled by a social order that has ceased to have a heart and soul." The impact of Expressionism made itself felt on literature (Stramm, Stadler, Trakl, Edschmid, Brecht, Werfel, Benn), in the theater (Max Reinhardt, Herbert Ihering), in the ballet (Kurt Jooss), the cinema (Robert Wiene, Fritz Lang, Paul Leni), in architecture (Behrens, Poelzig, Höger, Mendelsohn, Bartning), in sculpture (Jespers, Epstein, Zadkine), in woodcuts (Masereel) and in music (Alban Berg, Schönberg, Webern). In all these fields dissociation revealed the values of the night-side of life, while uprushes from the subliminal self testified to a frenzied inward drive. Successive political crises, attacks on human freedom and the menace of Fascism tended to propagate the phenomenon into all departments of culture, and this explains the importance of the role of Expressionism in the history of modern civilization. An essentially demotic movement, it had little appeal for the bourgeoisie whose guilt it proclaimed in no uncertain voice. All the same the middle class, though displeased by its painting, found a certain relish in expressionist films, plays and music, though without fully grasping their anti-bourgeois implications.

ÖGER (1877-1949).
LE HOUSE, HAMBURG, 1922-1923.

PABLO PICASSO (1881).
GUERNICA POSTSCRIPTUM, WEEPING WOMAN, 1937.
COURTESY OF THE FOGG ART MUSEUM,
HARVARD UNIVERSITY, CAMBRIDGE, MASS.

PETER BEHRENS (1868-1940).
HALL OF THE ADMINISTRATIVE BUILDINGS OF THE FARBWERKE.
HOECHST-FRANKFURT, 1920-1925.

PABLO PICASSO (1881). GUERNICA, 1937. OIL PAINTING.
ON EXTENDED LOAN TO THE MUSEUM OF MODERN ART, NEW YORK, FROM THE ARTIST, M. PABLO PICASSO.

DISMEMBERMENT OF THE IMAGE

By undermining the seemingly definitive conception of the plastic image that had prevailed in the western world for many generations, the new ideas that thus gained ground set the twentieth-century art historian one of his major problems. Before Cézanne no one dreamt of calling in question the relation between image and reality; the etymological root of *image* being the same as that of the Latin *imitari*, it followed that the artist's function was to copy, to imitate. To imitate what? Appearances, needless to say. But this answer lacked finality, for it led on to another question: *what* appearances? Those which accorded with the anthropomorphism of the Mediterranean lands and the world view implicit in it? Up to a point, yes. But the art founded on them was, so to say, a one-way art, guided and conditioned by an illusionist geometry. And here we come up against another problem, that of so-called "realism." For the quality of a work of art is obviously determined by the way in which the model is transposed by the artist's selective, appraising, strictly personal vision, and by his competence in rendering it. Under these circumstances the beholder is free to diagnose and interpret the work from one of two angles; he can fix his attention either on the thing re-presented (a sort of fetishism of the object) or on the image *qua* image. In both cases he can glean semantic information of a more or less rewarding order and also the affective satisfactions of an aesthetic experience or revelation.

The boldest ventures of the first decades of the present century seem to have been guided by a will to combat the dichotomy of significant and signified. This is what Klee had in mind when he said that "the picture with a subject confronts us with all the contradictions of the psycho-physiognomical dimension." To resolve these contradictions nothing short of a close investigation of the semantic process itself, a simultaneous attack on both the "code" and the subject, was needed. This goes far to explain why the new art was enthusiastically welcomed by some and scarified by others. And here we have perhaps a line of approach which may well lead to the discovery of one of the structural principles of all contemporary art. In any case the new type of art criticism it has inspired seems to promise fruitful and far-reaching discoveries in the aesthetic domain. In this context mention may be made of a recent work by Abraham Moles, dealing with the "physics of communication," which throws light, if indirectly, on the ideas underlying this new development in the field of aesthetics.

According to the author of *Théorie de l'Information et Perception esthétique* (1958) every message has two aspects. The first relates to the order of the intelligible and since this is an external, quantitative order, it can be formulated in terms of an aggregate of laws and standardized symbols. Thus the message is capable of being received and deciphered by a fairly large number of persons. Explicit, mobile and translatable, it can be transferred from place to place thanks to the techniques of reproduction, without any loss of the semantic information it contains. The theme, structure, linguistic elements and laws of syntax in the ordinary novel enter into this class of information. The same is true of the subject, scenographic layout, arrangement of planes, recessions, transitions, modeling and chiaroscuro of the classical picture. Conditioned thus by a "field" of disciplines, the semantic information it conveys can be more or less accurately evaluated.

But the other part of the message defies appraisals of this kind, for the element of "aesthetic information" is governed by no laws and allows free scope to individual predilections and responses. It belongs to the domain of expression: that is to say of the unique, ineffable, unanalysable and, consequently, untranslatable. It varies according to the temperament, sensibility, knowledge and culture of the recipient, and pits his private, particular response against the generalization (*de facto* or potential) of the semantic message. Needless to say, we here are giving the term "information" a wider than its normal sense. The meaning of the word has been extended by Gestalt psychology (Köhler, Wertheimer, Katz, de Schloezer) and Behaviorism (Watson), and now, in accordance with its etymology (Latin *in-formare*), it includes the active effect it may have on the recipient by shaping his behavior. This gives rise to a dialectic enabling us to envisage from a new angle the function of the work of art within its social context. Communication and its consequences can now be regarded as one of the ingredients of the "cement" to which (as Norbert Wiener holds) the social structure owes its cohesion; the implications of cybernetics take over from the theory of catharsis.

Since the Renaissance, the originality of a work of art has been commonly regarded as a criterion of its value. The present-day theory of information tends to show that this myth links up with the unforeseeableness of a message and an assumption that the novel, startling and original promises a wealth of information. On the other hand a probable, expected, foreseen message will give only meager, banal information, since it is bound to be full of commonplaces—in a word, redundant.

Redundancy may affect the aesthetic as well as the semantic aspect of the "information," when each of these aspects gives the impression of being an independent factor. "A stage play," Moles observes, "can have an incoherent, illogical, even senseless plot, and this may actually enhance its semantic originality. On the other hand the plot can be logical, solidly constructed, predictable, and this may diminish its semantic originality (while making it easier to follow) without affecting the element of aesthetic information—which likewise may be large or small, disproportionately large or small in relation to the maximum content that can be assimilated by the average spectator." The redundancy of a picture obviously derives from a monotonous technique, an insistence on certain color patterns, the repetition of motifs, the frequency of signs distinctive of a personal style, or else from the artist's fidelity to a period style (i.e. a style based on that of a familiar prototype), or perhaps from the use of outworn formulas (this covers all the forms of academicism). Thus we find in *The Soler Family* redundancies of a semantic order that were to be eliminated in *Guernica*. And it is not so much the verbal wealth

of *Ulysses* (Hanley lists 29,899 words as against the average vocabulary of an English writer, some 10,000 words) that gives this fabulous microcosm its magical allure, as the author's unconventional handling of syntax. Can it be due to chance that both Joyce and Picasso "move so spontaneously and effortlessly from one language to the other"? In both cases the disregard of conventional syntax increases the quotum of originality and opens up a new aesthetic dimension.

If the views set forth above are accepted, they suggest that the line of evolution linking Cézanne to Mathieu, Gonzalez to Schöffer, Joyce to Queneau and Schönberg to Boulez, interposes between the image and the world of things a relationship based on a type of thought that Lévi-Strauss describes as *sauvage*. It is the outcome of man's constant struggle, *qua* living being, to stem the tendency towards disorder which seems to be the "natural" condition of the universe—a process that, so far as can be judged, is irreversible. Entropy, the random element in the universe first posited by Clausius to account for its disorder, is the polar opposite of information, that measure or determinant of order which corresponds to a measure of probability (the more the message is probable, the less the "information" it contains). Whether visual, audible or verbal, the contemporary image appears *per se* to constitute an order which, paradoxically enough, tends to body forth the chaos of the universe. Its "realism," on this view, is total and the information it conveys equates a *negative* entropy. It bears traces of an analogical, global, intuitive mode of thought. This is why it appears to aim at dismantling the classical image, which answered to the conception of a stable, orderly universe, governed by reason. Thus once again science has supplied the formulas for an hypothesis of art, but conversely—and more resolutely than ever—art is now by way of staking out a place among the hypotheses of science.

For it is still the path of aesthetic information that links up the achievements of both science and art. As Croce has aptly pointed out, they are at one in this respect as well as in others. "Every scientific work is at the same time a work of art. The aesthetic nature of the former may be almost imperceptible when our mind is wholly absorbed in the effort to understand the scientist's thought and to test its validity. But it ceases being unnoticed when from the activity of understanding we move on to that of contemplation and find the thought in question taking form before us, clear-cut, limpid, well-arranged, without superfluous verbiage or words omitted, invested with the appropriate rhythm and intonation; or else confused, incoherent, restless, jumping from one idea to the other. Some great thinkers have made a name as great writers. Others have always been more or less 'scrappy' writers, even if their fragments, from the strictly scientific viewpoint, match up to harmonious, coherent, perfect works. Thinkers and scientists are excused for being indifferent writers; their fragmentary texts atone for everything, for it is easy to divine behind the inspired fragment what would have been a well-composed work had the author aimed at literary perfection. But how forgive pure artists for exhibiting inferior works? The poet or painter whose work lacks form, falls short in everything for *he himself* falls short" (*Aesthetic Breviary*).

It was not form that suffered when, at the turn of the century, Cézanne applied himself to reinterpreting visual experience in terms of knowledge; what was altered was the mold in which some of its elements had been docilely cast ever since the days of Giotto. Both the image of the world and the world of the image were now being called in question. Who could have foreseen that "nature," the "nature" figured forth by Poussin, would one day be so manhandled as to become hardly recognizable? Why did a concern for formal structure so quickly supersede the artist's fidelity to the thing seen, the tree lose its "signature" and the man his face? Why did things lose weight and stability, and take to moving freely in space, slipping through the distended meshes of a network no longer capable of holding them *in situ* or arresting their movement? And, finally, why did nature undergo so many metamorphoses in a series of works ranging from the *Grandes Baigneuses* to the *Cabanon de Jourdan* and the *Montagne Sainte-Victoire*? The link that had always existed between the image and its natural model was giving way, the image tending more and more towards the sign. The gap between significant and signified grew narrower at the very time when the mental space between the image and the beholder was dwindling and the latter being invited to plunge into the limbo of an unstable world. It may well have been in order to defeat any trend towards a "cult of the object" that figurative art now sought

to evade the illusionist device of a third dimension. Already the apple proffers itself to our scrutiny as no more than a translucent patch of color, prefiguring the time when the image will cease to embody a physical re-presentation of the "thing itself." The association of the curve of a shoulder with the curve of a hill serves only to unify the elements of a line of a new order, that arabesque whose function it was, in the later art of Matisse, to "modulate a pre-existent spatiality." Here we have perhaps a sort of *Ursprung*—a preliminary leap—towards that discovery of a reality behind and beyond the visible which at this same moment was being envisaged by the thinkers of the day. Thus the image of the world that unfurled itself before the intensely scrutinizing eye was regarded as no more than a portal of discovery opening on a new reality. And the reason why the world of the image—even if Cartesian logic might seem to rule this out—was shaken to its foundations was that the new demands of the thinking mind were rendering obsolete the premises on which the time-tried method of Leonardo had been founded.

It would be absurd to suppose that Cézanne's avowed aim—"to see nature as if no one had seen it before us"—was due to the adoption of a blindly speculative attitude towards the notions and practices of his day. The idea behind his remark is characteristic of all great creators, and relates to their power of expressing themselves while expressing the world they live in, a world which they have duly taken stock of and now propose to body forth and qualify (the notion of an artist's being "ahead of his time" is a romantic fallacy).

A point that calls for mention in this context is that, lying between the emancipation of poetry sponsored by Rimbaud and the disintegrated vision of a Dos Passos, the break with the semantic canon of the work of art signalized by Cézanne coincides with a displacement of the social center of gravity. The beginning of the century witnessed the rise of mass civilization; the status of the individual, forced to mingle with the crowd, was altered and the absolute challenged by the relative, the singular by the plural, the solitary gaze by a host of simultaneous gazes. And now the mutilated man, the cyclops schooled with so much care by the Renaissance ("Shut one eye," Leonardo told his pupils, "and keep your head still"), lost the advantage of that stable, single viewpoint (in the exact sense of the term) which, from the earliest days of capitalism, had been his proud prerogative. Once the return to a "normal vision" had freed the artist from the narrow disciplines of classical geometry, new fields of the perceptible were opened up, space became imaginary and the dimensions of the objects in it undefined. If when painting (c. 1895) *Millstone at Le Château-noir* Cézanne appears to waver between two attitudes, this very hesitation seems to contain the promise of a new dimension, in which (as Merleau-Ponty points out) "the invisible provides the relief and depth of the visible" (Schelling had voiced the same idea in much the same terms).

The disintegration of the painter's language that now took place spelt the end of illusionist *trompe-l'œil* art. It showed that the current static worldview was by way of being superseded by more flexible conceptions and that certain ways of handling and assembling ideas hitherto regarded as fundamental, needed to be profoundly modified. A particularly striking example is the weakening of the conception of "individuality" not only in the domains of sociology, art and literature (Walt Whitman, Jules Romains, Charles Vildrac, Emile Verhaeren, Charles Péguy, Romain Rolland), but also even in the field of scientific research. Physical science—Einstein and Infeld made this clear—was now to be directed "to formulating the laws governing groups, not individuals" and to defining, not properties, but probabilities. The task of quantum physics was to investigate "the laws determining changes of probability in time relatively to large aggregates of individual units." For this purpose it was necessary to abandon (as Cézanne had done to some extent) the postulates of Euclidean geometry. This involved the adoption of Riemann's topological schemas, schemas which Cézanne had intuitively lit on in his analysis of the phenomenon of extension in the visible world. The significance of this orientation can best be grasped if we bear in mind the fact that, as against Euclidean geometry based on the notion of distance, Riemann's topology, based on surfaces and elastic curves, tended to show that all fundamental relations can be expressed without recourse to any instrument of measurement. Since matter is extensible and distortable, a circle can become an ellipse or a sphere a convex surface without the loss, in either case, of its initial qualities. Ruling out the notions of rigidity, right angles, straight lines and

distance (hence of projective co-ordinates), this topology deals with forms that can be manipulated and reshaped at will. This explains why the many versions of *Montagne Sainte-Victoire* differ from each other far more than all the replicas or variants of a classical "Adoration of the Magi." Also why, following those of Cézanne, similar intuitions play a part in the works of all the great creative spirits of the twentieth century: of its painters (Matisse, Klee, Kandinsky, Braque, Bonnard, Picasso), and its sculptors (Lipchitz, Gonzalez, Laurens, Moore). This is less surprising in view of the discoveries of experimental psychology that the "spontaneous geometry" of the child leaves out of account proportions, measurements and co-ordinates and is based on purely topological data, such as proximity, remoteness, succession, interiority, envelopment (Piaget and Inhelder, *La représentation de l'espace chez l'enfant*, 1947).

It was inevitable that the development of contemporary scientific thought should lead artists completely to revise their attitude towards the world of visual experience. How could there be any idea of "imitating" nature once scientists had shown that nature was always and everywhere in movement (Rutherford, Planck), domain of a malleable geometry (J. H. Poincaré), of an evolutionary biology (Darwin, Mendel, Weismann), of radioactive chemistry (Becquerel, Curie), of a psychology of subliminal forces (Freud, Adler, Jung), and an ontology of perpetual becoming. Of such a "nature" Cézanne confessed he could grasp only "equivalents" at best. Equivalents "capable of evoking the thrill of its eternity with the elements, the aspects of all its changes"—a curiously Bergsonian turn of phrase! Cézanne knew he was opening vistas on the future: "I shall always remain the Primitive of the path I have opened up."

Short shrift was given to rhetorical mimesis; the problem of *creation* was now to dominate all other ends. For Matisse this meant "regaining the purity of our means"; in Derain's hands "tubes of paint become dynamite cartridges"; for Dufy "the thing is to create the world of things we do not see"; for Vlaminck "to show nature in freedom"; for Delaunay "to build up colored phrases, color acting almost as an independent agent"; while Kandinsky declared that "the hour has struck for a freedom conceivable only on the eve of a great epoch." The first step needed was to transmute appearances in the crucible of color, which, reinforced by recent discoveries in the field of industrial chemistry (alizarin red, cadmium and antimony blue), now proved to be rich and potent enough to create its own dimension and to be assigned a structural function. Following the lead given by Gauguin, and replacing the illusionism of modeling by signs capable *per se* of rendering spatial values, Fauvism made free play with "imaginary color," though without dispensing altogether with the perspective layout; for the Cézannian ambivalence persisted and was to last until the middle phase of Cubism. The violent colors of the Fauves gave the impression of a reaction against the chromatic impoverishment of the industrial and urban milieu. They also seem to voice a protest against the monochromy of the contemporary photograph. On the theoretical level, the ideas behind Fauvism may well have inspired Edward Bullough's magisterial work, *Perceptive Problem in the Aesthetic Appreciation of Single Colors* (1908), and David Katz's *Die Erscheinungsweise der Farben* (1911).

True, Van Gogh had already—probably before Gauguin—made an arbitrary use of color with a view to "expressing himself strongly." But, as a preliminary to the surging movement and frenzied agitation of his *Olive Trees*, he had explored the master rhythms of the cosmic flux, struck down to its hidden forces. Here color renders simultaneously space and energy. By ever more closely associating dynamic color with the line and dynamic line with color, Fauvism instilled into the picture the "energy dimension," the dimension which in the long run did away with its representative function. That this happened to coincide more or less with Maxwell's discovery of fields of force does not detract from the significance of the artists' achievement. Neither Cézanne nor Einstein, neither Matisse nor Planck could have envisaged a "new reality" without the intervention of this notion, clear to some, intuitive with others. Einstein himself admits that it lies at the base of his researches; reality manifested itself to him in a new light the moment he fully realized that the natural world is ruled by forces operating not *in* but *between* bodies. Thus in his first pronouncement of the Theory of Relativity (1905) he began by demonstrating that the geometric nature of our universe is the result of masses and their speeds. Decidedly "our universe" is non-Euclidean. In

setting forth the basic principles of Cubism, Braque was quite definite on this point. "The merely mechanical devices of traditional perspective can never give us a total mastery of things. It starts from a point of sight and keeps to it perpetually — like someone who all his life draws profiles on the assumption that man is one-eyed." Both Braque and Picasso defined the artist's task as that of creating *un fait pictural*. This falls in line with a remark (quite in the spirit of Paul Valéry) made by Jean Royère: "Poetry is verbal creation." At the time when Schönberg was beginning to dismantle the sound-image, the editor of *La Phalange* was advising poets "to do away with classical discourse" and Jules Romains speaking of his attempt to discover a mode of composition enabling the novelist "to break with the habit of centering his gaze on the individual." Already, in the field of literature, Henry James had shown the way to a treatment of the novel that abolished the single (perspectival) viewpoint. Like Braque and Picasso, the author of *The Turn of the Screw*, struck by the multiplicity of possible ways of seeing, applied himself to discerning one thing beyond another, then still others beyond the former. This involved the use of a sort of multiple perspective, focusing all possible viewpoints on the object of perception (a similar method was used in *La Source*, a poem by Raymond Roussel published in 1903). Only thus can the image provide "a synthesis of all the aspects of the living being" (Sartre), and become a record of an (often exciting) discovery rather than a mere re-presentation of a model that the artist has lit on "ready-made" and copied to the best of his ability. Thus the record of a direct experience was little by little to supersede the ostensible subject, or, rather, to relegate it to a point within the image where the significant and the signified coalesce. The gradual progress from the cubist fruit-dish to Van Doesburg's rectangle or Malevich's square is remarkably consistent and we can trace its course quite clearly in the successive permutations of Mondrian's famous "apple-tree."

Servitude to the visual datum was more and more replaced by what Malevich called "a feeling of the *absence* of the object," and this in less than two decades gave rise to "a system of qualities" which did away with the previous schema of magnitudes, overcame anthropocentrism, merged subject into sign and invested the "message," now become a-semantic, with an appeal that can only be described as magical. Hence the notion of an art which, employing its own means exclusively, modifies and modulates our vision of the world. From his discovery of the fact that "the life of a picture is independent of the life it imitates" Jean Cocteau drew the conclusion that "it is much less easy to fool the eye with an 'illegible' picture than with one that 'represents'." Somewhat the same idea must have been behind the theory of forms and a "structural aesthetic" which arose in Germany at the end of the nineteenth century, with Hildebrand and his successors, Wölfflin, Riegl, Schmarsow, as its exponents. These efforts to establish once for all the autonomy of the language of art involved far-reaching changes in the conception of "the beautiful." This ceased to have the functional quality attributed to it by Socratic tradition and the privileged domain it had occupied through the ages now became a field of signs and groups of signs.

But it would be a mistake to infer that the new art abolished the Euclidean mentality once for all. Rather it operated as a catalysing factor, one of whose consequences was an ambivalence destined to have momentous effects on the collective sensibility; I have in mind the parallel development of photography. Thanks to technical progress and the widening use of mass media, it gained ground in inverse proportion to the increasing "disfiguration" of the classical norms of art. Between 1890 and 1914 the photograph gradually took the place of handmade illustrations in newspapers and magazines. The photographic image, whether isolated or serially presented on the cinema screen, came more and more to be regarded as having an "objective" validity, and being somehow "truer" than the hypothetical, allusive, imaginary or inner realities implicit in the plastic image. (Yet all the camera actually does is to record a scene by means of lenses, devised on strictly Euclidean lines.) Thus for the first time in history two competing, diametrically opposed types of imagery shared simultaneously the approbation—or disapproval—of the public. And this dichotomy of taste persisted despite the mediating influence of the art of the poster, which often embodied the "folklore" of Cubism or another of the great movements of the period. Never in any previous age had the world of imagery thus been divided against itself.

IMAGINED COLOR

"The really important battles," Nolde said in a letter written in 1908, "were fought in France. Great Frenchmen, such as Cézanne, Van Gogh and Gauguin, played the part of ice-breakers. These men gave short shrift to all the old working methods—and this was the only way in which a new art, ranking beside the great art of the past, could be created." In other words it was between the years 1880 and 1905 that steps were taken to loosen up the imagery that had held its ground inflexibly since the days of Uccello, Van Eyck and Fouquet. Borne on by the tidal flux of history, the "ice-breakers" Nolde speaks of were the first to break up the established semantic arrangement of the picture, directing their attacks, particularly, at the accepted scenographic layout, with its paraphernalia of planes, coulisses, *transitions, modeling and chiaroscuro. Closely associated with the changes coming over the social system, the abandonment in physics of the principle of mechanistic laws and the emergence of "topological" mathematics, the convergent attacks of Van Gogh, Gauguin and Cézanne were aimed at eliciting no less a new experience of the world than the world of a new experience. Following them, the Fauves, without giving further thought to the distinction drawn by psychology between the real and the imaginary, set out to establish, between man and the world at large, a relation which no longer called for the intermediacy of any external object. Hence that recourse to the figurative potency of color-in-itself which we find in the early work of Braque, Matisse, Derain, Vlaminck, Rouault and Dufy who, all alike, found in the creative act* per se *a justification for the shocks they were imposing on the "renovated" eye of the spectator, who now was called on to collaborate actively with the artist. This taste for pure, strident colors led to the use of chromatic signs thrown into prominence by tracts of flat color, sometimes slightly modulated or emphasized by circumscribing lines—effects which were reinforced by a bold, untrammelled execution. This freedom in the* facture *was implemented by an equal freedom in the treatment of forms: mobile, elastic or curtailed fragments of a dematerialized "reality" sublimated in terms of a color which was endowed with a constructive, space-creating function. An autonomous, direct act of communication, the work of art derived its value from the over-all message conveyed by the indissoluble triad: form-color-expression, and the artist's sensibility directly controls the handling of the picture. Is this because both the picture itself and the evolution of the concept of the world implicit in it call in question the ancient notion of "the beautiful" or, on the other hand, has the very content of that concept released the work of art from the classical canons that used to dominate it? In any case this was a turning-point in art history; resuming all previous achievements, it opened the way to every possibility.*

HENRI MATISSE (1869-1954). GIPSY, 1906.
MUSÉE DE L'ANNONCIADE, SAINT-TROPEZ.

GEORGES ROUAULT (1871-1958). HEAD OF A CLOWN, ABOUT 1908.
COURTESY OF THE DUMBARTON OAKS COLLECTION, WASHINGTON, D.C.

GEORGES BRAQUE (1882-1963). L'ESTAQUE, 1907. COLLECTION COLONEL SAMUEL A. BERGER, NEW YORK.

ANDRÉ DERAIN (1880-1954). L'ESTAQUE, THREE TREES, 1906. COLLECTION OF AYALA AND SAM ZACKS, TORONTO.

AN AESTHETIC OF DISCONTINUITY

When a visitor to one of our museums pauses to examine, whether with an expert eye or as a thing of beauty, an Attic amphora, a Gupta Buddha, an effigy from El-Amarna, a Florentine Maestà or a romantic landscape, he tends, according to his viewpoint, to see in it an object made to give pleasure to the eye or a "document" of historical interest. The Kantian gaze converts it into an adornment, perhaps the fine flower, of a civilization, while the aesthetic apprehends it strictly as a work of art. In neither case is any account taken of the circumstances under which it emerged, its social and human background. At most the beholder may discover in it the reflection of a moment of time, an epoch, or a certain climate of sensibility.

But surely the inadequacy of such a view is evident; the *Demoiselles d'Avignon* did not in any sense reflect the social order of its day in the way that certain bodies reflect rays of light. Reflection is a phenomenon that takes place on the surface of an object. But the work of art is an end-product whose origins are deeply rooted in a "body," in this context a social body; it stems from a tissue, living, healthy or anaemic (depending on the historical predicament), and far from being a reflection is an *emanation*: that of an individual wholly integrated into an (active) social group. In other words it draws its sustenance from the very stuff of everyday life and for this reason gives specific, visible form to the concrete relations between members of a given social order. If these relations are strained, even antagonistic, the artist reveals them candidly, unflinchingly, just as they are, without a thought for the reception his work will get from the public. If expressionist rupture, cubist fragmentation, dodecaphonic dissonance, surrealist ambiguity seemed "intolerable" this was because they expressed the human situation (of the day) with such uncompromising accuracy. "People get annoyed," Adorno writes, "because art, if it has any element of vital actuality, makes ruthlessly apparent all that we would

prefer to forget." What our bourgeoisie wants to forget is the political and economic chaos of the world of today, its feudal servitudes and class barriers, the fusion of the concepts of production and domination. Also a mystique of obstructionism, the dregs of colonialism, an inability to adapt technological structures to an ever more complex social order, the constant menace of nationalism, of a new wave of fascist oppression—all so many charges of dynamite ready to be touched off at any moment and shatter the fabric of society. "Modern man," Maurice Blanchot observes, "is discontinuous, fragmented, and not just momentarily as in some earlier periods; discontinuity is implicit in the very texture of present-day life. And apparently we are expected to build up a coherent world, a whole with the maximum of unity and universality, out of scattered, dislocated, incoherent fragments of the personality—out of all the imperfections of modern man."

Discontinuity, a "speciality" of the twentieth century, pervades the social activities and problems of today (strikes, the demands of labor, divorces); politics (the party system, personal rivalries, conflicts); practical economics (models perpetually superseded, changes of taste, competition, publicity); industrial doctrines (Taylorism, Fordism, Stakhanovism, etc.); mental disciplines (logical procedures, patterns of thought, antinomies). And inevitably this disintegration affects the organization of the State, the city and the home.

In all these fields we see *praxis* giving new forms to major themes of thought. Thus for the notion of continuous evolution—*natura nihil facit per saltum*—basic to nineteenth-century natural philosophy, the quantum theory and present-day genetics have substituted the notion of a nature proceeding by leaps and bounds and in terms of elementary, clear-cut units. At the core of Marxist dialectic lies the notion of an interplay of contraries, source of all the changes and mutations that take place in nature and the social organism. The dynamic logic formulated by Lupasco takes for its premise the theory that "implicit in every event is a contrary event, with the result that the actualization of the one brings into play the potentiality of the other" (a theorem linking up with Heisenberg's principle of uncertainty). Similarly for Klee every force conjures up its complement and the components of the cosmos cannot be adequately symbolized without taking this into account. (In 1927 Niels Bohr found in the concept of "complementarity" a means of interpreting quantic phenomena.) Klee saw nature as "a subtly differentiated organism," consisting of "organisms within organisms, to such effect that each part is a begetter of other parts. To perceive this in even the smallest things is the first step to knowledge." When Braque said he did not believe "in *things* but in the *relations* between things," he had in mind the discontinuous nature of the "structuralism" which Jakobson posited as basic to the history of literature. Without a study of its structural characteristics, he said, "no connection can be established between the literary and the other domains of cultural phenomena" (1928).

Basing his argument on the pluralism of time implicit in the principle of relativity, Bachelard confutes the Bergsonian theory of continuity. "We have no right to posit continuity and we equally refuse to posit an organic unity in the world of matter, since each of its elements bears the imprint of diversity. Examining any series whatever of events, we observe that marginal to all of them is a time in which nothing happens. However many series are added, there is nothing to prove that you are getting down to a *continuous* duration. It is unwise to presuppose the existence of any such continuity when one remembers that mathematical systems exist which, though themselves discontinuous, have the potency of continuity... From the psychological viewpoint everything can be explained in terms of discontinuity."

That is well said. Once anthropomorphism loses ground, continuity collapses. Space becomes fragmented, matter becomes movement, time merges into a duration punctuated with "accidents." And since the sign is of its very nature discontinuous art was led ineluctably to have recourse to it and to visualize the world as "an archipelago of lacunae." Thus architecture has shattered the supporting

envelope sheltering a space reserved to silence; sculpture has ceased to give form to solid, opaque volumes; music now rejects the *vis inertiae* of harmony. The poem gives us "words in freedom," the novel disintegrates the mannerisms of classical prose, painting becomes a complex of abbreviations. Publicity exploits intermittences, the cinema "cutting," jazz the rhythms of feverish excitement. Collage ceases to be a mere recreation and "junk" to be relegated to the ashcan (as far back as 1885 some old, battered lanterns Van Gogh had noticed at a place where scavengers dumped refuse "had fired his enthusiasm").

Unquestionably it was due to the downfall of classical physics, to the mutations of biology and logic, to the triumph of structuralism (an outcome of *Gestalttheorie*) and the disruption of the social order, that discontinuity now made its appearance on all levels of communication. Segments, prisms, unlikely juxtapositions, cavities, lattices, perforated masses—"patches of poetry" as Marcel Raymond describes them—form connecting links between the works, seemingly poles apart, of Picasso and Matta, Stravinsky and Varèse, Joyce and Céline, Gargallo and Lippold, much as in earlier times a philosophy of continuity had sponsored a connecting link between Jacopo de' Barbari's still lifes and Chardin's, Dürer's portraits and Courbet's, Giorgione's landscapes and Corot's, the *Colleone* and the *Thinker*.

Where melody had exercised a charm akin to that of modeling, Schönberg emancipated counterpoint, Satie had parachuted the typewriter into the orchestra (in *Parade*, 1917), and Cézanne introduced the staccato into painting. Where perspectival layout called for fully stated form, harmony of outlines and modulated color, the new topology of art—from the *Montagne Sainte-Victoire* to Picasso's *Charnier*, with Matisse's *La Danse* as an intermediary—dwindled, expanded, twisted or flattened forms, while cubist geometry segmented facets along the sharp edges of a prism, toyed with "planes in depth," dismantled, fractionated, split up and regrouped "serializations" of an organic whole, viewed simultaneously from in front, from behind, from above and from below.

For some forty thousand years the sculptor's task had been to disengage from the mass of some material deemed "noble" (on good grounds, sociologically speaking) entities with clear-cut forms and pertaining to the order of the convex. Now, however, such men as Gargallo, Gonzalez and Tatlin ply their chisels on sheet metal and strip-iron or mold them in a forge, so as to lend the void a plastic value, to make the hollows "speak," to load surfaces with meaning, and to produce works hammered out, bolted or welded, that body forth a complex of conflicting tensions, ambivalences and contrasts.

Where formerly light glanced smoothly over the closed façade of Cretan houses or Florentine palaces, perfectly bringing out the uniform development of each plane and the static quality of the material, Perret, Le Corbusier and Mies van der Rohe manipulate, divide, and modulate transparent volumes poised precariously in the interstices of a metal framework subjected to the conflicting stresses of tension and compression.

Whereas the Roman letter gave its full value to the signs which Garamond standardized in the heyday of classical humanism, the *Bifur* alphabet (1928) assimilated typography to a galaxy of twinkling lights, inviting the beholder to reassemble mentally the *disjecta membra*.

Or, again, when we survey the long history of the novel, from *Tristan and Isolde* to the *Human Comedy*, we find that the narrative moved fluently, with smooth transitions, charged with fine shades of feeling, touches of verbal magic. To all this *Ulysses* peremptorily says "No." No to symmetry, to the classical unities, to romantic glamour, studied grace. The bleak, ironical precision of the "Ithaca" episode, from which the following passage is extracted, typifies this "negative" side of Joyce's genius.

"What in water did Bloom, waterlover, drawer of water, watercarrier returning to the range, admire?

"Its universality; its democratic equality and constancy to its nature in seeking its own level: its unplumbed profundity in the Sundam trench of the Pacific exceeding 8000 fathoms: the restlessness of its waves and surface particles visiting in turn all points of its seaboard: the independence of its units: the variability of states of sea: its hydrostatic quiescence in calm: its hydrokinetic turgidity in neap and spring tides: its subsidence after devasta-

tion: its sterility in the circumpolar icecaps, arctic and antarctic: its imperturbability in lagoons and highland tarns: its violence in seaquakes, waterspouts, artesian wells, eruptions, torrents, eddies, freshets, spates, groundswells, watersheds, waterpartings, geysers, cataracts, whirlpools, maelstroms, inundations, deluges, cloudbursts: its vast circumterrestrial ahorizontal curve: its secrecy in springs, and latent humidity, revealed by rhabdomantic or hygrometric instruments and exemplified by the hole in the wall at Ashtown gate, saturation of air, distillation of dew: the simplicity of its composition, two constituent parts of hydrogen with one constituent part of oxygen: its healing virtues..." In *Ulysses* (and still more in *Finnegans Wake*) we find spasmodic language, simultaneous contrasts, palpitating rhythms, verbal democracy, labyrinthine topology, spontaneous architecture. Joyce mobilized in his prose all the subversive forces stirring in the vanguard art of his time. In Joyce's creations Klee and Picasso, Apollinaire and Eluard, Braque and Schönberg, Mondrian and Webern, Armstrong and Eisenstein join forces, for his art is a geometric locus of "the aesthetic of counterpoint," of the autonomous sign, of staggered planes, of anacrusic rhythms, of a dynamic asymmetry in which any notion of orderly development is submerged by complexes of lines, words, colors, quavers—details each of which has a precise structural function. These "serial" arrangements are now creating a curious, unpredictable affinity between the present-day technician mentality and the basic operations of the primitive, untrained mind. Thus our contemporary creative activity is regaining something of the dynamism of the so-called "savage" mentality. As Lévi-Strauss has proved, primitive man tends to think in terms of contrasts, antinomies (which is also the method, *mutatis mutandis*, employed by our electronic computers). And this new type of creative activity may well stake a permanent claim on the future if, agreeing with the author of *Tristes Tropiques*, we hold that "primitive arts and the 'primitive' periods of sophisticated arts are the only ones that never age, since they utilize and integrate to the best of their ability the raw material of art and invest it, empirically, with significance."

True, the major sensory stimuli of the industrial age (rumblings of traffic, backfires, accelerations, slowing-downs, sudden halts, flashes, stridencies of the telephone) and its characteristic techniques (typewriting, structural prefabrication, newsreels, montages of films, flaring headlines and so forth) have gone far to disintegrate our ways of seeing and feeling, and by their impact to syncopate our trains of thought. But it was not by way of a compensation (as is commonly supposed) but by what might be called a complementary reflex that the western world began to show an active, ever-increasing interest, quite early in the century, in the cultures of Africa and Polynesia and, from about 1925 on, in pre-Columbian art. This phenomenon had an historical importance. On the eve of the First World War, France, England, Portugal, Belgium, Italy, Germany and Spain were annexing almost the totality of Africa on the pretext of "enlightening" the dark continent with their manners, their languages, their flags—and their weapons. But meanwhile the new interest in Negro and Oceanian art was preparing the way for a spiritual decolonization, a sympathetic comprehension, and denouncing with an unconscious flair for the future the myth of a "primitive mentality" (Lévy-Bruhl, 1922).

The Paris World's Fair of 1900 came as a revelation to the men who were soon to pioneer the Fauve and Expressionist movements, for they sensed the affinity between the tensions of the life of western man and those which make their presence felt in the structure of primitive communities and are symbolized in their cult objects. What could be seen in ethnological museums failed to satisfy the artists' curiosity; they wanted closer contacts. Picasso took to buying objects from Africa and the Marquesas from sailors in the seaports of the south of France. In 1903 Vlaminck ransacked the curio shops in small towns on the banks of the Seine and built up a collection of "wood carvings made by black artists in French Africa," and in 1905 he presented Derain with one of his Congolese masks. In Munich, in 1905, Kirchner and Pechstein purchased several Nigerian statuettes. Matisse, in 1906, formed a collection of some twenty pieces and a year later Braque acquired a mask from the Cameroons. "This taste," Apollinaire observed in 1912, "coming at the time when the Impressionists had at long last freed painting from the shackles of academicism, was to have a marked influence on the future of art."

We shall not dwell on the very different manners in which artists turned to account the lessons of African carving: for expressive ends in Germany and for plastic ends in France. Here we are less concerned with any question of "influence" than with the change of sensibility that ensued from these artistic contacts with a world of signs remarkably attuned to current trends of thought and technological developments. If painters and sculptors showed a lively interest in Negro art this was not only for the light it threw on the problems they were already facing; African carvings also led them to set themselves new problems—of convex-concave dialectic, of overlappings, of the breaking-up of masses and so forth: problems soon to be solved by the great creative spirits of the period. Moreover—and this was brilliantly attested by the "Orient-Occident" exhibition organized in 1958 in Paris, one of the outstanding cultural events of our time—whereas Impressionism utilized elements borrowed from oriental cultures (motifs, forms and colors) only in a relatively passive way, western twentieth-century art is tending, rather, to *integrate* exotic actualities into a way of seeing that is still in process of undergoing a far-reaching mutation.

Another factor, which must not be underestimated, has probably facilitated our access to non-European arts; this is the *caricature*, that form of critical expression which Daumier employed to lash his bête-noire, the bourgeoisie, and endowed with a new authority, a universal import. The schematization of the caricature involves a process of disjunction based on "a clash of positive and negative polarities." Inspired and conditioned by factors of a social and economic order—these have been admirably set forth by Max Raphael, to whom we owe the most pertinent sociological analysis of Picasso's œuvre so far available—it envisages man "as a contradictory being, at odds both with himself and with his environment." And since his morphogenetic dynamism keeps pace with the development of machinery, the twentieth-century artist "can outstrip Daumier by replacing the organic (both psychic and physical) aspect of man by analogies with the machine and a new system of general, abstract relations."

PABLO PICASSO (1881). LES DEMOISELLES D'AVIGNON, 1907. COLLECTION, THE MUSEUM OF MODERN ART, NEW YORK. ACQUIRED THROUGH THE LILLIE P. BLISS BEQUEST.

FRAGMENTED FIGURATION

When in the spring of 1907 Picasso gave the finishing touch to Les Demoiselles d'Avignon *he launched a challenge whose impact on the world of art equated that of Giotto's great* Maestà. *A brilliant prolegomenon to Cubism and a landmark of the age, this work broke with all the accepted disciplines of re-presentation, restated in new terms the crux of figurative art, confronted the current Bergsonianism with a drastic fragmentation, and severed the links which had been long taken for granted between things and the percipient mind. One is almost tempted to say that it dealt a death-blow to the Euclidean mentality. The discontinuity it evidences does more than merely parallel the disintegration then taking place on the social plane. It takes into account "the dislocated, discordant, fragmentary state of man himself." Thus at the time when the problems set by extra-European mentalities were beginning to attract the attention of sociologists, Picasso looked towards the future and sensed instinctively all that was to be learnt from archaic or "primitive" cultures. By way of the work of art, a sort of linguistic, morphological and plastic anamnesis now joined issue with the traditional bourgeois ideology. This offensive was startlingly sudden, though premonitory hints of it were visible in the most recent developments of Cézannesque aesthetic, for example the schematization of landscape practised by Braque at L'Estaque in 1908, in which the elements of the scene are reduced to a subtle, lightly modulated complex of planes which are stripped of their normal density, weight and colors with a view to abridging their allusions to the world of appearances. For the figure (or object) contemplated by the artist to be treated as "a synthesis of all its appearances" (the words are Sartre's), it was enough that the triangle which acted as the picture's structural basis should be multiplied and presented as a sequence of* Abschattungen. *This is the method adopted by Picasso in his* Accordionist *(1911), peak-point of the middle period of Cubism. But each phase of this process called for new discoveries, and here Juan Gris's contribution was decisive. In the* Smoker *we have the end-product of a long series of experiments. It marks, after several years of near-monochromy, the return to vivid, highkeyed color and the technique of painting in flat areas of local color replaces that of scattered touches and diffused tones. It stressed the rigidity of the plane, hitherto undulating and transparent. But already, in 1915, there was the threat of return to orthodoxy (e.g. the* Man with a Pipe*). So as to avert this Picasso took to employing dappled, rectangular planes, superimposed or interlocking. In proportion to the greater or lesser number of values they contain, they tend to repel each other, thus giving rise to a space in which no entire volumes are located and to which only fragmentary units—symbols of the social and psychic disruption of the age—have access.*

GEORGES BRAQUE (1882-1963). LANDSCAPE, 1908. KUNSTMUSEUM, BASEL. RAOUL LA ROCHE DONATION.

PABLO PICASSO (1881). ACCORDIONIST (PIERROT), 1911. THE SOLOMON R. GUGGENHEIM MUSEUM COLLECTION, NEW YORK.

PABLO PICASSO (1881). MAN WITH A PIPE, 1915. COURTESY OF THE ART INSTITUTE OF CHICAGO. GIFT OF MRS LEIGH B. BLOCK.

JACQUES LIPCHITZ (1891). STANDING WOMAN, 1918-1919. STONE. KUNSTMUSEUM, BASEL. RAOUL LA ROCHE DONATION.

JUAN GRIS (1887-1927). SMOKER, 1913. COLLECTION MR AND MRS ARMAND P. BARTOS, NEW YORK.

HENRI LAURENS (1885-1954). WOOD CONSTRUCTION, 1919. MAURICE RAYNAL COLLECTION, PARIS.

DYNAMISM AND DURATION

Although the Expressionists *appeared* to reject direct experience in order to reveal the dimensions of the world within, their images were nevertheless affected by contacts with tangible reality. Moreover, in their attempts to solve the equation between being and becoming, they clung to the Bergsonian notion of perspectival, three-dimensional space—which at least partly explains why by and large their art kept to the procedures of classical tradition. All the same they displayed some bold innovations in their handling of these procedures, notable being their introduction of the time factor, in the form of speed. These images already carried intimations of the emancipation which was to transform them, after the Second World War, into instruments for communicating a dramatic lyricism of a new order, pointing the way to action painting.

All expressionist painting teems with contradictions; this was probably inevitable, given its content. Not the least is the vehemence with which it reveals certain fundamental aspects of the contemporary sensibility—and this although the movement originated in a rejection of everyday life and had the air of a revolt against the tyranny of the machine and all-pervasive mechanization. This ambivalence led to affective and emotional reactions; hence the fleeting glimpses, unstable perspectives, unsure directions, spatial anomalies and telescopings distinctive of the major works of Kirchner, Schmidt-Rottluff, Heckel, Grosz and Campendonck. In such works Bergsonian duration is immersed in the "nerve-racking time" (Enrico Castelli) which dominates the life of man when he is reduced to performing "splintered tasks," condemned to "working in fragments" (Friedmann), because these activities have become a *sine qua non* of his existence. Here we have a language indirectly due to mechanization, the fervid revelation of a dynamic inner life experienced but never explicitly stated. This led up to the discovery of a sociological reality, that of the spirit of "anti-machinism," in which Emmanuel

Mounier has rightly discerned the influence of a widespread, instinctual drive—that reaction against a machine-made world which led a certain school of writers, from Carlyle to Gina Lombroso, from Ruskin to Georges Bernanos, to voice an oblique protest against the scheme of things.

Paul Garnier was probably right when he said that life becomes violent only when it is struggling against death. When it merely takes the world just as it finds it, it stands for an acceptation of things as they are, an adventure in the domain of sentience and finds its satisfactions in the time through which it travels. Once the absurd has been ruled out, hope becomes feasible and the glorified present seems rich in promise for the future. This was the case with Walt Whitman when he said that personally he asked for nothing better or more godlike than real life; with Guillaume Apollinaire ("Let us extol life whatever form it happens to take"); Emile Verhaeren ("Future, my heart is uplifted by you as once it was by God"); Blaise Cendrars ("This morning is the first day of the world"); Alfred Jarry ("That man yonder is the first man of the future"); Marinetti ("We wish at all costs to break back into life"); Umberto Boccioni and Fernand Léger ("As for me, I can get all I need in the street"). Similarly in the works of Erik Satie and Arthur Honegger we find a commitment to real life and a passion for its sights and sounds. All these ideas stemmed from the same mode of sensibility, the same historic situation, and counteracted the Romantic attitude which was beginning to threaten culture because it barred the way to recognition of the new realities.

These new realities were driving-shafts, pistons, gear-boxes, streetcars, the screech of axles and the blare of hooters. They were semaphores, "speed-mad locomotives," "rocketing telegraph-poles." They were international expresses, jazz, the foxtrot, high-tension pylons, traffic lights, hydraulic lifts and gramophones, assembly lines, endless streams of automobiles, flickering images on cinema screens, airplanes, typewriters, traction engines, children's kaleidoscopes, hurrying crowds, hurricanes of dust, a plethora of publicity and newsreels, "a never-ending din of crazy wheels sounding along the byways of the sky" (Blaise Cendrars).

Frantic speed, incessant shocks for eyes and ears, syncopated rhythms—here was an entirely new experience of mobility, of change and flux, imposed on the human sensibility by the mechanized environment in which man now was living. It could only be made assimilable by a more or less complete transformation of his perceptive equipment and by a feat of mental adaptation enabling him to maintain a precarious balance between all the diverse modes and incentives of thought and action. "We must prepare ourselves for the approaching and inevitable identification of man with the machine," wrote Marinetti in 1911, "by facilitating and perfecting an endless give-and-take between metallic intuitions, rhythms, instincts and disciplines of which most people are as yet quite unaware, and which only a few extra-lucid spirits have divined."

For the construction of duration by means of rhythms can be achieved only after a hard training in a special way of seeing and in terms of a sort of Bergsonian "reduction" which, as Merleau-Ponty has suggested, "tends to reappraise all things *sub specie durationis*." It was certainly not due to chance that, at the beginning of this century, Rainer Maria Rilke took to using the expression "learn to see."

The opening paragraphs of the *Notebooks of Malte Laurids Brigge* (written in Paris in 1904) record the birth of this awareness of a modification of the space-time relation. "Trams run clanging through my room. Motorcars race across my body. A door slams. Somewhere, a window-pane is smashed. The glass clatters down and I hear the loud guffaws of the big pieces, the tiny tinkle of the splinters. Then suddenly a low, dull sound comes from the other side, from within the house. Someone is on his way up the stairs. Coming nearer, steadily nearer. Is there, stays there, passes on. And then the street again. A woman cries, 'Do shut up! I've had enough of it.' The electric streetcar rushes by with a loud to-do, passes over them, submerges everything. Someone shouts. People are running helter-skelter. A dog barks. What a relief! A dog."

The passage is revealing, for this insistence on the actuality of the outside world shows how simultaneous impressions make themselves felt at the point of intersection of time and space and thus have much to tell us about the constant onslaughts of the machine world on our sensibility. Here there are striking analogies with the then new world of the cinema which was in process of inventing new ways of giving expression to its own kind of poetry. Méliès, for instance, had already used dissolvings, fade-outs, superimpositions, alternating planes and "traveling" in *La caverne maudite* and *Pygmalion et Galatée* (1898). And the Italian Futurist painters seem to have based many of the seeming paradoxes in their 1910 manifesto on an adaptation of these same "magic" procedures, stepped down to a lower key. "Our bodies become part of the sofa we are sitting on. And the sofa grows into ourselves. The bus charges into the houses as it hurtles past them, and the houses in turn rush at the bus and seep into it" (Marinetti).

Both the cinema and Futurism owed much to the dynamic aesthetic of metamorphosis that was coming into vogue at the same time as quantum theory was developing the idea that change is a corollary of movement. When objects break loose from the static vision and refuse to be segregated by the eye of the beholder, they lose their objective individuality. Their forms and aspects change, they break up or dissolve. Mobility, speed, vibrations, fluidity, translucence—all these new values could be registered only by an instrument of perception adjusted to the technique of "mobile vision." "Time flies and all things flow"—thus Bergson. Balla, Boccioni, Carrà, Russolo, Severini, Marinetti agreed that "everything is moving, hurrying on, being rapidly transformed." The outlines of the things we see are never stationary, but constantly appearing and disappearing. Given the persistence of the retinal image, moving objects become multiplied and their shapes change as they follow each other, in streams and eddies of vibrations, through the space they traverse.

The Futurists defined their aims as follows. "We wish to reproduce on canvas happenings that are no longer 'arrested moments' of the universal dynamism. Rather, they must convey the sensation of that dynamism in its pure state. It is high time to jettison the outworn themes and give expression to the tumult of this age of steel and feverish speed" (Marinetti). Likewise in Fernand Léger's art the metamorphoses of the object are closely bound up with the increasing usage of a mobile viewpoint. "The creative activity of the present-day artist is at once more condensed and more complex than it was in previous centuries. Images are less static, objects less fully and clearly defined than in the past. A landscape seen from a motorcar or a fast train loses in descriptive value but gains in synthetic value. The ordinary look of things changes when, traveling at high speed, we see them through a train window or a windscreen. Modern man registers far more impressions than did the artists of the eighteenth century, with the result that the language of modern art is full of diminutives and abbreviations." This means that ways of seeing and feeling, thinking and acting, making and creating, are always conditioned by an aggregate of stimuli projected by what Focillon calls "the formal frame of reference imposed on the artist." (This way of putting it is more dynamic than the notion of "environment" which Dewey and Lewis Mumford brought into fashion.)

In the physical and mental milieu of the twentieth century we are constantly forced to experience movement, or anyhow the presence of things in motion. For, as Merleau-Ponty has pointed out, "movement does not necessarily presuppose a 'mobile,' that is to say an object definable as an *ensemble* of predetermined properties." For movement all that is needed is "an element that moves," or at most "something colored or luminous" giving an effect of mobility.

It was a foregone conclusion that artists would now come to treat data of everyday sensory experience as a prime factor of their compositions, so as to furnish man with "models" helping him both to understand the significance of the visible world and by the same token to come to a better understanding of himself. Yet it was impossible to abandon, then and there, all the ancient categories on which art had so long relied. The new art had to content itself with loosening up the immobility of structural forms so as to render them translucent and amenable to the metamorphoses imposed by time.

THE SPACE-TIME DIMENSION

It has now become impossible to make the clear-cut distinctions between identity and difference, sequence and simultaneity, space and time, that were taken for granted until quite recently. At the turn of the century, Von Ehrenfels and Georg Cantor pointed out the lines on which indivisible wholes should be envisaged. Similarly, a day may well come when history, too, will cease dividing art into watertight compartments, trends and phases. Then perhaps we shall see the frontiers hitherto assigned to certain art "movements"—Fauvism, Expressionism, Cubism, Dada, Surrealism, Constructivism and the rest—merging into a continuous line of development, a single phenomenon comprising several active nuclei. Viewed thus, the art of our epoch will prove to be a conjuncture of events rather than a sequence in time of local, national or "nationalized" art movements. Their individual names will lose significance and they will be regarded as component parts of an organic, all-inclusive whole. Once assigned its own duration, this whole will prove to be a self-complete achievement and, what is more, a singularly momentous period in the history of world art. Momentous because it witnessed an effort to disintegrate a complex of outworn relations (felt as irrelevant to present needs), to break down accepted categories, to dispense with set rules of quantity and measurement, and to make the plunge from the known to the unknown, from stability to instability, from the conscious to the unconscious, from immobility to movement, from the visible world to a world invisible. This change of approach is all the more significant since, from Delaunay to Pollock, from Archipenko to Calder, from Sant'Elia to Le Corbusier, the new developments derived from, and revealed, an intuitive understanding of the vitally important researches which were then being conducted, on parallel lines, by physicists and mathematicians, taking as their point of departure Einstein's epoch-making theory of the indivisibility of time and space.

This recognition of the oneness of time and space involved an abandonment of the old notion of absolute time and the classical "co-ordinates of inertia," and thus *ipso facto* assimilated time to a fourth dimension: the movement dimension. The discovery of the space-time continuum (whose formula Hermann Minkowski had worked out in 1908) completely modified the conception of the universe that had prevailed throughout the western world since the Renaissance. Based on Aristotle's Categories and Euclidean geometry, that conception posited a world having a static conformation and measurable in terms of numbers. "From now on," Minkowski declared, "space and time, conceived separately, are mere phantoms; only a combination of the two can equate reality." Starting out from premises furnished by pure science, a tendency developed in all twentieth-century thought to envisage time in terms of space. Today there is not a single problem, biological, psychological, sociological or philosophic, which is not studied in the light of discoveries made in the realm of pure physics. Since the beginning of the century we find that almost every change that has taken place in literature, the fine arts and music has been effected to some extent by this new concept, the "spatialization of time."

No doubt, as Bergson recognized, the existence of a fourth dimension had always been taken for granted, if inexplicitly, both in science and in the language of the creative arts, and the incorporation of time in the latter does not give the impression of a new departure. The five-legged Assyrian bull anticipates the Futurist figurations of rapid movement and Egyptian offering-bearers advance to the same slow rhythm as the Apsara dancers. Yet rhythm is bound up with numbers and, consequently, measure, whereas measurement has no place in time viewed as a dimension. Time, here, becomes intensity, an integrated, non-measurable magnitude. In this context we would draw attention to the extreme importance of the experiments begun by Robert Delaunay in 1906, which led him in 1911-1912 to create an art of movement in its pure state: colored "phrases" functioning in undifferentiated space. Here, instead of objective time, we have a time that is integral and transparent. This step towards the dissolution of classical, three-dimensional space was an innovation with far-reaching consequences. It is in the works of Delaunay and in the experimental art of the Czech Frans Kupka and two Americans, Stanton Macdonald Wright and Morgan Russell, that we see what is in effect the first deliberate incorporation of the space-time dimension in the plastic arts. And this introduction of integral time into the rendering of space marks the starting point of a dynamic, non-perspectival treatment of the data of visual experience. Delaunay's *Simultaneous Disks* have the same dialectic and experimental value for twentieth-century art that Uccello's battle pieces had for Quattrocento art. It was as daring an act for Uccello to tamper with nature and translate it into analogized figurations, as it was to probe reality and to suggest it by means of "latent analogies." This is why the transition from a perspectival to an aperspectival world has given rise to as many tentative interpretations as in an earlier age the transition from a two-dimensional world to a putatively three-dimensional one. When we remember that even Vasari could still believe in 1568 that Uccello "wasted his time on marquetry-work," we need not be surprised if the mentality of our generation is not yet sufficiently attuned to the notion of a fourth dimension for it to be incorporated in our culture. There are still many who, as did Apollinaire, see in the space-time dimension a figment of the imagination. A day perhaps will come when it is recognized that the theories of Einstein and Bergson, allegedly incompatible, have found common ground in art.

Preliminary to the great discoveries that have thrown new light on the meaning of the world we live in was a specific change of sensibility. Before the space-time concept reached the speculative zone of philosophy, art and science, it had obscurely germinated at a lower level, that of the "collective unconscious." The progress of mechanization, the increasing strain of daily life, the new mobility of labor and even working conditions forced men to take stock of and to ponder on the problem of movement under all its aspects. For, once mechanization had begun to permeate the social system (in the second half of the nineteenth century), a need was felt to detect and analyse the elements of movement, to chart its phases and to isolate fragments of time in images; in other words, to translate into a visual language the successive moments of a phenomenon which by its very nature participates both in space and time. This was a departure of prime importance since, aside from its technical and social corollaries, it opened up possibilities of enriching the raw material of art and prepared the way for the invention of new means of expression.

Pace Jean Cocteau, Degas was no "victim" of photography. It would be truer to say that the snapshot did much to quicken the keen and (for the time) novel interest which he—like Constantin Guys and Toulouse-Lautrec—took in recording fleeting gestures, attitudes in process of taking form. A snapshot is the crystallization of a passing moment, petrified sign of an instant of becoming. And it could be startling enough to affect the artist's sensibility and radically to alter his way of seeing. It opened a path from the visible to the invisible, to the hard core of *reality* in the flux of appearances. Géricault's race-horses give a "simulation" of galloping, but Degas's horses, as Bergson pointed out, reveal the "real thing." Nor was it due to chance that scientific research was now directed to the problem of the "reproduction" of movement. It was by analysing the flight of birds, the motions of trotting and walking horses, that in 1882 a French physiologist Jules-Etienne Marey discovered the technique of the motion picture. Following up Lissajous's curious "swinging figures" (1847), Marey's "chronophotographs" aligned on a mobile film inaugurated the representation of movement in time and space. In 1890 Ehrenfels set forth his theory of form, demonstrating that movements in so far as they are visual data have *Gestaltqualitäten*. Meanwhile Eadweard Muybridge was carrying out research work in California on the same lines.

It was left to a disciple of Taylor, Frank B. Gilbreth, to perfect a complete visual record of movement; this was a by-product of his methodical study of the "economy of labor" with a view to eliminating useless or misdirected efforts and all unnecessary gestures. His "chronocyclograph" recorded movements as luminous curves and spirals, that is to say in abstract terms, isolated from the objects in motion. The models in wire which he used to illustrate his discoveries tended to prove that movement in its pure state could be an object of expression—and they would certainly have delighted Moholy-Nagy, Gabo and Pevsner. The day was to come when Picasso authorized the photographic reproduction of the illuminated and illuminating trajectory of his creative gesture. And the next step was to make sound *visible*, and enable us to *see* the waves of which it is composed; this too helped to an understanding of the dynamic factor operative in our perceptions.

It matters little whether or not Marcel Duchamp was aware of the discoveries of Marey, Muybridge and Gilbreth, had seen the films of Méliès, Griffith and Abel Gance, Boccioni's and Russolo's "arpeggios," and the animated cartoons made by Emile Courtet for his curious *Fantasmagorie* (deriving from techniques employed by Ducos in 1864), which blazed the trail for Fleischer, Pat Sullivan and Walt Disney. What is important for us here is that Duchamp's famous *Nude descending a Staircase* (1912) made its appearance at the right moment, translating as it did into analogical symbols the affective stimuli and motor automatisms called into play by the kinetic background of the period. For it symbolized a prevailing mode of sensibility and—what is still more significant—those "unstable attitudes in suspense between a Before and an After" which Edgerton's "stroboscope" was soon to make perceptible. Duchamp activated Cubism by the introduction of a dynamic element and effectively synthesized the phases of movement which the Futurists had dealt with summarily and had, so to say, left floating on the surface of their compositions. Guided by a sure instinct, he inserted into the space-time continuum a vital movement, a human quality which was lacking in Delaunay's over-schematized creations and which reappears in the brilliant rhythmic mimetism of Honegger's *Rugby*. Indeed Honegger's music may be said to be the sound equivalent of Duchamp's cataracts of movement. For in both works the space-time dimension equates a dimension of action. Some conception of the same kind forms a link, more direct than is generally supposed, between the theory of "cinematics" exploited by Fernand Léger in 1911-1912, Franz Marc's "super-impressions" (1912-1913), Kandinsky's "improvisations" (1911-1912), Larionov's "Rayonism" (1911-1914) and John Marin's "cataclysms" (1922). In all alike the desire

to break with the traditional repertoire of significants leads to a dramatization of form and color, a short-hand record, as it were, of the fluctuations of a reality constantly in motion within diaphanous, continuous space. But it was Paul Klee who excelled all others in the subtlety, profundity and, we may add, the fervor with which he transmuted the time dimension into spatial values. Klee (who had once been Einstein's neighbor at Bern) realized better than any that mass-society man has stepped down from the pinnacle to which the Renaissance had exalted him and from which he proudly contemplated the passing shows of life, its perturbations and its oases of calm. Man had become "a point in the cosmos," a mobile unit subject to the law of the relativity of movement. To Klee's thinking the artist has to place himself at a point which is for him, at the moment, "the organic center of all movement in space and time." A man pacing the deck of a steamship at night is conscious of (*a*) his own movement, (*b*) the movement of the ship, (*c*) the direction and speed of the oceanic currents, (*d*) the rotation of the earth, (*e*) its trajectory, (*f*) the trajectories of the moon and stars above him. The result, then, will be a complex of movements in the universe, whose central point is now the "I" on board the ship. This being so, and movement being a prime condition of the cosmos, movement must be basic to a work of art, and the work of art is itself in continuous movement. For, as Klee observes, the space-time continuum comes into play the moment a point moves and becomes a line. Similarly a surface results from movements of a line, a volume from displacements of a surface, and a circle from the rotatory movement of a suspended weight. These considerations bring us back to the origins of the natural world, and the development in time of the process of creative evolution, hidden in the mists of the past, can best be brought to light through the medium of art. Hence an increasing recourse to tenuous, almost furtive signs, to a wavering, unstable line, translucencies and tracts of iridescent light: an interplay of the forces and tensions that figure forth the transition from the significant to the signified, from the level of expression to that of content. This content is determined by all the psychological and scientific conceptions which, entering into the currency of contemporary thought, have largely done away with the boundaries fixed by Lessing between "the arts of time" and "the arts of space."

MARCEL DUCHAMP (1887). NUDE DESCENDING A STAIRCASE, NO. 2, 1912.
PHILADELPHIA MUSEUM OF ART, THE LOUISE AND WALTER ARENSBERG COLLECTION.

AN INTERPLAY OF TENSIONS

While for some three or four years Moscow had been the meeting-place of the revolutionary trends of western art, the International Exhibition of Modern Art (better known as "The Armory Show") in 1913 was an event of capital importance. On view first in New York, then in Chicago and Boston, it brought to a land which was already highly industrialized, but was only just beginning to acclimatize Impressionism, the revelation of a vanguard European art basically oriented by the directives of a technological civilization. In the evolution of taste and culture the Armory Show has as great a significance as, in political history, the entry of the United States into the First World War in 1917. The general outcry against the "Show" was followed, paradoxically enough, by the purchase of no less than three hundred and fifty works, the development of a national school of painting and the creation, at the height of the depression, of the Museum of Modern Art (1929).

It was around Nude descending a Staircase *that the battle raged. Midway between expressionist introversion and futurist extraversion, this picture directly links up with Cubism: here the active values are integrated into a stable, "classical" system, based nonetheless on latent movement. All the components of an identical reality are brought into play and interlock within a schematic duration in which chromatic and linear nuances subtly combine the mechanics of movement with the pure translucency of a state of tenuous vibration, and both alike incorporate experienced time into the fabric of an obsessive dream.*

The Futurists' sensorial response to the dynamic elements of the world around them was less arbitrary, and in a sense more factual. Severini's Blue Dancer *expresses rather than signifies the "plastic analogies of dynamism." The active give-and-take between the object and its environment is sophisticated, not to say impaired, by a conflict between a pointillist visual technique and a calculated fragmentation deriving from Cubism.*

We see more of the romantic side of Futurism in Boccioni's art. In the body in violent movement of his bronze Discus-thrower *(an embodiment of twentieth-century speed), the painter-sculptor sought to figure forth "the unique form of his (the figure's) continuity in space." Here a spiral fringed with flame and setting up a chain reaction of bulges and depressions introduces into sculpture topological allusions and the figure produces, symbolically, the effect of the developments in time of a prolonged athletic exercise. Delaunay and Picabia, Léger and Malevich proceeded on similar lines and, charged with the tensions of active movement, their works have a cinematic quality based on a simultaneous apprehension of a kinetic sequence. This art, in fact, gives actuality to Aristotle's dictum that "time is the quotient of movement."*

GINO SEVERINI (1883). BLUE DANCER, 1912. DR GIANNI MATTIOLI COLLECTION, MILAN.

UMBERTO BOCCIONI (1882-1916). UNIQUE FORM OF CONTINUITY IN SPACE, 1913. BRONZE.
CIVICA GALLERIA D'ARTE MODERNA, MILAN.

KASIMIR MALEVICH (1878-1935). WOMAN WITH WATER PAILS: DYNAMIC ARRANGEMENT, 1912.
THE MUSEUM OF MODERN ART, NEW YORK.

FRANCIS PICABIA (1879-1953). DANCES AT THE SPRING, 1912. PHILADELPHIA MUSEUM OF ART,
THE LOUISE AND WALTER ARENSBERG COLLECTION.

FERNAND LÉGER (1881-1955). WOMAN IN BLUE (SECOND STATE), 1912. KUNSTMUSEUM, BASEL.

ROBERT DELAUNAY (1885-1941). THE EIFFEL TOWER, 1910. THE SOLOMON R. GUGGENHEIM MUSEUM COLLECTION, NEW YORK.

4

VISION IN MOTION

Recent researches into the psychology of form have brought to light a faculty we have of discerning tensions or movements in unmoving constructs, in virtue of a "kinetic sense" of biological origin. This accounts for the existence, through the ages, of a visual intuition which conjures up images of movement, though the figuration itself contains no mobile elements. Thanks to this intuitive sense of movement, the idea of rhythm, primordially bound up with the dance—a total manifestation of man's *Dasein*, unconditioned by the historical process—has come to be as currently (and paradoxically) associated in the West with static art as the idea of depth with art in two dimensions.

Actually it was not until the beginning of the present century that, in a sufficiently developed scientific, technical and philosophic context, movement-in-itself was given a place in the vision of the creative artist. This was a phenomenon of no less importance than the contemporary discovery of the subconscious. Both played a vital part in the changes that now came over methods of expression and, separately or conjointly, provided art with a potential dimension capable of absorbing, or neutralizing, the accepted mystique of two or three dimensions.

It was in the 1920s that movement was given a place in the "physics" of creative art, and *ipso facto*

3).

HAUS, 1927.

3).

HAUS, 1927.

MARCEL DUCHAMP (1887).
ROTORELIEFS, OPTICAL DISKS, 1935.
COVER OF "MINOTAURE," NO. 6, WINTER 1935.

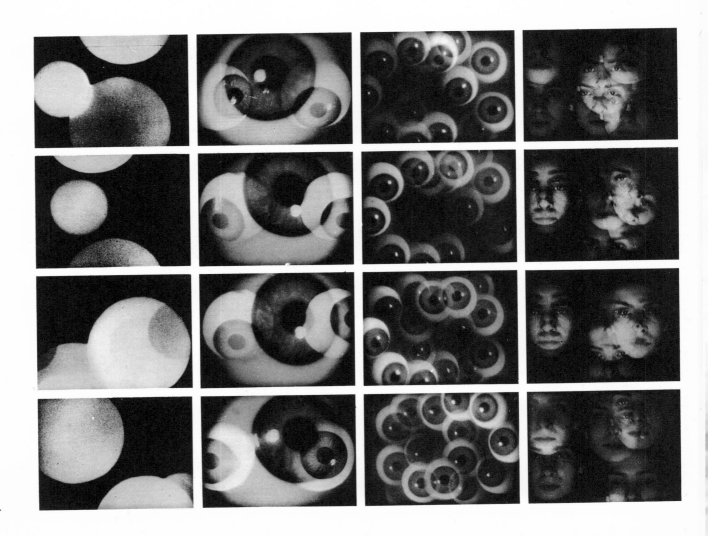

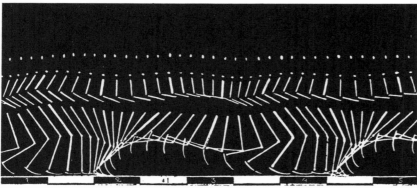

JULES-ETIENNE MAREY (1830-1904).
STUDY OF A MAN WALKING.
FROM THE MAGAZINE "LA NATURE" OF SEPTEMBER 29, 1883.

OSKAR SCHLEMMER (1888-19
DANCE OF CIRCLES.
EXPERIMENTAL THEATER OF THE BAU

UMBERTO BOCCIONI (1882-1916).
DRAWING AFTER "STATES OF MIND: THOSE WHO STAY," 1912.
COLLECTION OF MR AND MRS HERBERT M. ROTHSCHILD, NEW YORK.

HANS RICHTER (1888). FILM STUDY, 19

liberated the visual imagination from the old régime of purely rhythmical construction. It provided a new approach to the data of perception matching up to the vision of a period marked by a feverish desire for mobility, activity and speed. As defined by Moholy-Nagy, the concept of "vision in motion" stands for an attempt to relate and synthesize a host of social and technological phenomena simultaneously apprehended by the seeing eye and the sentient mind. It means seeing things in their relations to each other, no longer as isolated units, and promptly integrating simple elements and structures into a coherent whole. And it also means imaging objects in movement or as they appear when one is oneself in more or less rapid movement. This latter implies that the perception of objects varies with the speed at which the observer moves if the object is a stationary one, and with the speed of the object if the observer does not move. "Photography and the cinema," as Moholy-Nagy points out, "automatically recorded the changes of appearance due to speed, and anticipated the 'vision in motion' of a motorized world, long before there was any idea of the need for a re-education of our way of seeing." "Vision in motion," then, is the means *par excellence* of assimilating the space-time dimension and, as a result, of dispensing with the perspectival myth and evoking new forms which, generated as they are by mobile signs, entail an abolition of the traditional significants of the language of art. In other words, the new art assigns a functional value to mobility. An aesthetic is taking form which integrates the seemingly incompatible values of duration, change, simultaneity and succession, and the spectator is asked to share in the making of the work, to assimilate and absorb the optical substance of a scene in constant process of becoming.

Under the influence of accelerated means of transport and the motion picture, movement, for the first time in history, established a factual and cultural link between man and the machine, and thereby acquired an anthropological dimension. A mechanic art *par excellence*, that of the cinema was an end-product of the elaborate investigations of Jules-Etienne Marey into the component parts of movement. "It is today the only art that can represent with any degree of concreteness the emergent world-view that differentiates our culture from every preceding one... Utilizing our daily experience of motion in the railroad train and the motor car, the motion picture re-creates in symbolic form a world that is otherwise beyond our direct perception or grasp... This is no small triumph in cultural assimilation... It is an unfortunate social accident— as has happened in so many departments of technics —that this art should have been grossly diverted from its proper function by the commercial necessity for creating sentimental shows for an emotionally empty metropolitanized population, living vicariously on the kisses and cocktails and crimes and orgies and murders of their shadow-idols. For the motion picture symbolizes and expresses, better than do any of the traditional arts, our modern world picture and the essential conceptions of time and space which are already part of the unformulated experience of millions of people, to whom Einstein or Bohr or Bergson or Alexander are scarcely even names" (Lewis Mumford). The "linguistic" canon of the cinema and its specific vision differentiate it sharply from the arts of previous ages. True, according to a theory formulated first by Ragghianti and championed, notably, by Francastel, Agel and Léglise, traces can be found in literature, from Virgil to Mallarmé of "pre-filmic" texts—texts, that is to say, which seem to hint at a cinematographic way of seeing; but these are no more than analogies and in no sense precedents. In this context, mention may be made of the notable contribution of Diaghilev who, inspired by the example of Paul Fort and Lugné-Poe, offered painters a field of experimental action favorable to the emergence of a painting-in-motion. Nonetheless there is no question that it was the art of the cinema that provided the twentieth century with a backdrop for that "vision in motion" which now engrossed the attention of a group of vanguard artists. We must not underrate the stimulus given by the cinema to the kinetic perception of the Cubists, and the part it played in shaping the "activist" art of the Futurists (Boccioni's *States of Mind*) and Marcel Duchamp's dissections. Here we have anticipations of the conceptions which in the 1920s led to the production of works of art that actually moved; Duchamp's first rotoreliefs led up to the mobiles of Calder (1931), Moholy-Nagy (1930) and Bruno Munari (1933), while the light effects invented by Appia and Schlemmer incorporated signs of the machine age in stage performances and made of the actor a living symbol of the space-time dimension.

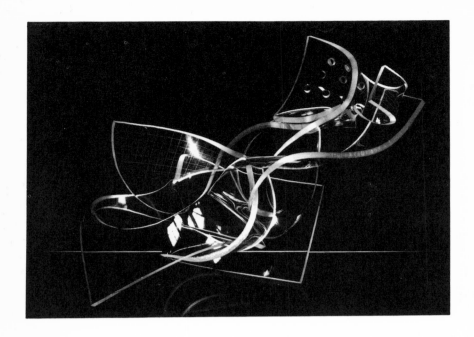

LASZLO MOHOLY-NAGY (1895-1946).
SPACE MODULATOR.
SCULPTURE IN PLEXIGLASS.
COLLECTION OF THE
DETROIT INSTITUTE OF ARTS.

HAROLD E. EDGERTON (1903).
SPLASH OF A DROP OF MILK
FALLING INTO A SAUCER OF MILK, 1936.
STROBOSCOPIC PHOTOGRAPH.
MASSACHUSETTS INSTITUTE OF TECHNOLOGY,
CAMBRIDGE, MASS.

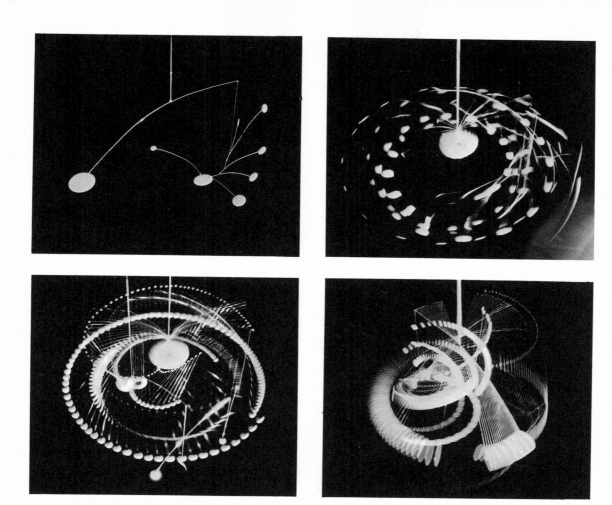

ALEXANDER CALDER (1898).
HANGING MOBILE, 1936. ALUMINUM AND STEEL WIRE.
MRS MARY CALLERY COLLECTION, PARIS.

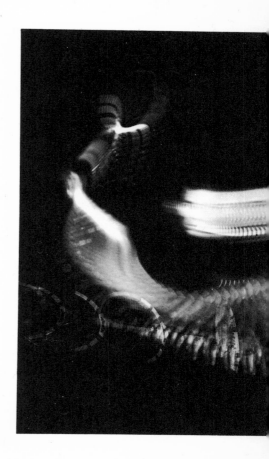

HAROLD E. EDGERTON (1903).
SWIRLS AND EDDIES OF A TENNIS STROKE, 1939.
STROBOSCOPIC PHOTOGRAPH.
MASSACHUSETTS INSTITUTE OF TECHNOLOGY,
CAMBRIDGE, MASS.

SIGNS, SIGNALS, SYMBOLS

Not enough attention has been given to the contacts and group periodicals which led to the deeply rooted affinities between the works of Eluard and Max Ernst, Matisse and Stravinsky, Cocteau and Picasso, Hans Richter and Busoni, Van Eesteren and Van Doesburg, Léger, Blaise Cendrars and many others. The fact that an avowed object of such movements as those promoted by *De Stijl* and *i 10* in Holland, *L'Esprit Nouveau* in France, and *7 Arts* in Belgium was to provide a sort of clearing-house, on the international level, between painters, sculptors, architects, composers, sociologists, philosophers and scientists, pointed to a new development in the history of culture, one which had nothing in common with the interdisciplinary relations that had prepared the way for humanism at the time of the Renaissance. Here we have a new departure based on a recognition of the common language, a sort of *lingua franca*, of a wide range of activities which, though *a priori* differing in kind, were committed to one and the same quest.

Why is it that we find the same problems coming to the fore, and on an unprecedented scale, in all parts of the world? Why are works being produced everywhere so much akin and conveying more or less equivalent messages, often transmitted by means of a quite novel order? It is, in our opinion, to the worldwide diffusion of mass media and to the great development of means of communication that we can assign the main reason for the contemporary trend towards a universalization of culture, intimations of which had been perceptible earlier in the century. True, the increasing use and constant enlargement of the field of action of the telephone, telegraph and radio, of written, spoken, printed and photographic vehicles of information and the general speeding up of means of transport—automobiles, planes, liners, railways—have suppressed distances and done away with isolation so effectively that our very existence *(Dasein)*, as Heidegger points out, has become "dilated" to such

an extent that we are now by way of becoming denizens of a world extending far beyond the world of our immediate surroundings. These changes in our means of communication have also led to the invention and proliferation of a host of signs, signals, symbols and abbreviations which have taken root in the mentality of present-day man, and often shaped the conduct of his life to the point of orienting the formation of certain forms of speech. In other words the conventional symbols of modern life—terrestrial, maritime or aerial, stable or mobile, permanent or intermittent, opaque or luminous, monochrome, bichrome or polychrome—which have been invented to serve practical ends, to regulate traffic, provide guidance where required and organize the reflexes of a mechanized civilization, have encouraged the invention of a system of pictorial signs which catch the eye and thus have a striking parallelism to the signs employed for strictly utilitarian ends. This is one of the reasons why in the first half of the twentieth century (before, that is to say, the coming of an audio-visual culture) technical appliances and their repercussions on literature and the arts did so much to stimulate the faculty of sight, a process that had begun as far back as the early seventeenth century.

Thus the need to act quickly, think quickly and to react no less quickly, has kept pace with the need to produce rapidly and to consume no less rapidly, and these exigencies have necessarily affected the manner of conceiving and executing works of art. Meanwhile, by way of compensation, the constraints of a mechanized way of life acted as a liberating factor since they furnished means of expressing the inner life in terms of simple, schematic units. Circles, disks, triangles, segments of curves, spirals, arrows, numbers, letters, zigzags, patches of color provided Klee, Kandinsky and Miró with the basic elements of an aesthetic which confided to "the imagination of the sign" a leading role in figuring forth both sensuous responses and the pleasures of the mind. Here we find "signals" with a conventional significance in practical life acquiring the value of aesthetic signs, the rational merging into the irrational, utilitarian functions merging into plastic functions, matter de-realized and the real dematerialized. The big capital letters—stock-in-trade of publicity—which figure in the compositions of Braque and Soffici, Gris and Léger, Picasso and Kubicki, Max Ernst and Malevich, Moholy-Nagy, Herbert Bayer, Raoul Hausmann and Kurt Schwitters, are stripped of their phonetic values, while Arabic numerals are similarly transmuted into pure visual entities. The language of sculpture is being transformed, even more profoundly, by a similar metabolism; from Brancusi to Pevsner, from Laurens to Gabo, we find sculptors, responsive to the spirit of their age and milieu, stripping signals of their logical, calculated values and replacing these with creations of the imagination at its purest, intent on "giving to see" (the expression is Paul Klee's) arresting forms, wholly or partially exempt from any representative function. This also goes to show that certain selected elements in his environment, otherwise uninspiring, could change the artist's way of seeing, react on his sensibility and lead him to counterbalance the processes of mechanic automatism by interventions of the active psyche. Challenging the bleak determinism that governs "the objective relations of exteriorized life," art calls into play signs that can give expression to spontaneous impulses of the inner self. Thus a "technocratic world" is not so completely "lost to freedom," as Bernanos thought. It seems to me more reasonable to believe, like Plekhanov, that "genius always makes its appearance at the place where the society that has prepared for its coming is ready to welcome it." Klee, Kandinsky, Arp, Baumeister and Lipchitz have as firm a foothold in art history as Picasso and Léger. And, viewed from this angle, their work is more "realistic" than is commonly supposed. It may also be regarded as an invaluable means of adapting the individual to our "electronic civilization" and bridging the gap between the world of man and that of the machine. By the same token it provides a connecting link between twentieth-century art and the worldwide adoption of stenography in business practice; a link no less operative than that between the system of "commercial" mathematics, which were introduced by Luca Pacioli in the fifteenth century, and our "classical" European art.

All this goes to show that the reduction of phenomena to the abstract concepts indispensable to science, theoretical and applied, need not involve a drying up of the artist's sensibility or restrain his flights of fancy. When Matisse said that "an artist cannot do no-matter-what; we are not masters of what we produce, it is imposed on us," he cited the determinist element only in order to emphasize the ultimate autonomy of the creative act. For constraint often evokes an urge to emancipation. And so oppressive was it in the period we are dealing with, that artists felt more than ever eager to assert their freedom and, with this in mind, to make a drastic revision of their techniques and adapt them to new-made codes of signs. Thus from the beginning of the century we find a tendency developing to seek for fresh, striking and spontaneous equivalents of ready-made ideas. Along with this a change came over the artist's attitude towards his "subject"; he was now led to attach a semantic (no longer ontological) value to the concept of beauty, and, on another plane, to try to release the technological mentality then in the ascendant from the drab conformity that threatened it. Yet, while covering all the rich variety of life, this new régime of signs seems to us to have led to a restriction and impoverishment of the "semantic field" invaded as it now was by a host of inflexible, functional signals.

Once the language of art was no longer directed to "re-presenting" the world but to "presenting" it, its freedom seemed boundless. An aesthetic of *analogia* opened up possibilities of invention which had been ruled out by the doctrine of mimesis. For in the absence of any objective, mythical, symbolic or religious criterion, analogy can justify the usage as a model of the activity of the creator—assuming that, following the Aristotelian tradition, we are to regard mimesis as relating exclusively to some clearly defined, specific object. Actually, however, following up, it would seem, a possibility sensed intuitively by Van Gogh, Paul Klee has shown that a mimesis of the imaginary can exist when art "goes beyond the object" and "imitates the forces which created and are still creating the world." Let us, then, briefly examine the path which Klee advises us to follow when, relying solely on pictorial signs, we seek to attain both "a deeper understanding of things" and an intuitive insight into "the world beyond the world."

"Breaking away from the dead center (point), we make our first move (line). After a while comes a pause to draw breath (broken or, after several pauses, articulated line). A backward glance to see how far we have come (counter-movement). Weigh the pros and cons of paths in several directions (cluster of lines). A river lies in the way, so we take a boat (wave movement). Upstream there may have been a bridge (series of arches). On the other side we meet a like-minded traveler, also bound for the land of deeper understanding. At first we are joyfully united (convergence), then gradually differences arise (divergence). We cut across a plowed field (planes crisscrossed by lines), then through dense woods. He loses his way, looks around and even goes through the stock movements of a running dog. I too am beginning to feel some qualms. Another river looms up, shrouded in fog (spatial element). But soon the weather clears. We meet some basket-makers on their way home in their cart (the wheel). One of their children has the funniest curls (spiral movement). Later it gets sultry and night comes on (spatial element). A flash of lightning on the horizon (zigzag line), though the stars are still twinkling overhead (scattered points)... Even so short a journey is very eventful. Lines of all kinds, dabs, dots. Smooth surfaces, hatched and dotted surfaces. Wave movement, delayed and articulated movement, counter-movement. Crisscrossing, interweaving. Walls scaling away. Monody, polyphony. Lines dying out or gathering strength (dynamics). The happy, even pace of the first leg of our journey; then come the obstacles." Thus, as Kandinsky said, "the true work of art is born of the artist. It breaks loose from him, acquires a life of its own, becomes an independent being, a living, breathing reality, a *creature* in its own right. Here any speculation as to whether it 'respects' a form deriving from the outside world is beside the mark." What matters is to assign to the artist "not only the right but the duty of handling forms in the way which he deems needful for his purpose." This implies "a total, unlimited freedom as regards the means employed," provided this freedom "is based on that inner compulsion which goes by the name of honesty." The *means* Kandinsky speaks of here fall into the same category as the *signs* described by Klee.

But, it may be asked, why are both artists so intent on codifying them? Why be at such pains to compile an inventory of these signs in which they are "listed and defined like the words of a language" (Kandinsky)? When Klee and Kandinsky undertook this task, it was not regarded by them as in any sense basic to their pedagogic function; the lectures they delivered at the Bauhaus in the 1920s were intended solely to meet the need for making the purport of their discoveries comprehensible to the younger generation. Thus Klee's *Pedagogical Sketchbook* (1925) and Kandinsky's essay *From Point and Line to Surface* (1926), along with Kandinsky's *On the Spiritual in Art* (1912) and Klee's *On Modern Art* (1924, published in 1945), should be regarded as contemporary equivalents of what the writings of Luca Pacioli, Jean Pélerin Viator, Alberti, Dürer and Leonardo were for the Renaissance; each group of works made known to the public of its day the origins of a *language*.

Are we justified in assigning to art the status of a language? According to linguistic specialists the term covers every system of signs capable of serving as a means of communication, and "communication" means emitting and receiving messages. The language we speak was devised with a view to conveying messages, in other words information. That, too, is the function of road warnings, railroad signals, buoys and so forth. And on the face of it does not the work of art do exactly the same thing? Yet we somehow feel that a plastic, especially a *pictorial* language can and must be differentiated from a *spoken* language. This fundamental problem, situated at the intersection of linguistics and semeiology, can perhaps be solved by relating it to a recent (1949) discovery. André Martinet has pointed out that, regarded as a system of signs *(semata)*, a spoken language is *articulated twice*. The first "articulation" gives words; thus taking the phrase *la flamme est faible* (the flame is weak) as an example, he notes that it consists of four words (linguistic signs), i.e. four significant units, morphemes, which the voice pronounces one by one. A second "articulation" leads to the breaking up of each word into a series of phonemes, non-significant units. (Thus the word *la* contains two phonemes $1 + a$, and *faible* five, f-ai-b-l-e).

The question next arises whether, among the various methods of communicating by signs, languages are the only cases where this "double articulation" is feasible and permits of the separation of significant from signified, vehicle from content, form from expression. Can the dot or point, used by Klee and Kandinsky as the primal unit of their plastic language, be assimilated, for example, to the letter B, a non-significant, purely mental unit of human language? Certainly not; once it is given form on a support it becomes a physical entity, having thickness and color (indeed bicolor, since it exists in virtue of both the color of the support and its own—unless, exceptionally, it becomes simply bidimensional, as is the case with Ben Nicholson's white dot on a white ground). Here the sign is self-sufficient, and apprehended as a sensorial reality. The signifying-signified factor is impossible to split in two as is the form-substance element. And when the letter B is included in a composition by Braque or Schwitters it loses *ipso facto* its non-significant character, quits the linguistic domain to which it "properly" belongs and acquires, in the plastic domain, the properties of the signifying-signified dyad.

Enlarged, the dot becomes a line or patch, impervious (in both cases) to analytic fragmentation. Each is *per se* an image denoting, at first sight anyhow, nothing except itself. Why, then, should a red patch in pictures by Klee, Kandinsky and Miró mean something quite different in each case? This is a result, for one thing, of the structural context, the proximity of the sign in question to other signs. It is also due to the psychological element, the affective content that has always been implicit both in certain forms (a right angle—tension, a curve—*détente*) and also in certain colors (red—tension, green—*détente*). And finally, it depends on the way in which an artist handles his brush or pen for outlining a form, laying in his color or bringing to birth in a flash of inspiration a colored sign. For basic to graphology is the connection between handwriting and character, a man's sensibility, his mode of being or, as Watson and Pavlov would say, his behavior. This explains how it is that the sign becomes symbolic and art may be regarded both as a symbol of emotion and also as a revelation of the inner life of a creator—a fact confirmed by psychoanalysis.

Thus, as used in contemporary art since the time of Klee, Kandinsky and Delaunay, the sign has a value in itself; it acts as a bridge between the creator and the beholder. It differs in this respect from the signal, which takes effect or communicates at a remove, in virtue of a conventional function arbitrarily assigned to it. Red, for example, means "Halt—danger ahead"; green authorizes movement. Moreover, such conventions are not always so arbitrary as they seem and sometimes owe their origin to proven psychological data such as the recent discovery of the existence of "focal" or "functional" colors. True, it may seem difficult to see how the signs used by our twentieth-century artists for indicating certain fundamental aspects of their vision of the world can, in the absence of any conventional link, render the image communicable and convey a message that is legible and understood. When the significance of its terminology remains a mystery to the public at large, can we talk of a "language" of art? Since, admittedly, nothing in the nature of a dictionary exists enabling the beholder to decipher the image, art might well seem to lack a *raison d'être* and to belong to Jules Romains's "archipelago of solitudes"—a scatter of islets out of touch with each other. In that case contemporary painting might be no more than a private language spoken by a single man or a very small coterie. This view is rightly rejected by Jakobson. "Private property does not exist in the domain of language."

In point of fact painters of the first half of this century did not discard figurative (objective) allusions, and if they simultaneously felt called on by the program they had set themselves to overstep the "grammatical" models consecrated by tradition, this was solely in order to give the symbols conjured up by the imagination freer scope and to elicit from their inner consciousness the antidotes of illusionist art. For, as Roland Barthes has pointed out, "the symbol is much less a codified form of communication than an (affective) instrument of participation." The symbol can make good only insofar as it is pertinent and apposite; that is to say justified by its psychological and psychic origin, and it is charged with expressive power only when it answers exactly to its motivation. The gap which formerly existed between the significant (the image) and the signified (what the image represents) is disappearing. The nexus "signifying-signified" calls, so to say, for the use of a lorgnette—direct, undeviated observation. Only yesterday the picture still presupposed a drama with three characters: painter, subject and spectator. Now it invites a dialogue between maker and spectator, is comprehended in virtue of a give-and-take between two personalities, and takes full effect only when there is active emotive co-operation by the person whom it bids "complete" it with his gaze.

A CONCRETE ART

The practice of treating collage *merely as a* trouvaille, *a procedure or a technical device, is apt to blind us to the fact that we have in it an artistic phenomenon of incalculable consequence. Implicit in the great upheavals of the beginning of the century, it supervened just at the time when a need was being felt to dispense, anyhow provisionally, with the time-honored stock-in-trade of schools of art, guilds and academies. The question whether Braque was the first to pick up a scrap of wallpaper and incorporate it in a cubist composition, or whether it was Picasso who first resorted to* collage *when he included a piece of "vulgar" oilcloth in a picture he was painting (in 1912) under his friend's approving eye, has less importance than the fact that both men simultaneously felt a need to react against what was then called* l'art savant *by introducing elements other than paint, with a view to implementing "the dialectic of discontinuity." For the surprise effect of this introduction of a humble, seemingly irrelevant fragment of everyday reality—a clipping from a daily paper—served, in the midst of Cubism's venturous course, at once to emphasize the distance covered between distortions of the real and non-dematerialized reality, and also to justify the gap between an ideographic (and idealist) operation and the "given" reality of things. This helped to safeguard the fundaments of a living culture by incorporating ways of seeing and appraising appropriate to the resources that nature has always made available: "a speculative re-organization and exploitation of the perceptible world in perceptible terms." Here we have a characteristic of that mythopoetic mode of thought which, as Lévi-Strauss has shown, is a sort of "intellectual tinkering" with a repertory of miscellaneous data. Hence the theory advanced by the brilliant author of* La Pensée sauvage; *the vogue for* collage *that developed at the time when handicrafts were dying out could, he said, be regarded as "a transposition of this manual dexterity into the field of contemplative ends."*

PABLO PICASSO (1881). PAPIER COLLÉ, 1913. MODERNA MUSEET, STOCKHOLM.

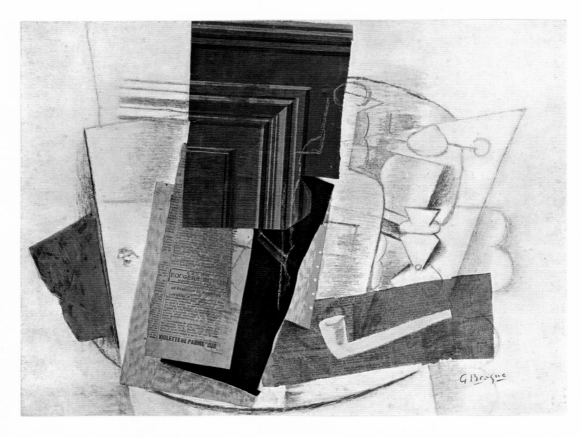

GEORGES BRAQUE (1882-1963). VIOLETTE DE PARME, 1914. SIR EDWARD HULTON COLLECTION, LONDON.

CARLO CARRÀ (1881). INTERVENTIONIST MANIFESTATION, 1914. COLLAGE. DR GIANNI MATTIOLI COLLECTION, MILAN.

KASIMIR MALEVICH (1878-1935). AN ENGLISHMAN IN MOSCOW, 1914. STEDELIJK MUSEUM, AMSTERDAM.

One of the postulates of collage *is the artist's freedom to handle signs like letters, to divide up nature's "words" in order to compose, and as it were to spell them out in separate units. Hence a fragmented pictorial structure built up of juxtaposed signs, groupings of antithetic elements, arrangements of "unlikely" details emphasized by their contiguity, displaced from their normal setting and located in an un-co-ordinated space. This procedure called for a return to the exact delineation of isolated objects, sometimes broken up into fragments and drained of their practical functions so as the better to merge them into "the mists of the dreaming psyche."*

A similar process of "cutting" is basic to the aesthetic of the Englishman in Moscow *(1914). Malevich's method of superimposing a written text on the man's shoulder, a fish on his face, a church on the fish, a sword on the candle, and letters on the coat shows that one and the same attitude governs the artist's visual and critical approach to fragments of reality, manhandled here with a calculated bravado. In this respect, too, Dadaism and Surrealism were to carry on the experiments initiated by the Cubists and Futurists. And the rhythmic, discontinuous discourse of Klee, Kandinsky and Miró, despite their seeming independence, is no less derivative from Braque's gesture when he took to utilizing a pair of scissors and a pot of paste.*

Hence, too, derived the trend towards an at once wider and stricter conception of the ultimate function of art, as a result of which the plastic "truth" of a picture or sculpture came to over-ride its representational "truth." Thus, reinvented and treated as an abstract value, the object acquired its "dignity of an existing thing." Examples are Brancusi's famous Mademoiselle Pogany *busts, with their pure, rhythmic and organic, yet finely sensual forms, and Giacometti's marble* Head, *which has something of the frozen spareness of a Cycladic idol. Giacometti's rigorously austere configuration stems from the same intentions as Kandinsky's curious* Points in an Arc, *whose splendid verve is complementary to the Rumanian sculptor's elegant stylization. In both cases the same stenography is introduced into "the language of forms"—with a view to the promotion of a style.*

WASSILY KANDINSKY (1866-1944). POINTS IN AN ARC, 1927. PRIVATE COLLECTION.

JOAN MIRÓ (1893). DUTCH INTERIOR I, 1928. COLLECTION, THE MUSEUM OF MODERN ART, NEW YORK. MRS SIMON GUGGENHEIM FUND.

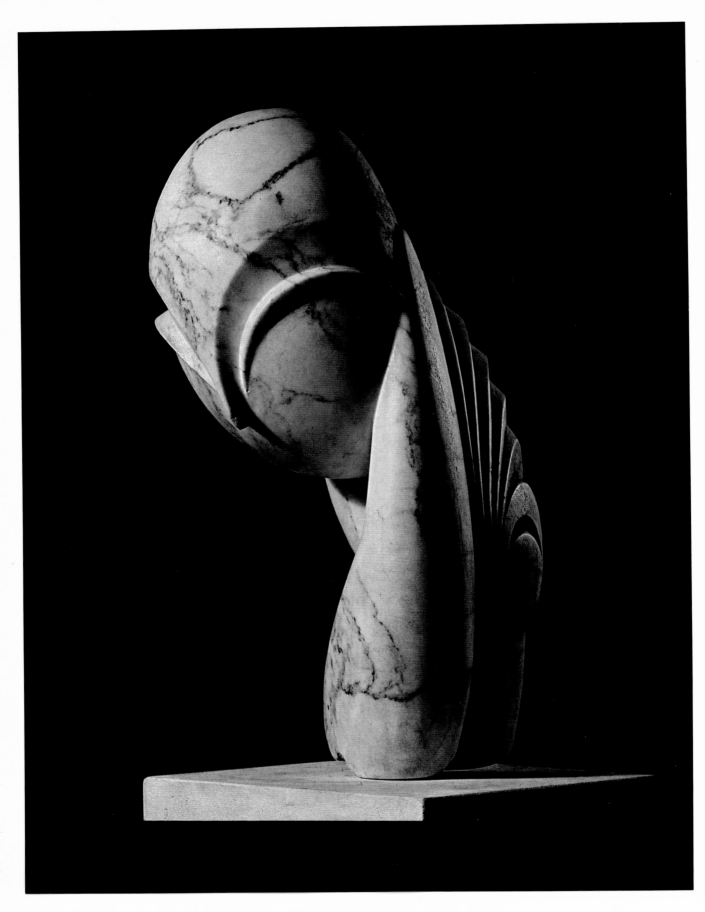

CONSTANTIN BRANCUSI (1876-1957). MADEMOISELLE POGANY, 1919. MARBLE. COLLECTION MR AND MRS LEE A. AULT, NEW YORK.

ALBERTO GIACOMETTI (1901). HEAD, 1932. MARBLE. STEDELIJK MUSEUM, AMSTERDAM.

III

THE PRINCIPLE
OF INDETERMINACY

CHANCE AND INDETERMINACY

Nothing could be more fully thought-out than the multiple portraits made by Picasso in the analytic phase of Cubism. Nothing more lucid than a composition by Van der Leck, El Lissitzky or Cesar Domela. Nothing more patiently and adroitly premeditated than a landscape by Jacques Villon. Braque made no secret of his views; like Brancusi ("art is not a brain-storm"), he approved of "the rule that corrects emotion." And since any element of chance or improvisation was thus eliminated, Valéry, following Poe and Mallarmé, might well have seen instances in all these works of what he called "the solemn exercise of reason." In 1921, referring to the sculpture of the young exponent of Vorticism, Gaudier-Brzeska, Ezra Pound remarked that it was now evident that such motifs as the circle or triangle, in their pure state, had quite as good a right to express, in terms of form, their own figure, their own "sonata," as a theme in music has the right to express itself—an observation that might well be given a place in the forefront of any survey of the evolution of contemporary taste.

Yet dare we say that the above-mentioned works were really so thoroughly "determined" as regards the language they employ as to leave no scope for the imaginary? Even before I approach them, they come towards me, conjure up all the perspectives they do not, overtly, contain, and transform themselves under my eyes. Losing their seeming inertia (or static function), they become active agents of communication. I find myself viewing them from different angles, and each time I do so they look somehow different and I experience a new pleasure. Could I have the same experience when confronted by a picture confined in the quadrangular strait-jacket of the perspectival plan, with the object "correctly" delineated? True, my eyes can rove with never-failing pleasure a Bruegel or a Claude Lorrain landscape—always providing they follow the course assigned them by the artist. And, by its strict immobility, *Madame Rivière* keeps me at a respectful

distance, the distance imposed on the beholder by the iron will of Dominique Ingres. On the other hand the admirable *Portrait of Daniel Henry Kahnweiler* does more than propose new vistas to successive contemplations. Its formal elements (triangles, trapezia, rectangles, parallelograms), fully integrated though they are into a structure pervaded by the discontinuity of dynamic signs and chromatic waves (by "waves" I mean the influx of colors resulting from the distribution of segmented corpuscules)—these formal elements make it clear that twentieth-century art calls for a *sympathy* (in the root meaning of the word, community of feeling) and for an active, creative co-operation on the part of the spectator. They clearly manifest, as Moulod puts it, "a more temporal awareness of the flux of being arrested and systematized" (in the picture), and they also show that the painted field, once it is opened up to "floating" structures, escapes conventional categories and can utilize to good effect such extra-pictorial, dissonant substances as sand, wood, paper, metal, string and so forth.

It was Cubism that took the lead in challenging the traditional means of expression, and the outcome was a development of prime importance in the history of art. The morphological innovations stemming from the creative imagination of Braque and Picasso, Klee and Delaunay, Kandinsky and Tatlin, put an end to all the clear-cut dividing lines drawn in the seventeenth century between the various genres: landscape, the portrait, still life, history painting. Between the years 1910 and 1940 an heterodox aesthetic developed—endorsed by the premises of Aristotelian logic—which gave free scope to all the "possibles" of art, no matter where this latitude might lead the artist, and obliterated the distinctions between the so-called major arts, even if this meant radical changes in the whole conception of the work of art. But this suppression of fixed categories did not lead to a realization of Wagner's dream of a union of all the arts. The result of the new awareness of indeterminacy was a linking up of rational with non-rational, stable with unstable, identity with non-identity, finite with infinite, the mobile with the immobile.

Boccioni was first, it seems, to apply cubist techniques to three-dimensional art (*Development of a Bottle in Space*, 1912). He had begun, a year earlier, by over-riding the traditional limitations of sculpture, playing fast and loose with classical dimensions and formal symbolism in his "plastic groups," in which he utilized not only color but extraneous materials (glass, plaster, iron, wood, hair, etc.) with a view to creating "objects which interlock in an infinite variety of stresses, attractions and repulsions" *(Technical Manifesto of Futurist Sculpture)*. From now on we find constant attempts, "on the level of a deliberate mobility of consciousness" (Husserl), to break down the tyranny of categories, the ossification of language, and the consecrated type-forms of the past. Examples are Auguste Agéro's hollowed-out and open-work statuettes (1911), speaking of which Apollinaire drew attention to "the constructive role assigned to air"; Picasso's experiments in sculpturesque architecture (*Women's Heads*, intended to serve as plans for houses to be erected on the Mediterranean coast); Tatlin's counter-reliefs (1912); Huidobro's *Painted Poems* and Apollinaire's *Calligrammes* (1912) in which he made a new use of Plantin's type by adjusting the typographical layout to the poetic image. A similar preoccupation accounts for the irruption of tracts of color in certain works by Blaise Cendrars, intended to be read and viewed simultaneously: *La prose du Transsibérien et de la petite Johanne de France*, 1913, with "painting" by Sonia Delaunay, and *The End of the World*, 1919, with "painting" by Fernand Léger. Some years earlier Scriabin had had the idea of incorporating spatial movement in a musical composition when the score of his *Prometheus* (1910) provided for a *clavier à lumière*, an instrument for projecting waves of light across the concert hall during the performance of his great tone-poem. Inspired by fireworks, luminous fountains, skysigns, and "those fairylands of vagrant light which in every exhibition are training our eyes to enjoy kaleidoscopic changes of color," the "color rhythms" invented by Léopold Survage just before the First World War stemmed from similar conceptions. Apollinaire saw in them the promise of a new, autonomous art "standing in

the same relation to painting as music does to literature... Thus, aside from static painting and the motion picture, we shall have an art which the public will soon get used to and which will win a following among all whose eyes are keenly sensitive to movements of colors, their interplay, their swift or gradual changes, approaches and recessions." Here we have a singular anticipation of the art described and illustrated by Moholy-Nagy at the Werkbund exhibition in Paris (1930): "a projection of luminous visions in the air, covering vast expanses, or on screens of an unusual shape, on patches of mist, on clouds." Thomas Wilfred was later to follow this up with his invention of the "clavilux" for the production of color music ("lumia"). In this new art form moving light is used as a direct medium of expression in the performance of "silent compositions" in which forms, colors and movement are projected by the operator in a dark hall. Since the composer-performer was free to follow the inspiration of the moment, the resultant composition was guided to some extent by chance, and this element of randomness or indeterminacy produced the most surprising effects. To the same type of experimental art belongs a group of motion pictures in which round about 1931-1932 Fischinger "translated" musical themes into graphic signs: dots, squares, lines and rhombuses. Some years later (1936-1939) Henry Valensi applied himself to "reinterpreting painting in cinematic terms." A Swedish painter, Viking Eggeling, had already done much the same thing (in 1921) in his motion picture, *Diagonal Symphony*, depicting "rhythmic movements of pure forms" and Walter Ruttmann successfully created "visual symphonies" (Opus 1, 2, 3, 4) inspired by geometric motifs. After studying counterpoint under Busoni, Hans Richter, in collaboration with Eggeling, "animated" groups of figures based on squares and rectangles, thus being among the first to launch the so-called abstract film *(Rhythm 21)*.

Never perhaps had there been such a spate of experimentation in all domains of art: Russolo's "Bruiteurs" (1913), Satie's *Parade* (1917), Nicholas Obuchow's machine-made sounds (1926), Tatlin's and Kurt Schwitters' relief-pictures (1913 and 1919), Dada's typographical extravaganzas (1916-1922), Max Jacob's "hazardous associations" (*Le Cornet à dés*, 1917), Picabia's poem-pictures (1918), Hugo Ball's phonetic poems (*Verse ohne Worte*,

1920), Man Ray's and Moholy-Nagy's photograms and photomontages (1920), the semantic and orthographic innovations of e. e. cummings (*Tulips and Chimneys*, 1923), Pierre Reverdy's "verbal sculptures" (*Les Epaves du ciel*, 1924), John Dos Passos' literary collages (*The 42nd Parallel*, 1930), Calder's mobiles (1933), Duchamp's "rotoreliefs" (1934), Joyce's neologisms and "portmanteau words" (*Finnegans Wake*, 1939), Fautrier's "erosions," Masson's "dream machines" (as H.G. Wells described them), Pollock's action painting, Mathieu's improvisations "starting out from a total *nada*." All alike postulated a new mobility of the mind and sensibility; all alike called on the materials in which they worked to point the way ("by the clash of their disparities they kindle with reflected gleams," Mallarmé), and all alike set out from a deliberate confusion of values ("one mode tends towards another and after merging into it reappears with borrowed elements," Mallarmé). And all alike see in *chance* a source of the creative activity, and this at the very time when physicists and mathematicians were regarding it not only as a scientific instrument but also, as Norbert Wiener noted, as immanent in the very structure and "nature of Nature." As far back as 1894 Strindberg had advocated a recourse to chance as a means of conjuring up "new arts" and it was chance that the Dadaists called on at their "jam sessions" to reveal the laws which, according to Arp, would enable them to "achieve a just balance between heaven and hell." It was chance, again, that the Surrealists canvassed when they took to automatic writing. In its scientific context chance was released from a system of inflexible laws only so as the better to acclimatize it in a realm where statistics reigned supreme, but it would be unwise to assume that scientific theories had any real bearing on the course of art. The gulf between the contemporary research work of Borel, Lebesgue, Boltzmann, Gibbs, Bohr and Heisenberg and the works of art described above is far too wide to justify any such approximation. This much, however, may be said: that men practising widely divergent disciplines were led to see in chance "a basic element of the structure of the universe" (Wiener) and that while some were discovering a microphysical universe which ruled out any simultaneous comprehension of its geometrical configuration and the movement of its atomic components, the others—the artists— were figuring forth open, indeterminate, multidimensional structures, charged with overlapping significances which demanded of the beholder a polysensorial response, while leaving him free to choose his path in a labyrinth of relations, probabilities, metamorphoses *ad infinitum*. Thus, agreeing with Umberto Eco, we may say that the methodological approach of the artist and that of the scientist have analogies enough to reveal a striking uniformity in their concepts of the scheme of things.

It took Ingres nearly as long as it took Bruegel to make his way to Rome. In the meantime, needless to say, art had evolved, responding to the pressure of social stresses, changes of the sensibility and the climate of taste. Yet, though between *Dulle Griet* (1564) and the *Turkish Bath* (1862) there had intervened a great political Revolution, a declaration of the Rights of Man and a *Code Civil* momentous in its consequences, these had caused no violent upheaval in men's ways of thinking in the West and little if at all affected the outlook of the peasantry, whose mentality had remained to all intents and purposes the same since the Roman conquest. Middle class and peasants alike saw the world around them with the same eyes as in the past and from the same angle of vision. This is why Delacroix speaks the same language as Rubens, and Courbet's "etymological" roots are the same as Pieter Aertsen's. Also why Turner would have diverged but little from Claude Lorrain's poetic landscape art, had he not glimpsed in a flash of clairvoyance the startling changes soon to take place in what was then the most industrialized country in the world. Clearly more genius, more courage and more zeal were needed to conceive and create—in the heyday of Romanticism—*Rain, Steam and Speed* than twenty years later Claude Monet needed to handle, on impressionist lines, his "portrait" of a railway station, the *Gare Saint-Lazare*. First depiction of a moving train, Turner's great picture has more than an iconographical and historical importance. By converting *rain* into a motif, by treating *steam* as a visual fact worthy of interpretation and, above all, by suggesting *speed* (if only by traditional methods) he heralded the vital role that "vision in movement" was to play in the pictorial, literary and musical domains during the next century. At the very time when Flaubert was protesting against the excessive speed of the railway train "which prevents the traveler from seeing anything and having any adventures en route," Turner's response to values of this order testifies

to a sensibility akin to that of Michelet who, in the same period, the mid-nineteenth century, made the journey from London to Liverpool. "Two hundred kilometers in four hours!" he writes. "No words can give an idea of the astounding rapidity with which the landscape flashes by. It's like living in a fairytale, our train seems, not to be running, but flying over fields, rocks and marshes, skimming across suspension bridges and aqueducts whose prodigious boldness and stability remind us at every moment of the great structures of the Romans and Etruscans. Sometimes we seem to hover high in air above yawning gulfs." Evidently Michelet was keenly alive to the effects of (relatively) high speed. But— and this is no less remarkable—he also observed with a singular acuteness the physical transformation the machine was by way of imposing on nature now that the first industrial revolution was striking root in "England's green and pleasant land."

As a result the space in which man lived, thought, felt and created was not only enlarged; it soon came to include the environment formed by a totality of natural and artificial stimuli and all the phenomena the active mind could grasp. Thus, apprehended as the sum of the perceptible and intelligible phenomena existing at a given moment, man's physical and intellectual surroundings, his concrete and his abstract milieux were now seen to be indissociable. This notion (more exactly formulated than the theories adumbrated by Montesquieu, Taine and intermediate thinkers) canceled out the dichotomy containing-content, exterior-interior and, consequently, the "geometric image" of man's environment. Thus the environment in which he lives, his milieu, has become a *collective* ambience, formed and formative, spurring him to action. "There are as good reasons," Mounier tells us, "for regarding the woodcutters as the 'milieu' of the forest as for regarding the forest as the 'milieu' of the woodcutters, since the forest too changes form under the action of the woodcutters."

It was the sociologist Georges Friedmann, brilliant successor of Vidal de la Blache, and (around 1900) founder of the French school of anthropogeography, who brought into prominence those basic concepts of a "natural environment" and a "technical environment" which bulk so large in modern thought. They throw light, in particular, on the psychosociological conditioning of the verbal or perceptible images in current use and thus on the problems bearing on the relations between man and the world he lives in. Implicit in the research-work of Lucien Febvre, this awareness of the interplay of environment and personality is characteristic of present-day thought; it responds to the challenge of the new "technological culture"—and it would have been unthinkable in the days when soldiers on campaign took cockerels with them to play the part of clocks.

At the risk of over-simplification, let us resume the issues. Source of all the primitive beliefs, the "natural environment" is the habitat of the rural way of life common to all pre-machine age civilizations. In every latitude, whether a plainsman or a mountaineer, whether he lives on a sea-coast or in a forest, man depends on and exploits the resources of nature. His mentality, his emotional responses, his behavior and his activities are determined by the slow rhythms of nature (rhythms of the seasons, the tides, of alternating light and darkness). "Nothing, in fact, seems to intervene between man and the elements; he is always in direct contact with them, with things and living creatures, animals, tools, plants, the winds, the land he tills—indeed he is at one with them. The tool he holds is a prolongation of his hand, to which it is adapted and familiar, and which shapes it as desired. The tool is an outcrop of his body, his skill, his art" (Friedmann). Dances, theatrical performances and games always take place in the open air; the materials of man's art are no less rooted in the soil than his foodstuffs, and the more limited and rudimentary are his means of acting on the raw material of nature, the more absolute is his dependence on the soil. A society of this type, whether urban or rural, is unequipped with the machines and techniques enabling a certain leisure. For some forty thousand years this way of life was common to all social groups, however diversified their structure, and traces of it survive even today in communities which have escaped the tyranny of the machine.

It was at the start of the nineteenth century that, seconded by an intensified extraction of steam-coal, the widespread use of machinery began to modify the relations between man and nature, and while nature's hold on man declined, man's power of bending nature to his will increased. But, rapid as were the technical advances, it is not until the 1880s that we find the conditions of daily life, both in Europe and in the United States, being profoundly affected by what may be described as the technological mentality. Henceforth the growing use of steam power changed the whole aspect of the countryside, shattered the links between the river and the factory, dominated the activities of the great ironworks and ribboned the landscape with railroads (in France the railway mileage rose from about 1,800 in 1850 to 28,000 in 1900). Another result of the industrial revolution has been the constant migration of workers from the country to the great hives of industry; between the years 1900 and 1950, Fourastié tells us, twenty-six of every hundred Americans abandoned agriculture and found employment in the cities. It has also led to the extinction, anyhow the partial extinction, of the rhythms of "natural" life, to an influx of machines and machine-made articles into the home, and a general speeding-up of productivity. Thus, to quote Fourastié again, whereas in 1900 two minutes were needed to reap a hundred square yards of wheat with a reaping and sheaf-binding machine, in 1945 it took only thirty-five seconds to harvest the same area with a reaping-and-threshing machine. And, what was even more significant, this mechanization confronted aristocratic humanism with the germs of a mass culture and fostered the development of "an urban way of life" (L. Wirth).

Just as Impressionism signalized the transition from the old order to the new, so Cézanne stood for the clean-cut break that took place at the very time when the railroad was becoming the axis of an industrial civilization. When, in the 1920s, electric power and the internal combustion engine took over from steam, our roads regained the prestige that was theirs in Roman times, and the link between residence and railroad was gradually severed, with the result that the population tended to overflow into the countryside, the old conception of the town lost its cogency and contemporary town-planners had to include in their survey far wider areas. By the same token the whole conception of organized labor has had to be revised in the light of woman's economic emancipation, the undermining of ethical (Christian) values, the loosening of the family tie (in 1945 there were almost 70,000 divorces in France as against 38,000 in 1938), the reduction of working hours under pressure from trade unions (between 1910 and 1939 working hours were reduced from 3,500 per annum to about 2,000). Tourism has come to the fore as a by-product of the facilities for leisure, transport, distribution of consumer goods. And, finally, "a culture nourished by sacred symbolism" is giving place to a culture alienated from the sacred and oriented towards a synthesis of social and technical myths, a balance between man and mechanized reality, between the individual and the community. A balance hard to integrate. For our age is submerged by the ever-rising tide of technological exploitation and intrusion, and our mental equipment, despite a constant metamorphosis, fails to keep pace with our technical equipment. Our modes of seeing and feeling change but never match up to the new modes of action. Does it follow that we can make nothing of this new "robot" civilization (to use the term invented in 1921 by Karel Capek) without accepting Bernanos' view that it is "a vast conspiracy against any and every form of inner life"? Does this mechanization of our environment necessarily signify "the transition from an age of humanism to a mechanistic age" (René Huyghe)? Views of this kind stem from a so-to-say Virgilian attitude, a resolute commitment to the values crystallized by the Renaissance. They voice an individualistic, aristocratic conception of culture based on logical and aesthetic canons held to be inviolable: a culture bound up with man's physical and figural presence, with symbols having an agricultural origin and with beliefs stemming from man's natural environment. Such views lend credence to the mistaken notion that mechanization has estranged man from nature, that technology and humanism are congenitally hostile to each other. For they fail to take into account the fact that every technical appliance bears the imprint of a human agent and that a "technological humanism" may well develop which will step into the place of the pretentious humanism of the past, a domain reserved to men of letters in their ivory towers. Moreover, thanks to technical advances in the fields of aviation, monoculture, microscopy, biochemistry, telescopic observation, submarine research, the very concept of nature has been given a vast extension, with the result that men in general and creative spirits in particular are now amenable to a prodigious range of wholly novel stimuli.

Organic nature and inorganic nature, as E. N. Anderson has pointed out, are closely linked together in our present-day civilization. A flower is still a flower but it now has also the status of an object of scientific research. We can give it other forms, proportions, colors. As for minerals, we subject them to still vaster transformations, since they are, more even than plants, under man's control, and we have learnt to shape them into objects of various kinds of beauty. Thus we can now have close personal relations with fragments of asbestos, flint, iron pyrites—relations unknown to the man of the pre-industrial age. For him, a stone was simply raw material for building or sculpture; for us, it has all sorts of qualities and serves so many different purposes that we regard it as one of the most flexible and adaptable accessories of our daily life. Sculptors, as Mr Anderson points out, have always sensed the individuality of each type of stone; from this angle, even when we make aesthetic blunders, we all are "sculptors" to some extent today.

Here attention may be drawn to a fact of prime importance: that all the art of the first half of the present century can be regarded as a response— direct or indirect, positive or negative, docile or combative—to the challenge of the technical environment, and to the moral, social and political values to which it has given rise.

We have only to examine in detail the objects created and produced in this period of intensive mechanization, to observe that what is most specific in them stems from their being factory-made and, generally speaking, the result of such mechanical operations as punching, folding, pressing, assembling and adjusting. No less characteristic is the fact that these objects are fitted together, not hand-molded, and that particular care is devoted to their finish— nickeled, chromed, polished, oxydized, etc. Thus a whole new world of fixed or glancing, mat or glossy colors came into being and we can readily appreciate why, evoking as it did a host of sensations of a quite novel type, it caught the attention of the forward-looking spirits of the age, the pioneers of taste, and provided aesthetic satisfactions based on relatively new criteria: precision, power, structural efficiency, surface effects of luster or opacity. We are now better placed to understand why it was that mechanization and its characteristic realizations so greatly affected the mentality and taste of artists and why they then developed a language which, at the time of the rise of Cubism, came to include concepts directly borrowed from science and technology. Hence the need for rapid execution and that urge towards an experimental art which was both to do away with the superstition of the "masterpiece" and (again with Cubism as its starting point) to lead to a spate of movements which, however varied, divergent, even contradictory they may seem at first sight, can be understood and reconciled when viewed as parts of an all-inclusive homogeneous whole: the psychological and material environment out of which they stemmed.

Does it, then, follow that the changes due to the prevalence of mechanization were "assimilated by the sensibility" (to use an expression coined by T. S. Eliot in 1929, reiterated by Mumford in 1934 and by Giedion in 1941)? The truculent Futurist manifestoes, "the horrid literature of the Factory," the rapier-thrusts of *L'Esprit Nouveau*, of *NOI* and *L'Effort Moderne*, the dialectics of *De Stijl* and the Bauhaus did not do so much to speed up the change of heart as the ecstatic paeans of the contemporary vanguard might lead us to believe. Elie Faure is more judicious. "Very few of us have really welcomed the machine. True, we cannot ignore the new mentality it is creating, the changes in our social *mores* it may bring about and the modifications it is imposing on our aesthetic values, modifications which are bound either to spell the end of art or to dominate it completely. Still, there's no point in denouncing the machine. It is here, it is here to stay, and we can no more expel it from history than we can obliterate the act of Prometheus or the words of Christ. We would do better to make it serve our turn. But as yet we are not mentally, nor even physically capable of doing so" (*L'Arbre d'Eden*, 1922). And this despite the fact that Voisin, Farman and Ettore Bugatti were far from being Philistines and had attended schools of art; that Gropius had applied himself to "humanizing" a motor fitted with a Diesel engine in 1913 and to styling the Adler automobile in 1931; that Mies van der Rohe (in 1929) forced on steel the (improbable) task of providing the twentieth century with—unique of its kind!—a truly and completely comfortable chair.

It is on the visual and auditory levels that we find the products of mechanization most extensively "domesticated," embodied in figurative interpretations or precise symbolic referents, and their influence is clearly operative in the works of Boccioni, Léger, Sevranckx, Le Corbusier, Honegger, Prokofiev, Cendrars, Kakabadze, Malevich, Chaplin, Baumeister and Kiesler—to name but a few of the pacemakers of our time. Have we here "a mechanization deliberately foisted on to life"? No doubt, yes, in certain cases. An "arithmetic of the feelings" or a music of the heart? Neither one nor the other. The truth is, rather, that in all these cases a "mechanistic sensibility" conditions the reflexes of perception. It assigns value to the trivial, the crude, the summary; to stridencies, orgies of cacophony. It accords a place in art to ratchets, ball-bearings, gear-boxes. Henceforth we have to agree with Lewis Mumford that the hand on the throttle of a car is no less admirable than the hand that held the scepter in the past.

To a very different plane, however, must be assigned the imagery systematically elaborated by Paul Klee, Brancusi, Delaunay, Braque, Picasso, Juan Gris, Kandinsky and Mondrian. It stems from a viewpoint that enables them to contemplate the same data from a distance great enough to dominate them, integrate them, and by a process of sedimentation to recreate an *equivalent* experience at a profounder level. In their works only discreet allusions to the object have survived, elements that hint, symbolically, at its structure. On the occasions when these are given emphasis and endowed with figurative power, this is because they are activated by the same urge (conscious or subconscious) as that which led Schlemmer, Brusselmans, Gromaire and Chirico to figure forth on the world stage the phantasms of mechanization—that mechanization which gave rise to the poetic forays of the Dadaists and the massive counterattack of the Surrealists.

The 1914-1918 war was far from arresting the progress of the experimental art which had been developing in the years 1905-1910. Rightly or wrongly that brutal demonstration of man's inhumanity to man strengthened the conviction that he was the puppet of forces beyond his control; that human acts are determined by a sort of mechanical, mindless automatism. Confronted by the war-machine and the denial of civic liberties, man seemed to be losing faith in his high prerogative. Yet there could be no denying that Galatea, symbolic heroine of the new age, was the work of man; that, while Pygmalion gloried in his handiwork and others frowned on it, all alike were impressed; and that the metamorphosis it embodied took effect on even the least congenial sensibilities. Chirico presents his Hector and Andromache *as lay figures drained of living substance, classical heroes invested with an anachronistic humanism, linked in the sterile gesture of a geometric embrace, and deriving, one surmises, from Bracelli's seventeenth-century cubic* bizarreries, *offspring of Cartesianism. Behind them we sense a protest, something of the same mood as that which led Marcel Duchamp to employ the weapons of burlesque and irony for denouncing the effects of mechanization on man's mores and behavior; even on the most constant, most universal thing in life, the act of love. In* The Bride stripped bare by her Bachelors, even *love is reduced to a mechanism of communication in "cold blood" and at long range. All the resources of the imaginary and a fine poetic fancy are mobilized with a view to burlesquing the machine; we have here a pictorial equivalent of Aldous Huxley's* Brave New World. *Nonetheless, to the thinking of Duchamp-Villon no less than that of Léger, these mechanic forms of "life" merited the artist's scrutiny; whether because they bore traces of a human gesture, as in Léger's* Motor, *or because, as in Duchamp-Villon's* Horse, *a member of the animal kingdom could be so presented as to convey the driving-power and strict precision of a highly complicated machine. Gonzalez's* Woman combing her Hair *is no less mechanized. This figure borrows from by-products of the industrial age, pieces of scrap-iron, the wherewithal for assembling, welding and projecting in space an effigy charged with mechanistic magic. An idol or a demon? In any case, harking back to the handicrafts of a bygone age, it has the farouche simplicity of an inspired improvisation.*

GIORGIO DE CHIRICO (1888). HECTOR AND ANDROMACHE, 1917. DR GIANNI MATTIOLI COLLECTION, MILAN.

RAYMOND DUCHAMP-VILLON (1876-1918). HORSE, 1914. BRONZE. MUSÉE NATIONAL D'ART MODERNE, PARIS.

FERNAND LÉGER (1881-1955). THE MOTOR, 1918. RENÉ GAFFÉ COLLECTION, CAGNES.

MARCEL DUCHAMP (1887). THE BRIDE STRIPPED BARE BY HER BACHELORS, EVEN (THE LARGE GLASS), 1915-1923.
PHILADELPHIA MUSEUM OF ART, THE LOUISE AND WALTER ARENSBERG COLLECTION.

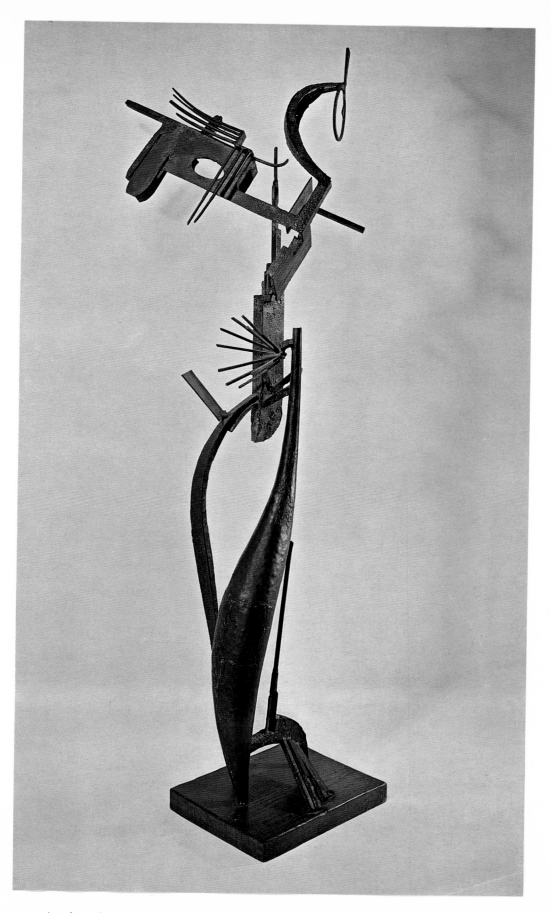

JULIO GONZALEZ (1876-1942). WOMAN COMBING HER HAIR, 1937. WROUGHT IRON. ROBERTA GONZALEZ COLLECTION, PARIS.

KURT SCHWITTERS (1887-1948). CONSTRUCTION FOR NOBLE LADY, 1919. COLLECTION OF LOS ANGELES COUNTY MUSEUM OF ART, MUSEUM PURCHASE FUND.

PROMOTION OF THE IMAGINARY

From the viewpoint of classical rationalism, artistic creativity was long associated with the master theory formulated by Baudelaire, a theory providing the art critic with an instrument still used extensively today, and one which has held its ground effectively despite the widespread influence of the pregnant psychoanalytic concepts advanced by Freud (*Traumdeutung*, 1900) and Merleau-Ponty's development of Husserl's philosophy (*Phénoménologie de la Perception*, 1945). "The whole visible universe," declared the brilliant epigone of La Font de Saint-Yenne, "is a vast storehouse of images and signs to each of which the imagination assigns a place and a relative value; it provides a pasture for the imagination to browse on, digest, metabolize." In other words nature is the artist's "dictionary" (the term employed by Delacroix), in which "those for whom imagination is the guiding principle can discover elements congenial to their inner vision." On the other hand those who lack imagination, "by dint of contemplating and copying, lose the knack of feeling and thinking" (*Curiosités esthétiques*, 1863). This, like the associationist psychology of a later day, meant assigning to the imagination the function of assembling, grouping and fitting together "with a certain art" mental records (duplicates, replicas, images) corresponding to things "given" by the real world, selected by the sensibility and transformed by thought. It was tantamount to saying of the visible that it sets in motion the imagination (the faculty of co-ordinating images). This is why Valéry believed so firmly that imagination is "a function of the real," and it is what Baudelaire meant when he said that if he wants to create an original work a man must have the gift of "seeing well."

According to Bachelard seeing well is fundamental to a realist culture for which perception "in broad daylight" is a *sine qua non*. Seeing well also calls for a distance between the percipient and the outside world: the distance which creates the interval between an achieved work of art and the reality which it transfigures. It was left to Nietzsche to inaugurate that depth psychology in which, at the beginning of the century, the traditional notion of the imagination was called in question. Thereafter Freud, Adler and Jung applied themselves to laying low the barriers, hitherto deemed impassable, between man and his inner self. Methods were devised for exploring in depth the human psyche, and some of its activities, wholly unknown to classical psychology, were brought out from dark recesses of the rational into the full light of irrationality, while new means of access to the non-physical pointed the way to a deeper, fuller understanding of the *animal rationale*. It was now that one of the most solid buttresses of the culture of the western world collapsed and it became evident that there existed behind the façade of the "I" a welter of unconscious urges, an unseen hinterland peopled with "imagined images." In this domain of the imaginary, field of the activities of the "imaging Ego," the imagination operated as "a function of the non-real" (Bachelard) and irrationality was found to be a new modality of being. Thus in effect a new dimension was added to man and his creations, accounting for lines of thought and conduct that are, strictly speaking, abnormal and absurd. Located in the heart of the imaginary, the imagination plays a vital and essential role, energizing the activities of the psyche.

Here we clearly have a reaction against a form of civilization bearing the mark of positivism and its corollaries: cultural (verbal, literary, plastic conventions, rules of logic); moral (attitudes to sex, sentiment of the inferiority of women); social (bourgeois privileges, paternalism, and so forth). It was inevitable that the attention now given to the phenomena of the personality—F.W.H. Myers's theory of the "subliminal self" (the self beneath the threshold), Bergson's theory of intuition and the *élan vital*, Freud's of the libido, the personal unconscious and the dream, and Jung's of a collective unconscious—should lead to the revelation of latent faculties in man, powers that were hitherto undreamt-of. It was as if humanity had waited till the twentieth century to make at long last Vulcan's liberating gesture when with his axe he clove the head of Zeus and thus set free his soul.

The impact of tangible realities was no less foreign than psychoanalysis (Marxism and the city-dwellers' claustrophobia) to the discardment of the masks of our machine-age culture. A world all in relief, the glamour of the positive, the glut of functional objects called forth their antidotes: the magic of emptiness, open spaces, absence—this overcrowded, obsessive, massive field of the visual was more than the eye could cope with. And this saturation of the sensibility—a direct consequence of science and mechanization—did much to further the opening-up of the domain of the imaginary, a domain on which psychoanalysis was now to cast a harsh, revealing, searing light. This cult of the imaginary, antibody of technical realities, was henceforth to promote what might be termed a psychic nudism and to strike down to the sources of the creative potency of the unconscious, scene of "teeming, powerful, super-abundant life," and to quicken the instinct of creation in untrammelled liberty. For the imaginary involves an adventure of the image *before* perception, a transposition of the stuff of dreams into the light of day, an affranchisement of the perceptible, an ecstasy of instinctual freedom, a summons from the world primeval, a consciousness of the unconscious and a commitment to History, the secret, fundamental history of all mankind.

An extension of the Ego into a fuller awareness of the world, the imaginary at its acme, tends to do away with such images as *Perseus cutting off the Gorgon's head*, where the mythological elements are based on and confined to data of visual reality, though the artist applies himself to evoking an archetypal image set in a complex of atavistic memories. In a fashion, this mythological image, objectified in clear-cut terms and conveying a message, is at once figuring and figurative. But the *absolute* imaginary provides the language of art with the means of figuring forth without a model. Thus "imagined images" cease to be merely sublimations of archetypes, and add a new experience to experience. "There is no model," Eluard writes, "for the man who seeks to body forth what he has never seen. Imagination has not the instinct of imitation; it is a

stream one swims *with*, but never swims *against*, towards the source" (*Donner à voir*, 1939). Envisaged from this angle, Ledoux's spheres go much further than Piranesi's *Prisons*. But it was left to the twentieth century to declare: "Let us deliberately be architects of the imaginary" (Bruno Taut, 1919). That "inner compulsion" of which Kandinsky spoke—and it is known that the painter of the *Improvisations* assigned the origin of this notion both to Maeterlinck and to Alfred Kubin, that great visionary whose novel *Die andere Seite* (1908) may be described as a prelude to Michaux's *Situations-Gouffres*—this compulsion joined forces with the affirmation of the November-Gruppe: "All visible architecture is a natural out-come of an inner architecture existing in the mind. The psychic qualities are more important than the architecture itself and, moreover, signify its origins" (Bruno Taut, 1920). Romanticism? Perhaps, if we insist on associating the imaginary with the categories imposed by Reason. In the dazzling collection of drawings in *Alpine Architektur* (1918) Taut's dreamworld reaches up to the stars. The fact remains, however, that the theories of the audacious town-planner of Magdeburg (to whom, along with his brother Max, is due the introduction of color—an acidic color—into architecture) tend to attune psychic dynamism to an architecture symbolizing social dynamism. We find the same theories, rigidly formulated, conditioned by technics and petrified by their utilitarian functions, in the "demythicized" architecture of Gropius, Breuer and Mies van der Rohe. Similarly, the imaginary city of Sant'Elia, whether or not deriving from the genius of Leonardo, found a modern instance in Le Corbusier's spatial mystique, before being incorporated, in a voluntarily attenuated form, in the layout of the grey, cold, opaque world of the American metropolis. In the imagery of Gaudí, however, the driving force of the imaginary never faltered. And if the "ideal palace" which the long patience of a French postman, Ferdinand Cheval, brought to fruition in 1912—a unique event in the functionalist desert—seems today to strike a whimsical note, this is only because it invests fretted stone with a fantasy whose origins lie in the atavistic past. As for Klee, Arp, Kandinsky, Miró and many others, we see them starting out from the zero point of plastic art, the dot and the line, when giving form to the images of their dreamworld—which proves that the artist's creative imagination can quite well dispense with the *bodies* of things. This was a gift that Chinese artists had possessed from time immemorial: a consummate art of expressing themselves without indicating either the thickness of a mountain or the hour of day.

Taking place as it did in the domain of the imaginary, where eyesight is placed in abeyance so as to give free rein to the imaging faculty, a phenomenon of prime importance for the art of the twentieth century—it signified at once a renewal of contact with the myth-making imagination and a rejection of all naturalistic criteria—calls for mention at this point; I have in mind the technique of *collage*. This term connotes an asyntactic, discontinuous method of expression whose purport Aragon was the first to analyse clearly and succinctly, in the magisterial monograph written by him in 1930 (for Camille Goemans) by way of introduction to a remarkable exhibition taking place that year. Including the earliest *papiers collés* by Braque and Picasso (1912), it not only challenged all contemporary painting but also, as we can better see today, outdid the Dadaist revolt in the sweeping changes it brought to the current conception of the work of art, and heralded the débâcle of "bourgeois aesthetic."

Not that *collage* was a twentieth-century invention. The mythological image referred to above was built up on similar lines and associated more or less heterogeneous elements, motifs stemming from different species and genera (especially where the imagery was of a fantastic order). As regards *papiers collés* in the strict sense, these were a form of art long current in Japan, and many of the major Japanese twelfth-century works can properly be described as *papiers collés*. In Europe this technique developed later, not until the eighteenth century, when it was used for New Year's cards—unless the insertion of letters of the alphabet into western paintings (in the sixteenth century) is to be regarded as a step in this direction.

To our thinking *collage* was an essentially *poetic* phenomenon (if we use the epithet in the root meaning of the Greek *poitikos*). In this connection mention may be made of a pre-Dada work by Raymond Queneau *What a Life!* in which the spirit of 1900 is combined with typically Anglo-Saxon humor. A sort of camouflaged autobiography, the joint work of two putative authors E.V.L. and G.M., this book consists of pages illustrated with pictures clipped from the catalogue of one of the big London stores (Whiteley's) and accompanied by brief printed comments. Queneau is quite right in describing this as "one of the first manifestations of the so-called modern mentality." The author of *Bâtons, chiffres et lettres* goes on to inform us that "this alliance of scissors and paste for disinterested ends" can be exactly dated—to August 17, 1911. The preface sets forth the program followed by the anonymous "authors." "One man leafed through Whiteley's catalogue and culled from it facts and prices; another discovered—what we ourselves had sensed in it—a profoundly moving human drama." Queneau, it seems, resorted to this procedure, soon taken over by literature and poetry, with a view to giving history "an imaginary dimension." *What a Life!* dates to August 1911. The first volume of *Fantomas* had just appeared. Cubism was beginning to create a flutter in the artistic dovecots. Apollinaire was tracking down "the modern" in a big department store and giving the final touches to his *Alcools*.

"But all this was only a matter of drawn and written signs, timid presages of that memorable year 1912 which witnessed three of the outstanding events of the century: the wreck of the *Titanic*, the theft of *Monna Lisa* and the outbreak of a new type of anarchism—all of them perfect illustrations of the contemporary predicament, guide-marks enabling us to classify subsequent developments. Thus the Russian revolution was an end-product of the last-named event, the inundations in the South of France were a reflection, so to say, of the first, and the World War can be associated, if at a far remove, with the second."

Queneau—to cite him again, for he is one of the most versatile and clairvoyant of our contemporaries —tells us that Jean Paulhan once quoted to him a passage in the writings of a Chinese sage telling of an emperor who, wishing to reform the morals of the day, began by changing the signs of the language. This was not so far-fetched as it sounds, though I know of no modern leader who took so bold, so drastic a step. Indeed the dictators of recent times— Napoleon, Hitler, Mussolini, Stalin—when they gave a patronizing hand to "culture" took a line diametrically opposed to that of the Chinese emperor. On the other hand, the leading, truly creative spirits of our age have put into practice—at the behest, perhaps, of the Zeitgeist—the intention of the ancient sage, undeterred by its subversive aims.

Apollinaire and Queneau, Breton and Michaux, Joyce and Ionesco, Ernst and Matta, Gaudi and Wright, Méliès and Bunuel, Schönberg and Boulez, Arp and Kemeny, the Douanier Rousseau and Aristide Caillaud are the poles between which, in "a world beyond the world," forgather all the forces which have made of *collage* a fundamental, privileged means of revolutionizing contemporary thought. This they have done by assigning to its antithetical dynamism, based on a clash of incompatibles, the function of neutralizing the postulate of non-contradiction, and projecting contradiction into ethics, and as a result (Lupasco would say) into the domains of epistemology and science.

Never, assuredly, would this trend of art and thought have had such widespread consequences had not the then political conditions acted as a stimulus. Nor would the "procedure" introduced by Braque have been so generally accepted, had not the social order proved itself "capable of slaughtering millions for selfish motives." Thus it was that in the midst of the First World War (that "metaphysical crack-up," as Musil called it), those Angry Young Men, the Dadaists, took to using *collage* as a therapeutic instrument, a shock treatment for crazed humanity, and a vehicle of revolutionary ideas. "Dada," Hülsenbeck proclaimed, "is the Germanic form of Bolshevism." Born in an age of "fire, steel and blood," Dada was more than merely nihilistic. It was in the imaginary—"a structure antithetical and complementary to so-called reality" (E. Morin)—that Tzara, Sophie Täuber, Richter, Ball and Janco (at Zurich), Raoul Hausmann, Franz Jung, Mehring, Höch, Hülsenbeck and Grosz (at Berlin), Arp, Ernst and Baargeld (at Cologne), Schwitters (in Hanover), Aragon, Picabia, Breton, Benjamin Péret, Eluard, Ribemont-Dessaignes, Théodore Fraenkel and Jacques Rigaud (in Paris), Paul Citroen (at Amsterdam) and Clément Pansaers (at Namur) sought and found the psychological staffage of their imagery, the connecting links of their associations and the fiery energy of their farouche, aggressive, diabolic configurations. By destroying the logical semantics of tradition and exploiting the nonsensical, they conjured up, for all the world to see, the signs of the new age.

Dada not only lay at the root of the political, moral and aesthetic ferment of Surrealism, but also, and above all, gave expression to the reflexes of the new mass culture. "The history of every form of art," as Walter Benjamin observed in 1935 (and what he said applies even more strongly to the art of today), "comprises critical periods in which art aspires to produce effects that can be achieved only after a drastic modification of the technical *status quo*, that is to say by a new form of art. This is why the seeming absurdities and extravagances that emerge in times of so-called decadence, far from being mere symptoms of decay, stem from what is most vital in the art forces of the period. This explains the 'preposterous' manifestations of the Dadaists less than two decades ago. We can now see what they were aiming at; they were trying to produce in terms of painting (and literature) effects the public now asks of the cinema... Before the triumph of the motion picture they promoted a movement that Chaplin was soon to launch on, so to say, more 'natural' lines." The social implications of Dadaism are excellently summed up by the same writer, a compatriot and friend of Bertolt Brecht and Theodor Adorno, in *Das Kunstwerk im Zeitalter seiner technischen Reproduzierbarkeit* (1959). "Whenever a radically new departure blazes a trail into the future, it tends to go beyond its stated program. So true was this of the Dadaists that, in pursuance of intentions of which (anyhow in the form we are here describing them) they were obviously unaware, they disregarded all the commercial values which have now come to bulk so large in the art of the motion picture. For they set far less store on the financial possibilities of their works than on the fact that they could not be treated as 'objects of contemplation.' One of the means they used with this in view was a systematic debasement of the *matière* employed. Thus their poems are often jumbles of words sprinkled with obscenities and every sort of verbal garbage. By the same token they stuck buttons and tickets on their pictures. Thus they deprived the works on which they imposed the stigmata of reproduction of any semblance of an 'aura.' Looking at a picture by Arp or reading one of Stramm's poems, we are not invited to linger and muse on it, as with a picture by Derain or a Rilke poem. For a decadent bourgeoisie this withdrawal into oneself had become a sort of anti-social gesture; with Dadaism, diversion from the self became a lesson in social comportment."

It was under the auspices of André Breton, great writer (without writings), unplumbed poet and hospital-trained psychiatrist, that in the heyday of philosophies of the absurd and of despair, the deep, sweltering underworld of the imaginary was opened up by a rebellious avant-garde.

Nothing is more revealing than the way in which, in the 1920s, in a climate of clairvoyant *Angst*, Surrealism supplanted Dadaism; the way in which it *organized* revolt and, drawing on the subconscious, undermined the cult of culture by providing man with a technique of finding himself anew, a method of subverting methods, rules for destroying rules, for disinterring buried instincts, releasing dormant reflexes, and abolishing the mental, intellectual and moral standards basic to the old order. Equally noteworthy is the way in which Surrealism set to neutralizing all social and academic prejudices, all norms and generally accepted rules of conduct. But, as we can see today, its aims were not merely negative and destructive. Like psychoanalysis, to which it owed so much, Surrealism sought to rediscover the path of *immediate* experience, leading to direct contacts with things, living beings and the outside world (the state of "being-in-the-world"). And in so far as its procedures aim at regaining contact with the "complete" man, they have so much in common with those of present-day phenomenology that we are justified in regarding Surrealism as a mode of existence or a way of life.

JEAN ARP (1887). BIG HEAD, LITTLE BODY, 1923. COLORED WOOD. JEAN ARP COLLECTION, MEUDON.

THE WILL TO METAMORPHOSIS

"You can photograph a landscape," Picabia once told his grandfather, who was a friend of Daguerre and an enthusiastic amateur photographer, "but you cannot photograph what I have in my head." His grandfather, firm believer in the camera and the motion picture, regarded them as a very real threat to his grandson's career. He saw only dangers where the younger men saw hopes of a new freedom. (A similar controversy was raging regarding the changes coming over the language of the arts.) Henceforth it was left to photography to take care of the myth of "the real"; the plastic arts could safely disregard it, and "realize" in the exact sense of the term—give form and substance to—images stemming from the imagination. Already, reacting against the pressures and provocations of the world around them, many artists had struck out on the path of freedom. Thus, once again, science enlarged, if indirectly, the powers of the image. Psychoanalysis relaxed the disciplines of Reason, opened the flood-gates of the subconscious, and broke the mirror of Narcissus which, from the fifteenth century on, had forced on the artist's eye a stable, invariable model. This encouraged him "to strike down to the mysterious forces latent in us, to probe their shifting nuclei and to draw on a wealth of undetermined possibilities, of hitherto forbidden hopes" (J. Baruzi, 1911). Physics, too, emboldened him to find in Chance "the universal rule." Hence the enchanting freedom of the art of Chagall, which leads us back, so delightfully, to the very dawn of human life. The illogical, dreamlike layout of The Poet *is rooted no less in the soil of atavistic culture than in the primordial psyche—though with less precision than in Paul Klee's* A Girl's Adventure, *fragment of a miniature wonderland, each element of which has the boldness of a new experiment and the perfection of complete achievement. Tanguy, Dali and Magritte took little interest in the "naivety" of direct experience, that is to say in the possibility of rendering it in a "primitive" style. They employ a sophisticated language, when harking back to the sources of human history, and often aim at effects of the absurd, or at startling the beholder with nightmarish visions. In* Surrealism and Painting *Max Ernst makes it clear that his purpose is not merely that of analysing "the flight of a non-Euclidean fly." One of the many merits of this work is its voluptuous counterpoint of full and empty spaces, positives and negatives—these are rendered with equal boldness in Henry Moore's* Helmet. *Arp, however, is always more discreet; in his work we see the compulsive magic of an art seemingly immune from the psychic and social disintegration of the age.*

MARC CHAGALL (1887). THE POET, 1911. PHILADELPHIA MUSEUM OF ART, THE LOUISE AND WALTER ARENSBERG COLLECTION.

PAUL KLEE (1879-1940). A GIRL'S ADVENTURE, 1922. BY COURTESY OF THE TRUSTEES, TATE GALLERY, LONDON.

RENÉ MAGRITTE (1898). PINK BELLS, SKY IN TATTERS, 1930. URVATER COLLECTION, BRUSSELS.

SALVADOR DALI (1904). DAY AND NIGHT OF THE BODY, 1936. GOUACHE. URVATER COLLECTION, BRUSSELS.

YVES TANGUY (1900-1955). A THOUSAND TIMES, 1933. URVATER COLLECTION. BRUSSELS.

HENRY MOORE (1898). THE HELMET, 1939-1940. BRONZE. MRS IRINA MOORE COLLECTION, MUCH HADHAM, HERTS., ENGLAND.

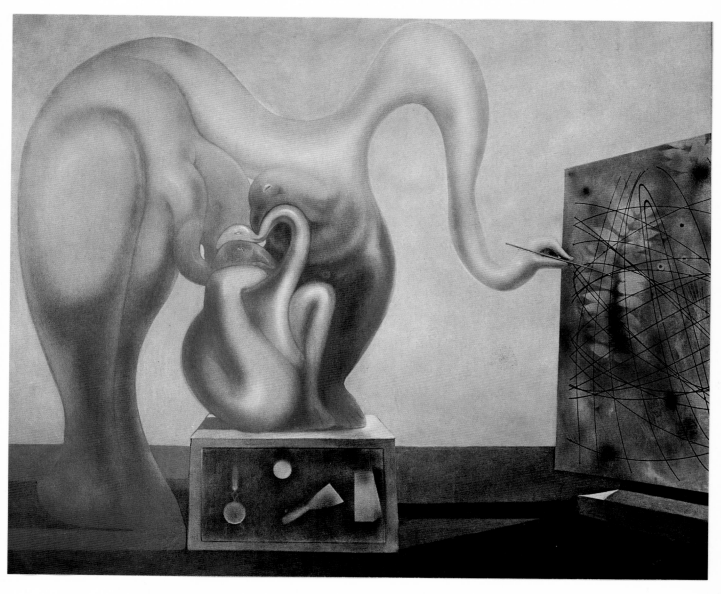

MAX ERNST (1891). SURREALISM AND PAINTING, 1942. COLLECTION WILLIAM N. COPLEY, NEW YORK.

5

THE CHALLENGE TO PAINTING

To December 10, 1896, when Alfred Jarry's play *Ubu Roi* made its sensational appearance on the stage of the Théâtre de l'Œuvre in Paris, may be dated the start of the revolt against all the "pre-established harmonies," the ossification of language, the decrepitude of official canons, the petrification of the sign and the resultant enfeeblement of the information provided by the traditional channels of communication. Like a high-powered bomb dropped by Jarry on the citadel of bourgeois propriety, *Ubu Roi* shattered, from within, the idols of the tribe, neutralized entropy and opened the way to an inrush of forceful and subversive values. With this famous play the work of art became a challenge, an act of provocation, even an indictment of its own criteria. Here, too, we have the beginning of an aesthetic of "shock tactics," founded on a phenomenon that Wiener and Shannon were to elucidate half a century later—the conveyance by signs (words, sounds or images) of information other than their ostensible, explicit message. Hence the rapid development of a tendency to utilize crude, brutally direct signs, to do away with traditional materials, the framed picture, set pieces, compact sculpture, melodic line, well-tempered sounds, "polite" words and "graceful" gestures. In all domains in which this revolutionary ferment was active, the techniques of *collage*, automatism and

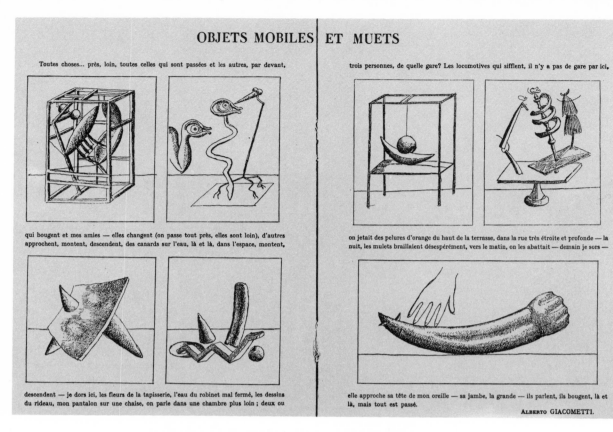

ALBERTO GIACOMETTI (1901). OBJECTS MUTE AND MOBILE.
FROM THE MAGAZINE "LE SURRÉALISME AU SERVICE DE LA RÉVOLUTION," NO. 3, PARIS, DECEMBER, 1931.

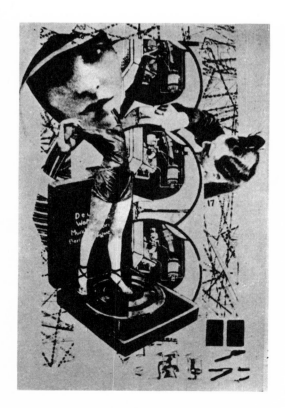

HANNAH HÖCH (1889). PHOTOMONTAGE, 1920.

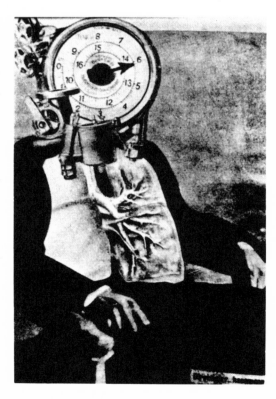

RAOUL HAUSMANN (1886). PHOTOMONTAGE, 1920.

MARCEL DUCHAMP (1887).
READY MADE: BICYCLE WHEEL.
THIRD VERSION, 1951. METAL AND WOOD.
SIDNEY JANIS GALLERY, NEW YORK.

FRANCIS PICABIA (1879-1953).
TITLE PAGE OF THE MAGAZINE "DADA," NO. 4-5.
ZURICH, MAY 15, 1919.

FILIPPO TOMMASO MARINETTI (1876-1944).
LETTER FROM A PRETTY GIRL TO AN OLD-FASHIONED GENTLEMAN.
FROM "LES MOTS EN LIBERTÉ FUTURISTE," MILAN, 1919.

astonishment seconded these ventures into a new-won freedom. From Erik Satie's *bruitisme* (noise music) in 1917 to Man Ray's spray-gun painting (1918) and Max Ernst's rubbings (1925)—for which the way had been prepared by Marcel Duchamp's ready-mades (1914)—artists aimed at bringing out the *dramatic* nature of perception and explored the most unlikely avenues with a view to tracking down (and destroying) clichés of style and language, demolishing cultural and social taboos, flouting the facile illusionism of familiar sounds and images. Humor became a standby of the artist's critical equipment, a keen-edged knife cutting to shreds the "uniform" of thought, enabling him to strip spurious values of their "glamour," and place the work of art on the orbit of demythification. Whimsical, ironical and aggressive, the work of art came to exercise a traumatic power owing something to the rising vogue of the cinema, since the motion picture, too, by its very nature, derives much of its efficacy from shock effects.

This practice of risking everything, even the work of art itself, stems from a will "to strike down to man's inmost being, in its state of incoherence or, more accurately, its primitive coherence" (Jacques Rivière, 1920). By what means? The only one which, according to Aragon, "can prevent the artist from indulging in narcissism, in art for art's sake, and lead him back to the magical procedures which are the source and justification of the plastic figurations sponsored by several religions"—in other words, to *collage*. This is the major form of expression of our age; the one which most clearly reveals "the revolt of the image" and presents the dismantled image as a symbol of the permanent revolution now in progress. It restores to creative art the quality of action, calls on the spectator to join in the destruction of his own myths, invites attention and co-operation instead of reverie or sentimental contemplation. With remarkable prescience Aragon, in his *Challenge to Painting* (1930) foresaw "a time when many recent developments in painting will seem as quaint, as out-of-date, as the rhapsodic laments of the poets of an earlier generation seem today. We can picture a time when our painters (who already have ceased grinding their colors with their own hands) will find the habit of laying in their colors with the brush childish and unworthy of them, and will see in that 'personal touch' which still is held to give value to their pictures only a matter of documentary interest, like that of a manuscript or holograph. A time may come when painters will not even get others to put on the colors, will not even draw—and *collage* gives us a foretaste of that time. Moreover it is certain that the painter's 'handwriting' or *facture* will follow the same course." Aragon's bold surmises have been justified in the event; but, more than this, they opened up uncharted fields, a zone charged with potential metamorphoses, which even today has not yielded all its content "in the way of human possibilities." Paul Valéry was meanwhile following up a train of thought which, if less committed, was suggested by the same order of events. "Our Fine Arts," he wrote (in 1929) in an announcement of *The Conquest of Ubiquity*, "were instituted, and their usages determined, in an age quite different from ours, by men whose powers of acting on things were trifling as compared with ours today. The amazing increase of our means, the efficacy and adaptability they have now acquired and the ideas and habits they engender make it clear that far-reaching changes will soon be taking place in the ancient industry of the Beautiful. All the arts contain a physical element which can no longer be envisaged or handled as in the past and which cannot fail to be affected by the developments of modern science... It is to be expected that the great discoveries of our age will radically transform the techniques of the arts, act on the creative spirit itself, even perhaps modify, amazingly, the very idea of art."

Modifying the idea of art involves both a new freedom of thought and a compulsive urge to achieve a new *praxis* in the closed, complacent, segregated world of aesthetics—an urge that has been operative since the beginning of the century. Following in the wake of *Ubu Roi*, Marcel Duchamp and Picabia were the first to play the part of Zeus—a Zeus of shreds and patches who hurled trumpery thunderbolts all the more "offensive" for being made of vulgar tin. And once the relativity of so-called precious metals was thus exposed, a whole category of standards collapsed. Next came Dada, born of the havoc of the First World War, and by a reckless use of high explosives imposed a régime of blatantly "unseemly" forms. For a while the Cabaret Voltaire at Zurich was Dada's headquarters and it was there that Arp, Sophie Täuber, Hugo Ball, Richard Hülsenbeck, Tristan Tzara, Hans Richter and Marcel Janco made a holocaust of the idols of the Platonic ideology, under the indifferent gaze of Lenin and Romain Rolland.

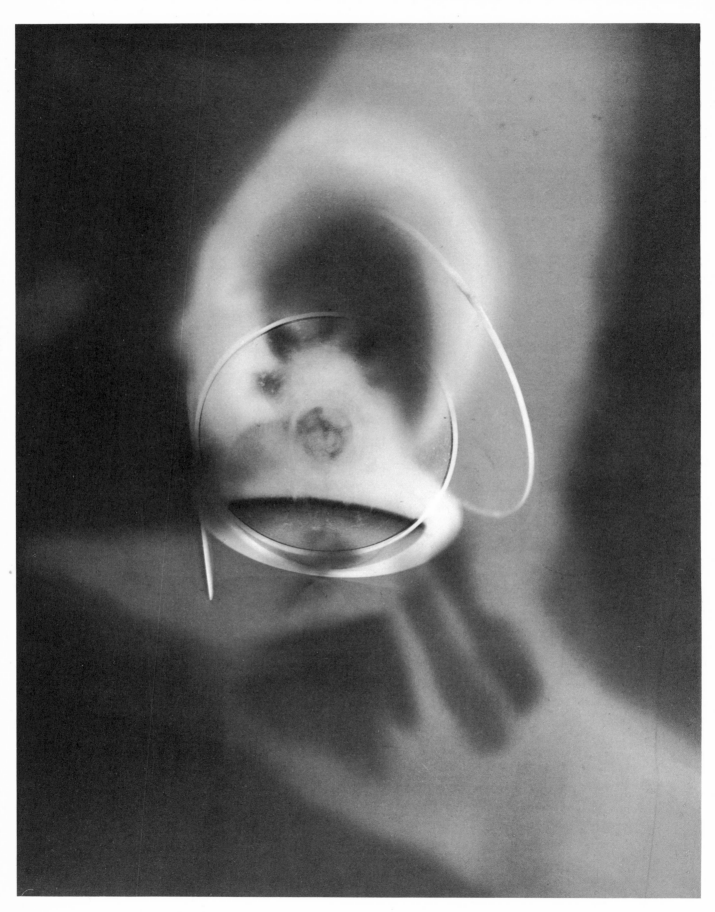

MAN RAY (1890). RAYOGRAPH, 1923. COLLECTION, THE MUSEUM OF MODERN ART, NEW YORK.

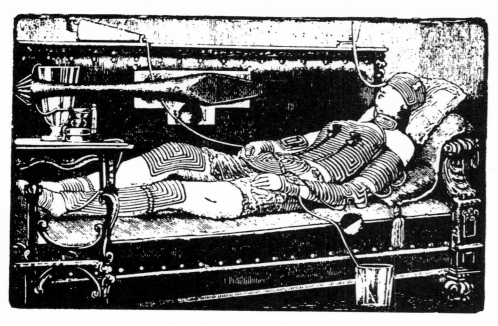

MAX ERNST (1891). THE PREPARATION OF BONE GLUE, 1921.
COLLAGE. FROM "DADA IN TIROL - DADA AU GRAND AIR,"
DATED SEPTEMBER, 1886.

ANDRÉ BRETON (1896). POEM-OBJECT. 1941.
COLLECTION, THE MUSEUM OF MODERN ART, NEW YORK.
RAY SAGE TANGUY BEQUEST.

KURT SCHWITTERS (1887-1948).
MERZ CONSTRUCTION (HANOVER), BEGUN IN 1924
AND DESTROYED IN THE SECOND WORLD WAR.

IV

THE REJECTION
OF PERSPECTIVAL VISION

FROM SURFACE TO SPACE

For several centuries the custom prevailed of associating "humanism"—or a certain conception of it—with the presence of the human figure represented lifesize and surrounded with more or less "heroic" tokens of the man's wisdom or achievements (unusual or familiar objects bringing to mind a presumably noble life and inviting our esteem). Prevalent throughout the western world, this practice gave rise to one of the most serious handicaps that hampered—and still hamper—the creative and critical activities of the European mind. It is as though a sign could not address itself *directly* to the beholder by incorporating referents stemming from an unconditioned impulse of the creative will. Plastic art is not necessarily bound up with what has been styled "the hermeneutics of the visage." Kandinsky once remarked that "a dot has sometimes more to tell us than a human figure," and not the only function of stone is its use as a commemorative material. Similarly a canvas or panel need not necessarily serve as a support for cultic, anecdotal, historical or decorative illustrations based on "a vocabulary of the identity of appearances." We now understand better than in the past that the plastic arts, *qua* language (like the arts of literature), rely on forms that play the part of *signs*.

This discovery, which has profoundly affected the art of the twentieth century, has led to the creation of a world in the image of the imaginary, no longer of a "reality" which has been proved to be elusive, not to say misleading, when contemplated from several simultaneous viewpoints. If, then, we agree that this type of creative activity stems from the manner in which the artist assembles, arranges, elaborates and articulates structures originating in his mind, it follows that all his creations (literary, plastic, musical and scientific) have a definite anthropological value, since they body forth "the man himself, his history, his situation, his freedom, and even the resistance Nature sets up to the operations of his mind" (Roland Barthes).

It is to the structuralist approach (implicit in Gestalt psychology and now identifiable as such *a posteriori*) that we must assign the *quality* of the ventures simultaneously launched in 1906-1907 by Picasso, Braque and Delaunay and later, between 1910 and 1925, by Klee, Kandinsky, Kupka, Malevich, Mondrian, Van Doesburg, Arp, Huszar, Van der Leck, Larionov, Lissitzky, Léger, Ozenfant and Le Corbusier with a view to creating an art of painting based as much on data of the imaginary as on the biological conditions of perception, and tending to restore to organic space its primacy over visible space. The time had come for the rediscovery, "beneath depth envisaged as a relation between things (and even planes), of a primordial depth equating the thickness of a medium without content" (Merleau-Ponty). This led to an abeyance of the subjects, themes, formulas and conventions exploited by an age when the world of things was held to be completely static or anyhow stable enough to be rendered in chronological or perspectival terms, that is to say in opaque blocks or inert volumes. "Materialist painters," Elie Faure wrote in 1926, "kept strictly to the appearances of matter and tried to give these appearances the force of law. They had forgotten the reality of *form*, as science had forgotten the reality of man. For there still existed a deeply rooted and widespread belief in the old scientific, static world-view and in the old political ideology, which regarded social ends as the sole criteria of good conduct. But meanwhile the idea of anatomical perfection which had dominated the western world since the age of Pheidias was giving place to the idea of that expressive symbolism which now is leading back the art of Europe to the oriental fountainhead of art and thought."

What, then, was needed was to integrate into a social order, which itself was cast into the melting-pot, a new order of art, an art that took full account of the values of mobility, tension, energy, and co-ordination and, by the same token, of the forces activating the science, philosophy and the great politico-social movements of the day. Thus only could the parameters of becoming replace the rigid configurations of the perspectival system. The effects of this bold innovation made themselves felt, successively, in the techniques of the cinema, of collage, and photomontage, and also reacted on the structure of the picture. At the same time—that is to say between 1913 and 1945—the art of photography, in the "absolute" creations of such men as Man Ray, Moholy-Nagy, Weston Brady, Edward Steichen and György Kepes, was breaking free from the trammels of illusionism. Meanwhile, following the trail blazed by Mallarmé, a number of French poets—Reverdy, Apollinaire, Max Jacob, Philippe Soupault, Breton, Aragon and Eluard—were similarly testing out techniques enabling them to create, vis-à-vis perspectival "appearances," a distance equivalent to the one interposed by the prose writers of the day, Joyce, Kafka, Faulkner and Dos Passos, between themselves and the data of reality.

Thus—to confine ourselves for the moment to the problems of pictorial art—we can see why the course of painting was so largely shaped by the famous, often-quoted formula enounced by Maurice Denis in 1890: "We must never forget that a picture, before being a warhorse, a nude woman, an anecdote or whatnot, is essentially a flat surface covered with colors arranged in a certain order." Aside from its historical applications, this axiom seemed to justify (a justification sometimes exploited to excess) the "gratuitous act," "dead" painting, aimless art. For the notion of regarding the "flat surface" not merely as the passive support of a figuration but as the receptacle of a *composition* acted on and acting in its own right, stemmed directly from the human situation. Only when this is recognized can the new painting claim fully to exercise "our pure power of expressing, transcending things already seen or said." In this respect, as Merleau-Ponty rightly observes, "it sets a problem quite other than that of the return to the individual *qua* individual: the problem of knowing how it is possible to communicate without recourse to a pre-established Nature, accessible to all our senses; and how we are integrated into the universal by those very elements which are most personal, peculiar to ourselves." Undoubtedly it was the solutions given to this problem by Delaunay and Mondrian, Klee and Kandinsky, Kupka and Malevich, that led

Merleau-Ponty to write (in *Signes*) that "modern painting like modern thought in general, compels us to accept a 'truth' that does not resemble things, and has no model in the outside world." That truth was glimpsed by Cubism, which without eliminating it altogether gradually compelled the "model in the outside world" to flatten itself on a plane surface, a plane immediately dynamized by the interplay of signs charged with non-perspectival spatial allusions. The chief interest, in my opinion, of the procedures inaugurated by Braque and Picasso and brought to fruition by Juan Gris lies in the fact that they called in question the decorative significance of the traditional plastic "screen" by subjecting the object to a multilateral analysis. This entailed the rupture of the perspectival axis and *ipso facto* did away with the co-ordination of the three dimensions of classical space. But the use of a "model in the outside world" gives rise to an ambiguous situation, of which Juan Gris was well aware. "When," he wrote, "I particularize pictorial relations to the point of actually *representing* objects, it is to prevent the man who is looking at the picture from doing this himself and to make sure that my arrangement of colored forms will not suggest to him a reality other than the one I have in mind." But it is, rather, to Delaunay that we must give credit for having discovered (as far back as 1906) the possibility of eliciting from "an imaginary reality" the elements of an art capable of bringing out the significances and values deriving from the new conception of the universe, envisaged as a field of forces in constant activity. This explains why his *Colored Rhythms* figure forth "a truth that does not resemble things," by presenting them in the form of "directed simulacra." In other words, Delaunay (in whom Klee saw "one of the finest spirits of our time") ceased to concern himself with individual objects accessible to direct observation and applied himself to depicting phenomena of a more general order, representative of the universal flux of things, and recording those rhythms and vibrations of the cosmos which could be made manifest only by tensions of colors handled as self-sufficing units. It was with a view to "providing intuitions of certain properties of the material or mental cosmos" that Delaunay sought to create a "plastic entity" which, by the use of "colored phrases," brought to life the surface of the canvas and in so doing generated a "phenomenal space" appropriate to the existential condition of contemporary man.

Thus there took form, in the very structure of the picture, a new image of the universe, in which, within the seeming unreality of a non-visual space, the psychic values of experienced depth replaced (provisionally) the physical values of the geometry of dimensions. It was this same geometry that Mondrian, in 1912-1913, sought to do away with by stressing the dynamic function of the plane, thus challenging the *ancien régime* of dimensions echeloned in circumambient space. Here we see a more radical solution of the problem Delaunay set himself when, so as to meet the demands of a highly novel type of sensations, he thought up a new handling of color "unimpaired by images seen in the real world." Mondrian, however, perceived the possibility, suggested by Cubism, of disposing pure plastic units (squares, rectangles) in such a way that—with a view to indicating rhythm, movement and lines of force—they are dynamized by an asymmetrical arrangement based on right angles and the use of the three primary colors. For many centuries, Mondrian declared, painters had expressed relations in their works in terms of "natural" forms and colors; not until the present day had there been any question of a plastic art based purely and simply on relations. Similarly, for many centuries the artist had "composed" with forms and colors; only now had the composition itself become *per se* the act of "plastic expression," i.e. the image. These methods—"a plastic art based purely and simply on relations," a presentation of rhythm in its purest state, a limitation of the resources of the painter's language by the strictest possible economy of forms, a practice of eliciting from these forms a dynamic of associations and oppositions and of integrating them in "a compositional continuum"—all these methods are fundamental to structuralist art.

True, extreme insistence on the formal element is tantamount to "making composition the protagonist," as Léger put it. But it would be wrong to see in this a sterile emphasis on formal structure for its own sake, a desire to make the painter's means autonomous, or a mere assemblage of "linear harmonies, cadences of forms sufficient-in-themselves." The structural design conveys far more than this, and is charged with intimations. In the case we are here considering it reveals not only that a flat surface organized in non-perspective terms can answer to human activity in general and convey a certain quantity of information, but also that it can comprise, apart from any semantic referent, spatio-temporal virtualities of such a kind that—to borrow Noël Moulod's apt description—"it matches up to our profound awareness of spatial existence." This is equivalent to saying that a formally bi-dimensional artefact (of the type produced by Mondrian, Van Doesburg, Albers, Klee and Malevich) tends, in itself, to act on surrounding space and to modify man's relations with the universe. Alexander Doerner, Siegfried Giedion and Max Bill were, I believe, the first to draw attention to this phenomenon. To Pierre Francastel we owe a lucid description of it. "Mondrian's space," he says, "opens out on several imaginary spaces, other than the figurative surface carrying geometrized signs. Hang a Mondrian on a wall and you immediately discover (provided this is one of the artist's successful works) that the picture *organizes* all the space around it. Its linear, but non-symmetrical forms lead the spectator to geometrize (and activate) this space. Here we have a sort of extension of the genetic values of lines and surfaces. The way opened up by Mondrian was fructuous because it made artists aware that their works played an active part as guide-marks in the realm of the imaginary."

There can be no question—and this is a point we would insist on—that the painter's imaginary space, created by a balanced disposition of planes of color, provided contemporary architecture with "models" which the new building techniques (steel or concrete skeletons, slabs, screens, etc.) were quick to incorporate. In this respect Mondrian's creations (with which we naturally associate those of Van Doesburg, Kupka and Malevich) contributed largely to the modification of architectural space, which was, similarly, liberated from the constraints of axial perspective, frontal layout, opaque façades, structure designed in terms of masses. For though it is rightly said that "painting is closely bound up with the developments of contemporary architecture," this does not mean (as is sometimes over-hastily assumed) that architecture gave the lead—we have only to compare the dates. In point of fact it was the painters' structuralist approach that activated the new architecture, by presenting to it units that could be handled in a persistently and thoroughly dynamic, aperspectival manner.

It fell to Cubism to inaugurate a structural aesthetic embodying a theory of visual perception in its purest state. (Is this why it was accused in Paris, during the 1914-1918 war, of being of Germanic inspiration?) Cubism blazed two trails: one leading northwards (to Holland) and the other eastwards (to Russia). The idea behind this art was, in its fashion, simple: that of figuring forth in painting the existential condition of contemporary man, without resorting to any method of re-presentation. To Mondrian's thinking, straight lines and color amply sufficed to convey to the beholder the rhythms of life under their most dynamic aspects. Following Malevich, Van Doesburg and El Lissitzky—in this agreeing with the psychologists of the subconscious—believed that simple formal relations "can indicate the shape of a thing, an event or a situation." Hence there was no longer any need for the figuration of objects, since a plastic construct could bypass, so to say, our everyday perceptions and nonetheless convey the sense of that primordial, fathomless depth which gives a meaning to existence. Like Klee and Kandinsky, Moholy-Nagy and Popova were conscious of the need we have (as Merleau-Ponty puts it) for "an absolute in the relative, for a space that does not glide over appearances, is not 'given' with them, in the realist manner, and can outlast their disintegration." This explains why the classical conception of space as a locus of relations between things is replaced by the notion of space as a phenomenon—"phenomenal space"—, an imaginary ambiance in which tectonic values, tensions, articulations and groupings of forms disclose "certain equilibria basic to the scheme of things, to both the natural and the spiritual world" (Moulod). Thus the spatial potentialities of color are associated with the tectonic organization of the picture and the montage of the signs—lines, squares, triangles, circles—which, repelling or attracting each other, combine to build up plastic poems at once translucent and unlimited in scope. Sculpture, however, could not borrow from the picture its tensions, lines of force, transparences. The potential volumes implied in Pevsner's major works are indicated by concave or convex inflexions of a surface; these correspond to spatial potentialities and may be likened to the linear tensions which convey the spiritual element in Kandinsky's art.

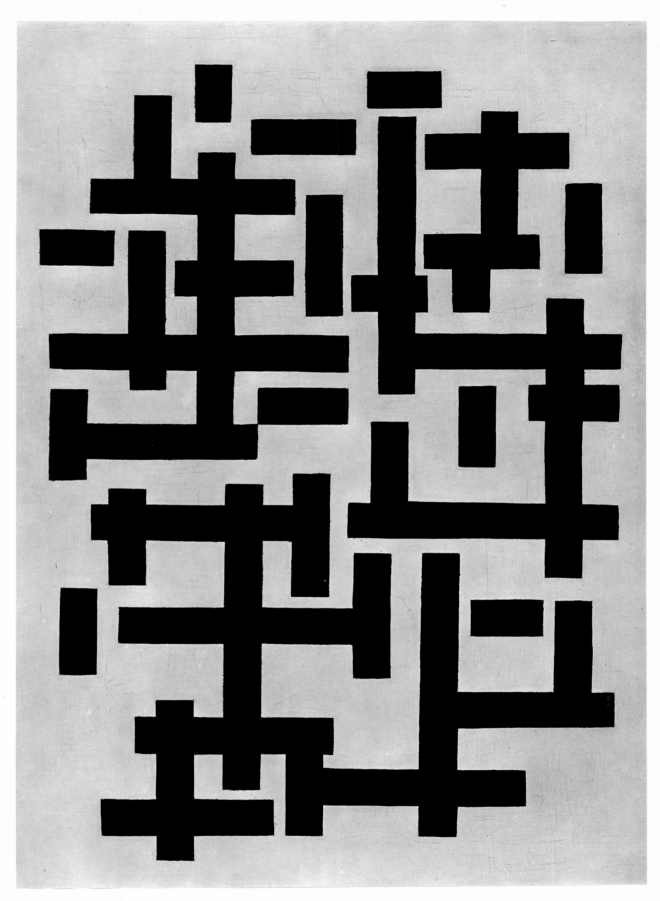

THEO VAN DOESBURG (1883-1931). COMPOSITION IN BLACK AND WHITE, 1918.
KUNSTMUSEUM, BASEL (ON LOAN FROM THE EMANUEL HOFFMANN FOUNDATION).

PIET MONDRIAN (1872-1944). COMPOSITION IN YELLOW, RED, BLUE AND BLACK, 1921. GEMEENTEMUSEUM, THE HAGUE.

1930 R.3 Farbtafel (auf maiorem Grau)

PAUL KLEE (1879-1940). COLOR SCALE (GREY DOMINANT), 1930. PAUL KLEE FOUNDATION, BERN.

LYUBOV SERGEIEVNA POPOVA (1889-1924). ARCHITECTONIC PAINTING, 1917.
COLLECTION, THE MUSEUM OF MODERN ART, NEW YORK. ACQUIRED THROUGH THE LILLIE P. BLISS BEQUEST.

LASZLO MOHOLY-NAGY (1895-1946). A.II, 1924.
THE SOLOMON R. GUGGENHEIM MUSEUM COLLECTION, NEW YORK.

JACQUES VILLON (1875-1963). SPACE, 1932. COLLECTION GALERIE LOUIS CARRÉ, PARIS.

EL LISSITZKY (1890-1941). PROUN 99, 1924. COLLECTION SOCIÉTÉ ANONYME, YALE UNIVERSITY ART GALLERY, NEW HAVEN, CONN.

WASSILY KANDINSKY (1866-1944). FLOATING, 1927. MARLBOROUGH-GERSON GALLERY, INC., NEW YORK.

ANTOINE PEVSNER (1884-1962). DEVELOPABLE SURFACE CONSTRUCTION, 1938. PRIVATE COLLECTION, BASEL.

Supreme moments of our western culture, the paintings in the Ducal Palace of Urbino and the Château de Versailles, the Sistine Chapel and the Marie de' Medici cycle rank rightly as majestic landmarks in the domain of "classical" art. Distinctive of all is the total mastery of the perspectival system which may be said to symbolize the concept of a well-ordered world mapped out in categories so clear-cut that it can reveal its unity only under an aspect of immobility, for thus alone do we perceive its cohesion, density and grandeur, and the immanence of (putatively) boundless space. The Petit Trianon is as closely linked up with the schema of the three dimensions as Molière's *Le Misanthrope* with the three unities, the *Comédie Humaine* with chronology, the *Missa Solemnis* with tonality and *Le Lac* with rhyme and meter. Since Space and Time were envisaged independently of each other, History necessarily assumed the form of a sequence of isolated entities. And similarly physics, incapable of giving an overall image of the cosmos, preferred to represent it as "a sort of picture gallery, with each class of phenomena treated in a different manner" (Max Planck).

The fact that tonality came into vogue in the period that witnessed the invention of perspective was due to a conjuncture like that which led Racine to retrieve and formulate the law of the three unities at the same time as Poussin inaugurated that of the three planes. And likewise the fact that the monarchical centralization of the age found in the perspectival mode and its harmonic corollaries an implement of "order" and royal "pomp and circumstance" links up with the triumph of an essentially closed system capable of producing spectacular illusionist effects and governed by rules of proportion—that "tremendous trifle" which establishes a meaningful, irreversible relation between things *inter se* and between things and their environment. From Michelangelo's vertiginous *trompe-l'œil* effects to the maze of mirrors in the castle of Herrenchiemsee, all art conspired "to render marvelously perceptible the space which every ensemble at once divides and unifies." Does this mean that, as Jean Starobinski suggests, this attitude "justified the acceptance of external appearances without troubling whether they might be deceptive"? In any case the practice of "associating eye-dazzling effects with truth" was not destined to stand up against the challenge to appearances launched simultaneously by James Watt and Robespierre, the challenge voiced long ago by Corneille:

> ... these misleading externals
> Have all too oft bedazzled my ill-enlightened eye,

and in our time by Paul Eluard:

> I feel Space coming to an end
> And Time growing out in all directions.

For both the French Revolution and the Industrial Revolution following on the invention of the steam engine were early symptoms of a phenomenon which, in the twentieth century, was to shatter the framework of our agrarian civilization by incorporating the time factor in both practical life and speculative thought. Already in the nineteenth century an effort was in progress to break free from the shackles of traditional values, preliminary to the major effort that has brought to fruition our present-day a-perspectival vision. Its pioneers were Cézanne and Bergson, Freud and Planck, Mallarmé and Apollinaire, Einstein and Minkowski, and it was founded on the negation of a quantitative space and a measurable time external to man. We see its culmination in Picasso's major works (such as *Guernica*), in Musil's *Man without Qualities*, Joyce's *Ulysses*, Max Ernst's *La Porte Saint-Denis*, André Breton's *Nadja*, Matisse's *La Danse*, Le Corbusier's Villa Savoye, Schönberg's *Pierrot Lunaire*, Pevsner's *Developable Surface Construction*, Klee's *The Cupboard*, René Clair's film *Entr'acte*, Queneau's *Les Enfants du limon*, Mies van der Rohe's Barcelona Pavilion and Mondrian's *Boogie Woogie*. Different as these works are, all alike treat the time element as biological duration, discontinuity, a manifestation of the life force, a factor of transparency. Now that it has become the non-categorical dimension *par excellence*, time-as-intensity conveys, *per se*, spatial intensity, brings before us all the values of diaphaneity, acquires and exercises the function of a fourth dimension. Hence the fundamental unity associating Kafka with Jaroslav Hasek, Böll with Moravia, Hemingway with Thomas Mann, Gide with Steinbeck, Joyce with Faulkner, Eluard with Friedrich Hagen. For all these men made no secret of their wish to bring to light the antinomies of the age, all alike sought to discover relations implicit in the time dimension and to comprise the totality of human experience without resorting to any hard-and-fast code of "laws." It was as though each of them feared the emergence of a system containing both the threat of a stereotyped spatialization and of a sterilization of information. This is why Picasso was an adept of "perpetual metamorphosis," Queneau the pioneer of a language in constant process of becoming, Schönberg high priest of atonality, Breton the advocate of "a state of savagery." With all these men this will to liberation led to what has been called a state of "achronism," where time ceased to count, where free scope was given to open, multidirectional forms—open in the sense of being accessible to all the vagaries of chance, all simultaneities. "Blocks of sound" dissolve in the same way as architectural masses, the opaque textures of sculpture and of modeling in painting are done away with. Klee's and Kandinsky's "constellations" herald Tobey's and Pollock's "nebulae," Archipenko's "lacunae," Moholy-Nagy's and Gabo's diaphanous modulations. Meanwhile the time dimension was permeating planes and a whole new topology taking form in the translucency of images. The poet Pierre Reverdy had a similar idea in mind when he wrote:

> Les yeux à peine ouverts
> La main sur l'autre rive
> Le ciel
> Et tout ce qui arrive
> La porte s'inclinait
> Une tête dépasse...

Apollinaire, too, in his famous poem *Zone* (1913):

> Tu te moques de toi et comme le feu de l'enfer ton rire
> pétille
> Les étincelles de ton rire dorent le fonds de ta vie

> C'est un tableau pendu dans un sombre musée
> Et quelquefois tu vas le regarder de près...
> Maintenant tu es au bord de la Méditerranée
> Sous les citronniers qui sont en fleur toute l'année
> Avec tes amis tu te promènes en barque...
> Tu es dans le jardin d'une auberge aux environs de
> Prague
> Tu te sens tout heureux une rose est sur la table.

Of this poem Marcel Raymond has aptly said that "it belongs to the genre of so-called 'cubist' pieces, synthetic or 'simultaneist,' in which are juxtaposed, without perspective, without transition, often without any apparent logic, incongruous elements, sensations, observations and memories, which intermingle in the flux of the stream of consciousness." Gertrude Stein displayed an equal liberty in *Tender Buttons: Objects, Foods, Rooms* (1914). But Benjamin Péret does more than merely draw up from the dark underworld of the unconscious "piping hot words that he sets to cool in daylight" (Ribemont-Dessaignes); he strikes down to the heart of the aperspectival world, to the point where the geometry of Time plays havoc with the rationalist usage of metaphor:

> En arrivant au baromètre tordu comme un vieux jeton
> l'homme en or de barre fixe
> réclame l'ascenseur qui fuit comme un haricot
> pour éteindre le feu de sa végétation tropicale
> qui s'use comme un édredon dans une salière.

A willful escape into the irrational? Certainly not. This semantic "bombardment" plunges us into an irrationality of structures that can properly be described as non-dimensional: they are the same structures as those which always hover in the background of contemporary physics and biology. Had not J. K. Huysmans, Isidore Ducasse and Alfred Jarry foreseen that, sooner or later, Reason would be compelled to quit her ivory tower and listen in to other voices?

There is another, even more striking phenomenon which helps to give a new meaning to the world. The transmutation of matter—that old dream of the alchemists—is being achieved at the very same time as the fusion of psychic space and psychic time is taking place, distinctions between finite and infinite are being obliterated and the barriers between the external and the internal wearing thin. These are among the major consequences of the rejection of perspectival vision, and here too we see some of the new possibilities it has opened up.

Their antecedents can be seen in the pioneer work of Mies van der Rohe, first in the western world to invite the spatial environment to join forces with architectural space—I have in mind the "Pavilion of Germany" built in 1929 to figure in the Barcelona Exhibition. If this had so great an influence on architecture throughout the world (Californian in particular) this was because it suggested that it was possible to "abstract" a wall by indicating the presence *in posse* of an absent surface, or expanding space by the use of large transparent planes. Here we surely have intimations of a composition without frames or boundaries, extensible (mathematically) *ad infinitum*, whose prototype may be traced to the art of Mondrian. At about the same time Le Corbusier freed architecture from the strait-jacket of classical perspective and opened it up to the "accidents" of discontinuity. Thus in the Villa Savoye (now in a state of sad decrepitude despite the fact that it is under the aegis of the French authority for the preservation of Historic Monuments) we can see a superb disregard of the three dimensions. Time is spatialized, space absorbed into it from every point of the compass and we are asked to read into it four sides without façades—so closely does its transparency seem to derive from Picasso's Cubism. Pevsner, too, succeeded in imparting to empty space the *quality* of a volume, vouched for by the imaginary and actualizing the intensity of the Time factor, vital element of the human condition, without recourse to any of the devices of illusionism. Even André Breton was momentarily fascinated by the possibilities of this new, startling synthesis, when he exclaimed: "How beautiful are parallels under God's perpendicular! Time is miraculously fading out behind its snow-flake sandals!" But where am I? In yesterday, today, tomorrow? The dyad synchrony-diaphony is transporting me into that diaphanous vista where all moments are the present moment, that vista which Gide had in mind when, in writing *The Counterfeiters*, he diagnosed the shortcomings of the "naturalist" (we would say "perspectival") school. "The great defect of this school is to cut its

slice (its slice of life) always in the same direction: in the direction of time, in length. Why not in width, or in depth? Personally I'd prefer not to cut at all. Meaning that I'd like to make *everything* enter into it, into my novel." A grandiose program, never brought to fruition. But where Gide failed Musil succeeded. His *Man without Qualities* is assuredly the finest example, in our generation, of the aperspectival, philosophical, topological novel and as far removed from the linear, horizontal style as is, in the domain of painting, the art of Delaunay, Picasso, Braque, and Léger. In this masterwork of "modern" literature an urge to total understanding and a feverish dialectic of ideas are implemented by a novel and perturbing feeling for the "liberty of time." Typical is this passage in the center of the book, marking the point at which begins the protagonist's experience of "the other state." "The journey had been long and particles of the general conversation which had sunk into him floated up to the surface... He now was posted in that sort of breathing-space which supervenes when tumult is replaced by silence... He had in his pocket his father's curious telegram, which he knew by heart, 'This is to inform you of my death,' words that the old gentleman had had written to him—or should he say 'had written'? The telegram itself gave the answer, since it was signed 'Your father.'" Farther on, we find this remark by Ulrich: "Memories grow old along with those who have them and even the most thrilling incidents acquire a faintly comic air, as if one were viewing them through a series of ninety-nine doors opening on to each other. But sometimes, when memories are fraught with intense emotion, they do not age and whole strata of the personality remain attached to them." And when this powerful, illuminating, disconcerting "romance of absence" evokes the special state of mind which induces "the amazing feeling, shared by love and mysticism, that the outside world and the world within have lost their frontiers and become limitless," it reveals the exact dimensions of the mutation that is taking place in present-day man.

It was doubtless necessary to begin by breaking up the image, before remaking it in another language. Despite the seeming conflicts in the art trends of the first half of the century, all alike may be regarded as leading up to what we have called the aperspectival vision. Viewed from this angle, every procedure is acceptable provided it is used as a means for testing out new theories and not as an end in itself. Also provided it carries conviction in virtue of the coherence and "truth" of its message. But when the limits of the possible are done away with, is this coherence really easier to achieve? In art, as in morals, do not "rules" provide the criterion—or illusion—of "good work"? And does not the permissibility of choosing freely between an unlimited number of possibles have a bewildering effect? The artist proposes, the "consumer" disposes. But who, then, chooses? One may even wonder whether, at this point of history, the public is not more responsible for the creative act than is the creator himself. Of all the possibles the one for which Picasso, Braque and Matisse elected was an outcome of the discovery that the human figure loses nothing of its humanity by being relegated to the surface of a given tract of space. Line and color have per se *the power of creating all manner of illusions. Also, is "knowledge" needed by the artist to actualize the knowledge of the scientist? When he draws the outlines of a sleeping figure, does he know that the arabesque he utilizes with such freedom to represent the model viewed full face and in profile, in density and in surface, in a brief moment of repose—does he know that this arabesque embodies a new concept of geometry? This is no direct concern of his, even though science confirms the veracity of his intuitions. The coincidence has value for us, observers of the historical process, but none for the artist; his sole aim is to convince us "on his own," by the "striking force" of his work. That striking force at its highest pitch can be seen in all Picasso's work, whatever he turns his hand to. How amazing is the psychical and physical plenitude he achieves where Matisse, using the same topological data, discreetly stylizes! Braque, however, taking a position midway between his Fauve and Cubist colleagues, always has recourse to fragmentation; his art is more a recapitulation than a synthesis— hence his obsession with the still life. He always seems to cut short his experiments when it comes to pressing them to their logical conclusions.*

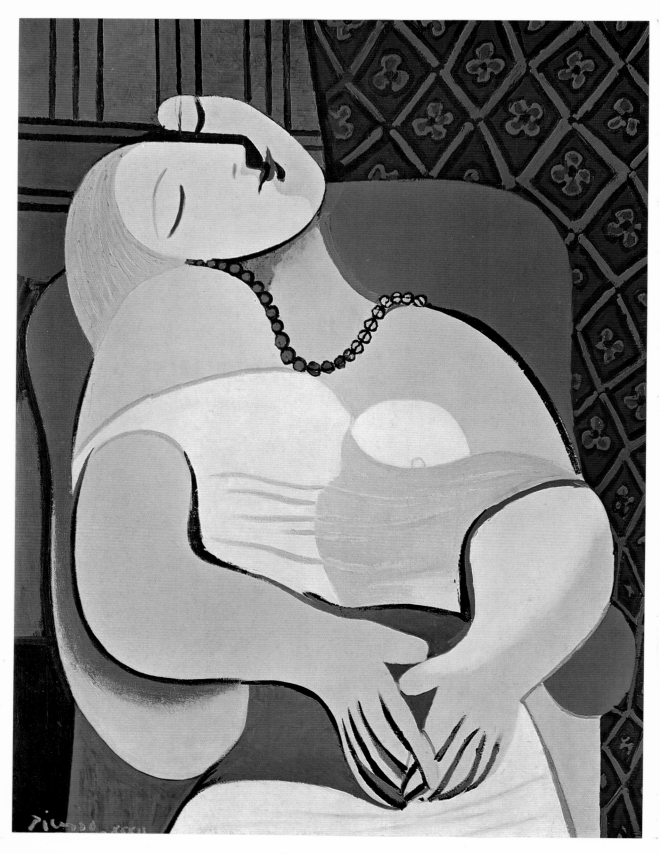

PABLO PICASSO (1881). WOMAN ASLEEP IN A RED ARMCHAIR, 1932. MR AND MRS VICTOR W. GANZ COLLECTION, NEW YORK.

HENRI MATISSE (1869-1954). THE DREAM, 1940. PRIVATE COLLECTION.

GEORGES BRAQUE (1882-1963). WASHSTAND IN FRONT OF A WINDOW, 1942. LOUVRE, PARIS. BRAQUE BEQUEST.

6

TOWARDS AN ARCHITECTURE

In appraising the vast changes that came over architecture in the first half of this century, it is not enough to assume that these were due to the use of new materials (concrete, steel and glass). Nor is it enough to say that the growth of a French and Austrian, Dutch and German Purism was the result of a certain ethical attitude or a cultural and historical conjunction. Nor is it enough to speak of the social upheavals of the age and the resultant metamorphosis of living conditions, and to see in their compulsions a prime factor of the new discoveries. It is of quite equal interest to note that architecture once again applied itself "to creating spaces, not to designing façades" (Berlage, 1908), and no less interesting to observe the growing tendency toward a universalization of its language, due both to the industrial nature of the material employed and to the rapid extension of means of communication. But it is no less important to point out that, seconded by both these factors, a new creative urge made itself felt, an urge whose origins seem to lie in the release of forces intuitively directed to elevating the problems and functions of the architect to the level of the speculative and scientific discoveries of such men as Planck and Einstein. This can be demonstrated only if we abandon the critical method which aims, primarily, at tabulating a series of "styles." We would do better to follow up the line

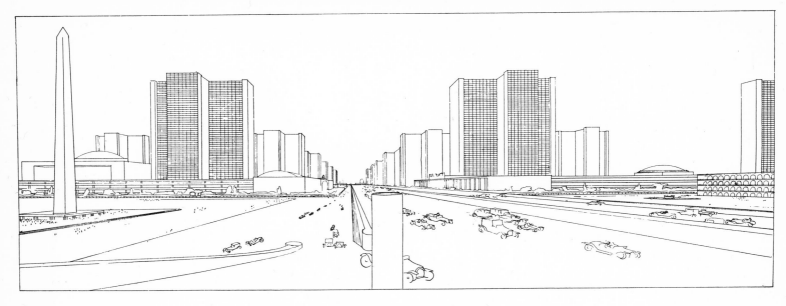

LE CORBUSIER (1887-1965).
STUDY FOR A CONTEMPORARY CITY OF THREE MILLION INHABITANTS, WITH THROUGH TRAFFIC LANES, 1922.

LUDWIG MIES VAN DER ROHE (1886).
PROJECT FOR AN OFFICE BUILDING WITH A CONCRETE SKELETON, 1922.

'951).
PROJECT, ABOUT 1930.
EMPORARY ARCHITECTURE," 1931.

LUDWIG MIES VAN DER ROHE (1886).
MODEL OF A GLASS SKYSCRAPER
WITH A METAL SKELETON, 1919.

VLADIMIR TATLIN (1885-1956).
PROJECT FOR A MONUMENT TO THE
THIRD INTERNATIONAL, MOSCOW, 1920.

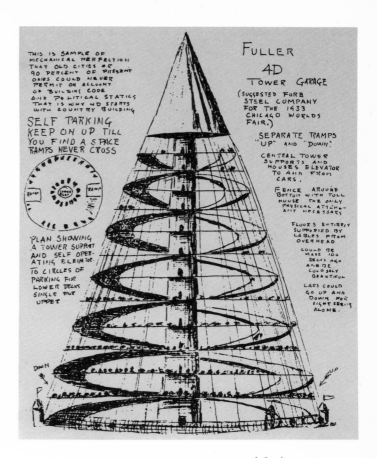

RICHARD BUCKMINSTER FULLER (1895).
DESIGN FOR A TOWER GARAGE, 1927.

IAKOW CHERNIKOV (1887-
CONSTRUCTIVIST RESEARCH
FROM "ELEMENTS OF CON"

of research which tends to bring out the fact that, apart from the pioneer achievements of Gropius and Wright, nothing was built before 1920 which dispensed with the perspectival vision, and that the few buildings which may be said to count (those designed by Perret, Van de Velde and Loos) still adhered to the post-impressionist tradition. The change did not take place until the discoveries made in France, from 1906 on, in the domain of painting— needless to say, I have Cubism in mind—and followed up in Holland (De Stijl) and Russia (Suprematism, Constructivism), had been assimilated and it was found possible to give them expression in terms of solids located in space, that is to say in architecture. Examples are the Villa Schröder at Utrecht (Rietveld, 1924), the Bauhaus buildings at Dessau (Gropius, 1925-1926), the Lovell Health House in Los Angeles (Neutra, 1927-1929), the Villa Savoye at Poissy (Le Corbusier, 1928), the Schocken Department Store at Chemnitz (Mendelsohn, 1928), the Van Nelle Tobacco Factory at Rotterdam (Brinkmann and Van der Vlugt, 1929-1930), the German Pavilion at the Barcelona Exhibition (Mies van der Rohe, 1929), the Paimio Sanatorium (Aalto, 1929-1933) and the open-air school built by Duiker in Amsterdam (1930-1932). These are the first places where we see the new aesthetic at its magnificent best; of cubist inspiration, it introduces the time factor into space, develops the plan organically, starting out from a central focus, and transforms the building into a non-perspectival dwelling open in all directions to the gaze and to the free play of hitherto unthought-of dimensions. But the antecedents of this aesthetic remain something of a mystery; doubtless because the course taken by the pathfinders is indicated only by signs, and they personally have little to say about it. By and large it emanated from the draftsman's office or the experimentalist's workshop; in other words, from innumerable projects, sketches and models made in the first decades of the century in Russia (Malevich, El Lissitzky, Tatlin, Leonidov, Wesnin), in Germany (Bruno and Max Taut, Finsterlin, Scharoun, the Luckhardts, Kohtz, Gropius, Mies van der Rohe), in Austria (Kiesler), in Holland (Rietveld, Van Eesteren, Van Doesburg, Vantongerloo), in France (Tony Garnier, Le Corbusier, Mallet-Stevens), in Italy (Sant'Elia, Virgilio Marchi), and in the United States (Burnham, Buckminster Fuller and several others). Everywhere, in the work of the vanguard spirits of the period, we find an urge

ERICH MENDELSOHN (1887-1953).
THE SCHOCKEN DEPARTMENT STORE, CHEMNITZ, 1928.

JOHANNES ANDREAS BRINKMANN (19
VAN NELLE TOBACC

FRANK LLOYD WRIGHT (1869-1959).
CAR PARK OF THE JOHNSON WAX COMPANY, RACINE (WISCONSIN), 1939.

H

L.C. VAN DER VLUGT (1896-1936).
ROTTERDAM, 1930.

ROCKEFELLER CENTER, NEW YORK, 1931-1939.
EXECUTED BY THEER ARCHITECTURAL FIRMS:
REINHARD AND HOFMEISTER; CORBETT,
RRISON AND MACMURRAY; HOOD AND FOUILHOUX.
COURTESY OF ROCKEFELLER CENTER, INC.

to do away with academic canons, a will to think freely, untrammelled by traditional procedures, to create large-scale urban centers, and fully to explore the formal and aesthetic possibilities of the new materials available. All agreed that there was an urgent need for the "modern" architect to turn his back on the past, to fix his eyes on the future and to think out projects suited to the new living conditions and symbolizing the way of life both of the individual and of collectivities. For this he had to take into account the latent or expressed requirements of the social organism, the ever-rising potential of production, the technical, economic, scientific and demographic background of a new, mass civilization explicable only in terms of the social sciences and the socio-cultural climate. To this intense speculative activity is largely due the modern insistence on the notion of design. Gropius saw in design an integral part of "the stuff of life"; to his thinking it stood for a philosophy preserving daily life from crystallization and art from stagnation. And it was the publication of so-called utopian projects of this order, draft plans of dream cities, an imaginary architecture having few direct contacts with the life of the moment but rich in promise for the future that signalized, well before they were given opportunities of putting their plans into execution, the genius of men like Le Corbusier, Mies van der Rohe, Gropius, Van Doesburg, Sant'Elia, Buckminster Fuller, Mart Stam, Chernikov and Hilberseimer.

Our twentieth-century avatars of Piranesi differed from their predecessor in that their utopian dreams were to be realized in the near future. For very soon their projects took form and meaning: a symbolic meaning and a form composed of steel and glass and concrete, both less derivative from any logically worked-out theory than from a way of seeing adumbrated in the preliminary experimental phase: a compulsive, frankly aperspectival vision. This vision was realized, on a grandiose scale, in the Rockefeller Center which "requires comprehension in space and time... analogous to what has been achieved in modern scientific research as well as in modern painting" (Siegfried Giedion). The Center, which consists of fifteen slabs of different heights constituting a self-complete urban zone within the orthogonal complex of New York, seems to stem as much from the experimental art of Malevich and Van Doesburg as from the prophetic views put forward by Le Corbusier in 1922.

THE CITY OF A DREAM

We get an impression that when Sant'Elia found himself enrolled in the ranks of the Futurists this was far from pleasing him. In May 1914, under the auspices of the "Nuove Tendenze" group, he had exhibited at Milan a remarkable set of plans for a "New City," accompanied by a declaration of faith with the simplest possible title: Messaggio. *Marinetti promptly made use of this text, embodying its themes and substance, enlarged and pressed to extremes, in the Manifesto of Futurist Architecture (July 1914). Sant'Elia died on the battle-field, October 10, 1916, at the age of twenty-eight. We can see today how far removed were the political and ideological conceptions of this young descendant of the Saint-Simonians, a militant socialist and whole-hearted pacifist, from Marinetti's bellicose nationalism.*

Even assuming that he knew of them (and this is highly doubtful), it was not from the projects of Otto Wagner or Tony Garnier's experiments that Sant'Elia got the makings of his amazing vision of the city of the future. Actually he found the premises of his ideal city in the prescient, brilliantly imaginative sketches of Leonardo (Manuscript B, 1480-1490): lofty residential towers, stepped buildings, roads hung in mid-air at different levels, separation of pedestrian and vehicular traffic—a whole program which has been rightly described as a uniquely brilliant anticipation of twentieth-century town-planning. Sant'Elia's imagination may well have been oriented by the new trends of American architecture when he conjured up this vision of the Milan of the future, basing his forecasts on the facts of demographic expansion, technical advances and their social corollaries. A concern for monumental values and a half-unconscious craving for theatrical effect are no less bound up with this concept of a Città nuova, *than a basic preoccupation with figuring forth a great urban center in which active recognition is given to the time factor—in other words a scene animated through and through by the "principle of movement." "We have to conceive and to construct the modern city in terms of a new plan. It must be like an enormous ship-builder's yard, full of sound and movement and resemble a gigantic machine. There will no longer be any concealment of the elevators—those melancholy earthworms—in dark shafts within the building. Having become superfluous, staircases will be dispensed with and lifts will wind their way, long snakes of glass and iron, up and down the façades. Built of concrete, steel and glass, houses will be erected flush with the edge of the street, stark and sheer in their simplicity, without any painted or sculptured ornaments."*

ANTONIO SANT'ELIA (1888-1916). PROJECT FOR "THE NEW CITY," 1914. WATERCOLOR. MARGHERITA G. SARFATTI COLLECTION, ROME.

When over forty years ago Auguste Perret built the church of Notre-Dame at Le Raincy, on the traditional basilical plan, he gave an early, brilliant demonstration of the possibilities of slightly reinforced concrete. In this respect the edifice marks an important date in the evolution of the first new artificial building material. But, though Perret's handling shows a full appreciation of the nature of this new material, he kept to a structural system inspired by Gothic architecture, which (as has been aptly said) was an art of "making the bearing points sing out." The lightly curving vault rests on slender, fluted pillars which only faintly indicate the divisions of the nave, bathed in a light discreetly modulated by neutral and colored windows pierced in the prefabricated slabs, mounted on a solid base, that serve as walls.

It fell to a Swiss engineer, Robert Maillart, who had studied under François Hennebique, to be the first to "think in concrete" as efficiently as Eiffel "thought in steel." Maillart's remarkable structural vision ("we must start out by perceiving the function of the whole before that of the parts") led him to a monolithic conception of his materials that involved the integration of pillars, beams and flooring slab into a structural unit in which supporting beams are eliminated, their function being resolved into the concrete slab. All his designs are conceived in a strictly functionalist spirit—as we see in his bridge across the river Thur near St Gall (though here a heavy parapet subsequently replaced an elegant balustrade). An interesting feature of this bridge is the way upright slabs are used as vertical ties between the roadway of the bridge and the pointed arch beneath it. The curious appearance of this arch is due to the fact that each half was cast separately in the same shuttering. Here the industrial method of mass production was applied for the first time to bridge construction.

As for the dwelling-house planned as—to quote Sant' Elia's formula—"a machine for living in," this was treated by Rietveld at Utrecht and Wright at Bear Run on lines that are less divergent than is often thought from those of our present-day "rational" and "organic" architecture. Both Falling Water and the Villa Schröder derive from the Cubist dialectic; both alike, breaking with the perspectival façade, convey an impression of fluid, multidirectional space.

AUGUSTE PERRET (1874-1954). NAVE OF THE CHURCH OF NOTRE-DAME AT LE RAINCY, NEAR PARIS, 1922.

ROBERT MAILLART (1872-1940). BRIDGE OVER THE RIVER THUR AT FELSEGG, NEAR ST GALL (SWITZERLAND), 1933.

GERRIT RIETVELD (1888-1964). THE VILLA SCHRÖDER AT UTRECHT, 1924.

FRANK LLOYD WRIGHT (1869-1959). THE KAUFMAN HOUSE, "FALLING WATER," AT BEAR RUN (PA.), 1936.

THE MINISTRY OF EDUCATION AT RIO DE JANEIRO, 1937-1943.

FROM THE INVISIBLE
TO THE VISIBLE

It was once said of Kandinsky that, beginning in the 1920s, he built up a repertory of "self-sufficient forms" having no reference to anything in the "real world." The same thing has been said, and still is often said, of the "inventions" of Klee and Miró, of Fautrier and Wols, of Tchelitchew and Matta, of Masson and Gorky, of Estève, Bazaine and other practitioners of so-called non-figurative art. It is suggested that as a result of hostility to the experienced visible, a weariness of the perceptive faculty or a saturation of the artists' sensibility, much of the art of the first half of the present century deliberately turned away from nature and took to searching out, in the dreamworld of the imaginary, those "imponderable phantasms" to which Apollinaire bade the creator "give reality." And this rupture of the dialogue with the visible has often been held to account for several of the main trends of contemporary art.

Nothing, in our opinion, could be falser. The truth is, rather, that our present-day artists find the stimuli for their most noteworthy creations in a sublimation of the perceptible—but a preternaturally intensified "perceptible," having little in common with the data of normal visual experience. Is this tantamount to saying that the painter—in particular —applies himself (as Fromentin once said of Rembrandt) "to making visible the invisible"? And does it mean that, so as to gain access to the world, *his* world, he deprived himself of the use of the exploring eye, of reference to the observable object and "the totality of the thing perceived"? No, on the contrary, it was at energizing the act of perception that he aimed when he directed his gaze towards the inmost core of realities, that latent substratum which was now in process of being rendered visible by the progress of scientific discoveries, for example the remarkable advances in the techniques of microscopy. For these were bringing within the range of eyesight new phenomena, revelations of the inner "life" of matter, geometric and chromatic figurations

of intangible entities, of structures or minute elements which now were made directly perceptible to the observer, or indirectly by means of microphotography. Here was a world in which, seen from the biological angle, forms often seem little adapted to any precise end and relations between forms and functions to defy analysis.

But that this world was brought into visibility did not suffice; nor was it enough that it should enter merely into the domain of purely scientific research. The sensibility of the artist needed to be attuned to it, for here there clearly was something capable of firing the enthusiasm of the creative mind and providing visual material of a new and fascinating order, rich in aesthetic possibilities. Here, in short, was a privileged domain of the visible having a direct appeal to the collective (socialized) mentality of modern man. It is to Klee, Kandinsky and Franz Marc that we must, it seems, assign the merit of being the first not only to have discovered here new sources of emotion but, what is more, to have provided this new-found world with a galaxy of forms so apt and meaningful as to constitute a system of intelligible signs, charged with both emotive and intellectual values. Where Cézanne rearranged three apples, Kandinsky uncovered the cryptic geometry of diatoms, and while Picasso sought for stereometric effects inspired by Negro plastic art, Klee uncovered histological cross-sections. The fact that here we can see one of the immediate sources of Klee's inspiration does not affect in the least the poetic quality of his genius. A passage in his Jena lecture (1924) testifies to his keen interest in microscopy. "Can it be disputed," he asks, "that a mere glance at any object through a microscope is enough to reveal images that we would surely describe as bizarre, indeed preposterous, if they happened to meet our eye in the ordinary way, without our knowing how they were arrived at? The first reaction of the ordinary man seeing a reproduction of one of these in a popular magazine is to exclaim, 'Forms of nature—

what nonsense! Just another sample of ugly modern decorative art!' Is the artist, then, concerned with microscopy, histology, paleontology? Solely for purposes of comparison, and to ensure a mobile vision, not with an eye to scientifically checking his fidelity to nature." Ten years earlier (in 1914) Franz Marc had thrown light on one of the fundamental relations between twentieth-century art and the scientific discoveries then in progress. "The art of the near future will be an incarnation of our scientific world view. We are breaking down nature—elusive and misleading nature—on the lines of our new discoveries. For we now can see through matter and surely the day is near when we shall penetrate it as easily as air. Matter is an entity that man still is forced to accept, but he is changing it out of recognition; instead of contenting ourselves with gazing at the world we scan it with X-rays."

But History does not always conform exactly to the image we would like it to present to us. In point of fact the works spoken of in the preceding pages tend to invalidate, partially, the theory that "the discovery of the infinitely small was made by artists whose starting point was of a purely pictorial order, and who, though their work ran parallel with that of the scientists, had no direct contacts with them" (Pierre Francastel). I say "partially" for the simple reason that we have to recognize that many artists applied themselves to constructing *imagined* images which did not derive from figural objects found in the transparent field of microscopic or X-ray observations, but were directly inspired by "models" created by Klee and Kandinsky. It is clear, in any case, that both groups of artists took guidance from the intuitions of those who, on the level of the imaginary, were now producing works which, when compared with the realities revealed by the microscope, show highly striking "coincidences." By and large—and even if these "coincidences" tend to give us up to a certain point "the illusion of seeing what we do not see"— they should not be regarded merely as pointing the way to a particularized evolution of taste and sensibility, but also as factors capable of introducing vital and pregnant elements into the culture and sensibility of the age.

Though not all contemporary artists have stated this explicitly, whether in writing or by word of mouth, we cannot fail to recognize that one of their chief concerns is manifested in an underlying tendency to enlarge by all possible means the visual domain and to break free from the thrall of worn-out "themes," "subjects" and "objects." Hence a will to figure forth hitherto unheeded or unseen events and, by the same token, to discover the elements of a new language in keeping with our times. Rare, in this context, is the frankness evinced by Paul Klee in his *Journal*, which tells us that in 1908 (the year he started painting) he made use of field-glasses, when sketching, "so as to break free from 'real' perspective, but without lapsing into the arbitrary." From the same source we learn that in 1910, when making studies from nature, he employed a magnifying glass, pending the time when, in the Bauhaus period and along with Kandinsky, he explored the possibilities of microscopy. This does not mean that scientific and technical devices demolished the wall of the visible; rather, they moved further back the wall of appearances. And since, as is common knowledge, appearances are misleading, the desire to get behind them also became more and more insistent. Hence the common urge, noted by Jean Gebser, to make visible the structures that lie behind things and thoughts. "It is not the outer aspect of things," Picasso said, "that interests us, but their secret, inner life." Franz Marc, too, some months before his death said: "I am now beginning to see further and further *behind* and, better still, *across* things." Seeing behind and across means dispensing with the perspectival system; by giving access to a measureless reality, transparences do away with the abstraction constituted, in the last analysis, by the three-dimensional perspective schema. Here depth is the sole dimension—and depth, as Merleau-Ponty has aptly remarked, is "the dimension, *par excellence*, of the hidden." This explains why the invisible takes the form of relief and depth in a composition rendered in the "aperspectival mode." And also explains why, from Proust to Michaux, from Rilke to Francis Ponge, from Klee to Wols, from Mackintosh to Le Corbusier, this half century has witnessed the rise of an art in direct contact with the illimitable "world behind the world."

When one of Tobey's friends, a Chinese artist, told him that most of the works of western painters were simply "framed holes," it is clear that, placing himself in the position of the European spectator, he was protesting against the opacity of an art that was based on a naive faith in geometrical abstraction. Tang Kwei could speak thus all the more freely since the man he was talking to was one of the few interpreters of the contemporary world who, in attempting to establish a cleavage between East and West, had for some time been applying himself to building up a vision of reality from which all homocentric attitudes and as a corollary all "rational" operations were excluded. Thus, following Paul Klee, Tobey found in a calligraphy freed from representational service a means of creating works addressed rather to the sensibility than to the eye. For Tobey "writing" the picture had become a sine qua non. *Not that he aimed at assimilating Oriental calligraphy—that would have been a superficial, crude and pointless endeavor; what he wanted was to record as instantaneously as possible the dramatic, often conflicting, always mobile elements of city life. It is in the "Broadway" sequence that his experiments in "white writing" culminate; these are graphic snapshots of the monstrous city, a tangled linear paroxysm, a vibrant carnival of signs. A fluctuating, fleecy line flickers over dim nocturnal grounds and figures forth, without describing or precisely specifying, crowds, light, space and traffic.*

Masson, on the other hand, had not needed any promptings from the world around him to perceive the hallucinative power of that free, uncalculated line which round about 1924 was to liberate Surrealism from its addiction to geometry, its morphological and literary erudition. Starting out from the possibilities of automatism, Masson lit on the idea—a happy one in the event—of a "whirlwind writing" which in itself and in the very moment of its execution, gave glimpses of a world beyond the world of visual experience. Hence this archipelago of embryonic forms, "tears of the imaginary," uprushes of the subliminal self, which make the picture a recipient of forces lacking any central axis and endlessly proliferating.

Have we not in this summoning-up of the invisible to the surface of the visible, this release of the subconscious, a challenge to the claims of objectivity, an abandonment of perspectival vision and, as Merleau-Ponty would say, an incorporation in the category of "the real" of the contacts between observer and observed, between the artist and his work? This, too, is why a phenomenology of the invisible lies at the base of Gorky's creative line—and this despite the fact that the fluid, dreamlike, not to say perverse design of The Unattainable *clearly owes much to Miró's archetypes, and seems relatively innocuous when compared to the torrential line that sweeps along Wols's* Bateau Ivre.

MARK TOBEY (1890). BROADWAY, 1935. THE METROPOLITAN MUSEUM OF ART, NEW YORK. ARTHUR H. HEARN FUND, 1942.

ANDRÉ MASSON (1896). TANGLE, 1941. ANDRÉ MASSON COLLECTION, PARIS.

ARSHILE GORKY (1905-1948). THE UNATTAINABLE, 1945. THE BALTIMORE MUSEUM OF ART, FRIENDS OF ART FUNDS.

WOLS (1913-1951). LE BATEAU IVRE, ABOUT 1945. KUNSTHAUS, ZURICH.

It is no doubt to the very structure of American Society, its internal organization, its apocalyptic way of life, its dynamic rhythm and a certain rudimentary eroticism, that we should ascribe the sudden and immense success of psychoanalysis after the arrival in New York (in 1933) of Freud and Ernest Jones. This probably goes far to explain the vogue for Surrealism in the years 1940-1945, a vogue that led to the ready acceptance of the work of that authentically American genius Jackson Pollock (1912-1956). If Pollock in his first phase endorsed the ascendancy of Picasso and Miró, Matta and Masson, this was only because he found in their art the most effective justification of his own raison d'être. *He seems similarly to have accepted the dictum that "all the great painting of the last hundred years had been done in France" only because it helped to a clearer understanding of what was now being achieved in the American art world. And if during the Second World War he responded to the stimulus of some of the leaders of European art who had settled for the time being in Manhattan—Ernst, Masson, Léger, Mondrian, Chagall, Breton, Lipchitz and Zadkine— this was chiefly in order to test out the possibility of building up an œuvre that both gave the measure of his private world and at the same time embodied the specific traits of an indigenous culture. The series of "Totems" that he then embarked on evidences an intention to associate a rapid calligraphy, subjected to the hazards of automatism and the incantations of the sign, with themes deriving from Indian folklore, revelations of a "primitive" mentality that had come to fruition in a natural environment. Here, then, we have an art deliberately antagonistic to the myths of a mechanistic civilization. Soon, with a view to wresting a meaning from the* Lebenswelt, *he resorted to the purest possible expression of the creative act, to instinctive gestures which challenged in their pregnant spontaneity the superstition of "the finished work of art." He called in question both the means and all the dimensions of painting by sublimating* The Cry, *whose message a* Totem *breaks up, under the stress of actuality, into a flux of ricochets expressive of the predicament of modern man, harassed both by the instant problems of the day and dark forebodings of the future.*

JACKSON POLLOCK (1912-1956). TOTEM LESSON II, 1945. COLLECTION OF LEE KRASNER POLLOCK,
BY COURTESY OF MARLBOROUGH-GERSON GALLERY, INC., NEW YORK.

BIBLIOGRAPHY

The following list is limited to the principal sources consulted in the writing of this book.

ADORNO T.W., *Philosophie der neuen Musik*, Tübingen 1949.

AGEL H., *Le cinéma*, Paris 1954.
– *Esthétique du cinéma*, Paris 1957.

ALAIN, *Système des Beaux-Arts*, Paris 1920.

ALQUIÉ F., *Philosophie du surréalisme*, Paris 1955.

ANDERSON E.N., *Apologie pour l'industrialisme*, Diogène, No. 11, 1955.

APOLLINAIRE G., *Les peintres cubistes, Méditations esthétiques*, Paris 1913; 2nd edition, Paris 1922; 3rd edition, Geneva 1950.
– *Chroniques d'Art (1902-1918)*, Paris 1960.

ARGAN G.C., *Salvezza e caduta nell'arte moderna*, Milan 1964.

BACHELARD G., *Le nouvel esprit scientifique*, Paris 1934.
– *Dialectique de la durée*, Paris 1950.
– *La philosophie du Non*, Paris 1962.

BANHAM R., *Theory and Design in the First Machine Age*, London 1960.

BARR A.H., *Cubism and Abstract Art*, New York 1936.

BARTHES R., *Mythologies*, Paris 1957.
– *Eléments de sémiologie*, Communications, No. 4, Paris 1964.
– *Essais critiques*, Paris 1964.

BENJAMIN W., *Schriften*, 2 vols., Frankfort 1955.

BENSE Max, *Aesthetica*, 4 vols., Stuttgart, Krefeld, Baden-Baden 1954, 1956, 1958, 1960.

BERGSON H., *Essai sur les données immédiates de la conscience*, Paris 1906.
– *Durée et simultanéité*, Paris 1922.
– *Matière et mémoire*, 30th edition, Paris 1939.

BOCCIONI U., *Pittura, scultura futuriste*, Milan 1914.

BOREL E., *L'espace et le temps*, Paris 1949.

BRETON A., *Manifeste du surréalisme*, Paris 1924.
– *Second manifeste du surréalisme*, Paris 1930.
– *Le surréalisme et la peinture*, New York 1945.

BRION M., *Art abstrait*, Paris 1956.

BUCHHEIM L.G., *Die Künstlergemeinschaft Die Brücke*, Feldafing 1956.

BUTOR M., *Le carré et son habitant*, Nouvelle Revue Française, No. 97, 1961.

CAMUS A., *Le mythe de Sisyphe*, Paris 1942.
– *L'homme révolté*, Paris 1951.

CARROUGES M., *André Breton et les données fondamentales du surréalisme*, Paris 1950.

CENDRARS B., *Le profond aujourd'hui*, Paris 1931.

COSTA DE BEAUREGARD O., *La notion du temps*, Paris 1963.

DANIEL-HENRY (D. H. Kahnweiler), *Der Weg zum Kubismus*, Munich 1920.

DELAUNAY R., *Du cubisme à l'art abstrait*, Introduction and Notes by P. Francastel, Paris 1957.

DEWEY J., *Art as Experience*, New York 1934.

DORFLES G., *Simbolo, comunicazione, consumo*, Turin 1962.

DUFRENNE M., *Phénoménologie de l'expérience esthétique*, 2 vols., Paris 1953.

DUVIGNAUD J., *Pour entrer dans le XXᵉ siècle*, Paris 1960.

ECO U., *Opera aperta*, Milan 1962.
– *Apocalittici e integrati*, Milan 1964.

EINSTEIN A., and INFELD L., *Die Evolution der Physik*, rowohlts deutsche enzyklopädie 12, Hamburg 1956.

EISNER L. H., *L'écran démoniaque*, Paris 1952.

ELIADE M., *Le mythe de l'éternel retour*, Paris 1949.
– *Traité d'histoire des religions*, Paris 1949.
– *Images et symboles*, Paris 1952.

ELLUL J., *La technique ou l'enjeu du siècle*, Paris 1954.

FAURE E., *L'arbre d'Eden*, Paris 1922.

FOCILLON H., *La vie des formes*, Paris 1939.

FOURASTIÉ J., *Le grand espoir du XXᵉ siècle*, Paris 1963 (definitive edition).

FRANCASTEL P., *Peinture et Société*, Lyon 1951.
– *Art et Technique*, Paris 1956.
– *Aspects sociaux de la symétrie*, Les Temps Modernes, No. 202, 1963.

FREUD S., *Vorlesungen zur Einführung in die Psychoanalyse*, Vienna 1916.

FRIEDMANN G. (editor), *Villes et campagnes, Civilisation urbaine et civilisation rurale en France*, Paris 1953.
– *Réévaluation des sociétés modernes*, Diogène, No. 31, 1960.
– *Le travail en miettes*, 2nd edition, Paris 1964.

GARNIER I. and P., *L'expressionnisme allemand*, Paris 1962.

GEBSER J., *Ursprung und Gegenwart*, II, Stuttgart 1953.

GEORGE A. (editor), *Louis de Broglie, physicien et penseur*, Paris 1953.

GEORGE P., *La ville*, Paris 1952.

GIEDION S., *Space, Time and Architecture*, 3rd edition, Cambridge (Mass.) 1954.
– *Mechanization Takes Command*, New York 1955.

GIEDION-WELCKER C., *Plastik des 20. Jahrhunderts*, Stuttgart 1955.

GILSON E., *Peinture et réalité*, Paris 1958.

GLEIZES A., and METZINGER J., *Du cubisme*, Paris 1912.

GODEAUX L., *Les géométries*, Paris 1937.

GOLÉA A., *Esthétique de la musique contemporaine*, Paris 1954.

GRANGER G. G., *Logique, langage, communication*, in *Hommage à Gaston Bachelard*, Paris 1957.

GRAY C., *The Great Experiment: Russian Art, 1863-1922*, London 1962.

GROPIUS W., *Scope of Total Architecture*, New York 1943.

GUILLAUME P., *La psychologie de la forme*, Paris 1937.

HAECHT L. van., *Les racines communes de la phénoménologie, de la psychanalyse et de l'art contemporain*, Revue philosophique de Louvain, Vol. 51, 1953, pp. 568-590.

HAFTMANN W., *Malerei im 20. Jahrhundert*, Munich 1954-1955.

HEISENBERG W., *Physics and Philosophy*, New York 1958.
– *La nature dans la physique contemporaine*, Paris 1962.

HITCHCOCK H. R., *Architecture, Nineteenth and Twentieth Centuries*, London 1958.

HUGNET G., *L'aventure Dada (1916-1922)*, Paris 1957.

JAKOBSON R., *Essais de linguistique générale*, Paris 1963.

JEAN M., *Histoire de la peinture surréaliste*, Paris 1959.

JUNG C.G., *Die Beziehungen zwischen dem Ich und dem Unbewussten*, Zurich 1933.

KAHNWEILER D.H., *Juan Gris*, Paris 1946.
– *Confessions esthétiques*, Paris 1963.

KANDINSKY W., *Über das Geistige in der Kunst*, Munich 1911-1912.

KATZ D., *Gestaltpsychologie*, Basel 1944.

KLEE P., *Pädagogisches Skizzenbuch*, Bauhausbücher No. 2, Munich 1925.
– *Über die moderne Kunst*, Bern 1945.

KLEE F., *Paul Klee, Leben und Werk in Dokumenten*, Zurich 1963.

KÖHLER W., *Gestalt Psychology*, London 1930.

LANGER S.K., *Feeling and Form*, New York 1953.

LE BON G., *La psychologie des foules*, Paris 1895.

LE CORBUSIER, *L'art décoratif d'aujourd'hui*, Paris 1925.
– *Quand les cathédrales étaient blanches*, Paris 1937.
– *Des canons? Des munitions? Merci! Des logis s.v.p.*, Boulogne-sur-Seine 1938.
– *La charte d'Athènes*, Paris 1943.
– *Les trois établissements humains*, Paris 1945.
– *Manière de penser l'urbanisme*, Boulogne-sur-Seine 1946.

LEFEBVRE H., *Contribution à l'esthétique*, Paris 1953.
– *Critique de la vie quotidienne*, II, Paris 1961.

LÉVI-STRAUSS C., *La pensée sauvage*, Paris 1962.

LUPASCO S., *L'expérience microphysique et la pensée humaine*, Paris 1941.
– *Logique et contradiction*, Paris 1947.
– *Science et art abstrait*, Paris 1963.

MALEVICH K., *Die gegenstandslose Welt*, Munich 1927.

MARINETTI F.T., *Le Futurisme*, Paris 1911.

MATORÉ G., *L'espace humain*, Paris 1962.

MERLEAU-PONTY M., *Phénoménologie de la perception*, Paris 1945.
– *Sens et non-sens*, Paris 1948.
– *Signes*, Paris 1960.
– *Le visible et l'invisible*, Paris 1964.

MILLER G.A., *Language and Communication*, New York 1951.

MOHOLY-NAGY L., *The New Vision*, New York 1928.
– *Vision in Motion*, Chicago 1947.

MOLES A., *Théorie de l'information et perception esthétique*, Paris 1958.

MOULOD N., *La peinture et l'espace*, Paris 1964.

MOUNIER E., *Traité du caractère*, Paris 1947.
– *La petite peur du XXe siècle*, Neuchâtel 1948.

MORIN E., *Le cinéma ou l'homme imaginaire*, Paris 1956.
– *L'esprit du temps*, Paris 1962.

MORRIS C., *Signs, Language and Behaviour*, New York 1946.

MUMFORD L., *Technics and Civilization*, New York 1934.
– *The City in History*, New York 1961.

MYERS B.S., *Expressionism*, London 1957.

NADEAU M., *Histoire du surréalisme*, Paris 1945.

NOVOTNY F., *Cézanne und das Ende der wissenschaftlichen Perspektive*, Vienna 1938.

OZENFANT A., *Art*, Paris 1928.

OZENFANT A. and JEANNERET C.E. (Le Corbusier), *La peinture moderne*, Paris 1927.

PANOFSKY E., *Die Perspektive als symbolische Form*, Vorträge der Bibliothek Warburg, IV, 1924-1925.
– *Meaning in the Visual Arts*, New York 1955.

PEVSNER N., *Pioneers of Modern Design*, New York 1949.

PIAGET J. and INHELDER B., *La représentation de l'espace chez l'enfant*, Paris 1947.

PIERCE J.R., *Symbols, Signals and Noise*, New York 1962.

PLANCK M., *Vorträge und Erinnerungen*, Stuttgart 1949.

PLEKHANOV G., *L'art et la vie sociale*, Paris 1949.

PONENTE N., *Contemporary Trends*, Geneva 1960.

QUENEAU R., *Bâtons, chiffres et lettres*, Paris 1950.

RAPHAEL M., *Proudhon, Marx, Picasso*, Paris 1933.

RAYMOND M., *De Baudelaire au surréalisme*, Paris 1940.

READ H., *Art Now*, London 1933.

ROGNONI L., *Espressionismo e dodecafonia*, Turin 1964.

ROSTAND J., *Biologie et humanisme*, Paris 1964.

ROUGIER L., *Les paralogismes du rationalisme*, Paris 1920.

RUYER R., *La cybernétique et l'origine de l'information*, Paris 1954.

SADOUL G., *Histoire du cinéma*, Paris 1962.

SARTRE J.P., *L'imaginaire*, Paris 1940.

SCHMIDT G., SCHENK R. and PORTMANN A. *Form in Art and Nature*, Basel 1960.

SCHUHL P.M., *Machinisme et philosophie*, Paris 1947.

SEUPHOR M., *L'art abstrait, ses origines, ses premiers maîtres*, Paris 1949.
– *La sculpture de ce siècle*, Neuchâtel 1959.

SEVERINI G., *Du cubisme au classicisme*, Paris 1921.

SFAELLOS C.A., *Le fonctionnalisme dans l'architecture contemporaine*, Paris 1952.

SHANNON C.E. and WEAVER W., *The Mathematical Theory of Communication*, Urbana (Ill.) 1949.

SIMONDON G., *Du mode d'existence des objets techniques*, Paris 1958.

SOURIAU P., *La beauté rationnelle*, Paris 1904.

STAROBINSKI J., *L'oeil vivant*, Paris 1961.

STERNBERG F., *Kapitalismus und Sozialismus vor dem Weltgericht*, Hamburg 1951.

TAYLOR J.C., *Futurism*, New York 1961.

ULLMO J., *La pensée scientifique moderne*, Paris 1958.

VALÉRY P., *Variété*, Paris 1924.
– *Regards sur le monde actuel*, Paris 1931.
– *Pièces sur l'art*, Paris 1934.

VAN DE VELDE H., *Les formules d'une esthétique moderne*, Brussels 1932.

VERKAUF W., *Dada, Monograph of a Movement*, New York 1957.

WEIL S., *L'enracinement*, Paris 1949.

WHITROW, *The Structure of the Universe*, New York 1948.

WIENER N., *The Human Use of Human Beings*, revised edition, New York 1954.

WINGLER H.M., *Das Bauhaus*, Bramsche and Cologne 1962.

ZEVI B., *Storia dell'architettura moderna*, Turin 1955.

INDEX OF NAMES

AALTO Alvar (1898) 37, 190.
ADLER Alfred (1870-1937) 74, 145.
ADORNO Theodor W. (1903) 82, 148.
AERTSEN Pieter (1508-1575) 134.
AGEL Henri 113.
AGÉRO Auguste 132.
ALAIN FOURNIER (1886-1914) 17.
ALBERS Josef (1888) 171.
ALBERTI Leon Battista (1404-1472) 117.
ALEXANDER Samuel (1859-1938) 113.
ANDERSON E. N. 136.
APOLLINAIRE Guillaume (1880-1918) 55, 84, 85, 94, 98, 132, 147, 148, 170, 182, 183, 205.
APPIA Adolphe (1862-1928) 14, 113.
ARAGON Louis (1897) 147, 148, 160, 165, 170.
ARCHIPENKO Alexander (1887) 97, 183.
ARGAN Giulio Carlo (1909) 26.
ARMSTRONG Louis (1900) 84.
ARP Jean (1887) 37, 116, 133, 146, 148, 150, 151, 165, 169.

BAARGELD Johannes Theodor (†1927) 148.
BACHELARD Gaston (1884-1962) 24, 83, 145.
BALL Hugo (1886-1927) 132, 148, 165.
BALLA Giacomo (1871-1958) 95.
BARBARI Jacopo de' (c. 1445-1516?) 83.
BARLACH Ernst (1870-1938) 57.
BARTHES Roland 14, 118, 169.
BARTNING Otto (1883-1959) 69.
BARTOK Bela (1881-1945) 17.
BARUZI Joseph 151.
BAUDELAIRE Charles (1821-1867) 10, 12, 145.
BAUMEISTER Willi (1889-1955) 116, 137.
BAYER Herbert (1900) 116.
BAZAINE Jean (1904) 205.
BEARDSLEY Aubrey (1872-1898) 15, 33.
BECQUEREL Henri (1896) 74.
BEHRENS Peter (1868-1940) 35, 36, 45, 67, 69.
BENELLI Sem (1875) 31.
BENJAMIN Walter (1892-1940) 148.
BENN Gottfried (1886-1956) 56, 69.
BENSE Max 16.
BERDYAEV Nicolas (1874-1948) 41.
BERG Alban (1885-1935) 55, 69.
BERGSON Henri (1859-1941) 13, 16, 25, 74, 83, 87, 94, 95, 97, 98, 113, 145, 182.
BERLAGE Hendrik Petrus (1856-1934) 189.
BERNANOS Georges (1888-1948) 94, 116, 136.
BERNHARDT Sarah (1844-1923) 15.
BILL Max (1908) 171.
BING Samuel 45.
BISSIÈRE Roger (1888-1964) 43.
BISTOLFI Leonardo (1859-1933) 31.
BLANCHOT Maurice 82.

BLOOM Hyman (1913) 69.
BOCCIONI Umberto (1882-1916) 37, 94, 95, 99, 101, 103, 109, 113, 132, 137.
BOHR Niels (1885-1962) 83, 113, 133.
BÖLL Heinrich (1917) 183.
BOLTZMANN Ludwig (1844-1906) 16, 133.
BONNARD Pierre (1867-1947) 13, 16, 18, 20, 30, 33, 74.
BOREL Emile (1871-1956) 133.
BOULEZ Pierre (1925) 72, 148.
BRACELLI Giovanni Battista (1584-1609) 138.
BRADY Weston 170.
BRANCUSI Constantin (1876-1957) 116, 123, 126, 131, 137.
BRAQUE Georges (1882-1963) 42, 74, 75, 77, 80, 83/85, 87, 88, 116, 118/120, 123, 131, 137, 147, 148, 169, 170, 172, 184, 188.
BRECHT Bertolt (1898-1956) 57, 69, 148.
BRETON André (1896) 148, 163, 170, 182/184, 212.
BREUER Marcel (1902) 146.
BRINKMANN Johannes Andreas (1902-1949) 190, 193, 194.
BROCH Hermann (1886-1951) 57.
BRUANT Aristide (1851-1925) 15.
BRUEGEL Pieter (c. 1525-1569) 131, 134.
BRUSSELMANS Jean (1884-1953) 137.
BUGATTI Ettore (1881-1947) 137.
BULLOUGH Edward 75.
BUNUEL Luis (1900) 148.
BURCHFIELD Charles (1893) 69.
BURNHAM Daniel Hudson (1846-1912) 190.
BUSONI Ferruccio (1866-1924) 57, 115, 132.

CAILLAUD Aristide (1902) 148.
CALDER Alexander (1898) 97, 111, 113, 133.
CAMPENDONCK Heinrich (1889-1957) 94.
CAMUS Albert (1913-1960) 15, 56.
CANOVAS DEL CASTILLO (1828-1897) 15.
CANTOR Georg (1845-1918) 97.
CAPEK Karel (1890-1938) 136.
CAPIELLO Leonito (1875-1942) 16, 28.
CARLYLE Thomas (1795-1881) 94.
CARNOT Sadi (1837-1894) 15.
CARRÀ Carlo (1881) 95, 121.
CASSANDRE, Jean-Marie Mouron (1901) 33.
CASSIRER Ernst (1874-1945) 14.
CASTELLI Enrico 94.
CÉLINE, Louis-Ferdinand Destouches (1894) 83.
CENDRARS Blaise (1887-1961) 94, 95, 115, 132, 137.
CÉZANNE Paul (1839-1906) 11, 13, 14, 17, 43, 71/75, 77, 83, 87, 135, 182, 205.
CHAGALL Marc (1887) 151, 152, 212.

CHAPLIN Charlie (1889) 137.
CHARDIN Jean-Siméon (1699-1779) 83.
CHÉRET Jules (1836-1932) 16, 28, 31.
CHERNIKOV Iakov (1887-1951) 191, 195.
CHEVAL Ferdinand (1836-1924) 146.
CHIRICO Giorgio de (1888) 137/139.
CHOISY Auguste (1841-1909) 10, 44.
Citizen Kane (Orson Welles) 57.
CITROEN Paul (1896) 148.
CLAIR René (1898) 182.
CLARK Colin 24.
CLAUDE LORRAIN (1600-1682) 131, 134.
CLAUDEL Paul (1868-1955) 11.
CLAUSIUS Rudolph (1822-1888) 72.
COCTEAU Jean (1889-1964) 76, 98, 115.
COHEN Gustave 10.
Colleone (Verrocchio) 83.
Comédie humaine (Balzac) 84, 182.
CONTAMIN (1840-1893) 25.
CORBETT 194.
CORNEILLE Pierre (1606-1684) 182.
COROT Camille (1796-1875) 83.
COURBET Gustave (1819-1877) 83, 134.
COURTET Emile 99.
CRAIG Gordon (1872) 14.
CROCE Benedetto (1866-1952) 72.
CUMMINGS E. E. (1894) 133.
CURIE Pierre (1859-1906) 74.
Curiosités esthétiques (Baudelaire) 145.

DAGUERRE Jacques (1787-1851) 151.
DALI Salvador (1904) 151, 154.
DARWIN Charles (1809-1882) 74.
DAUDET Alphonse (1840-1897) 12.
DAUMIER Honoré (1808-1879) 85.
DEGAS Edgar (1834-1917) 98.
DELACROIX Eugène (1798-1863) 10, 11, 134, 145.
DELAUNAY Robert (1885-1941) 74, 97/99, 101, 106, 118, 131, 137, 169/171, 184.
DELAUNAY Sonja (1885) 132.
DENIS Maurice (1870-1943) 17, 170.
DERAIN André (1880-1954) 74, 77, 81, 85, 148.
DESCARTES René (1596-1650) 11, 16, 24, 41, 73, 138.
DEWEY John (1859-1952) 96.
DIAGHILEV Sergei (1872-1929) 113.
DIDEROT Denis (1713-1784) 10.
DILTHEY Wilhelm (1833-1911) 16.
DISNEY Walt (1901) 99.
DOERNER Alexander 171.
DOMELA César (1900) 131.
DORIVAL Bernard 10.
DOS PASSOS John (1896) 73, 133, 170.
DONATELLO (1386-1466) 11.
DOSTOEVSKY Feodor (1821-1881) 12.
DREYFUS Alfred (1859-1935) 13.
DUCASSE Isidore, Count of Lautréamont (1846-1870) 11, 183.

DUCHAMP Marcel (1887) 99, 100, 110, 113, 133, 138, 142, 160, 161, 165.
DUCHAMP-VILLON Raymond (1876-1918) 138, 140.
DUCOS DU HAURON Louis (1837-1920) 99.
DUDOVICH Marcello (1878) 16, 31.
DUFY Raoul (1877-1953) 74, 77.
DUIKER Johannes (1890-1935) 190.
DURAND-RUEL Paul (1831-1922) 14.
DÜRER Albrecht (1471-1528) 83, 117.
DUTERT Charles-Louis-Ferdinand (1845-1906) 25.

ECO Umberto 133.
EDGERTON Harold E. (1903) 99, 111, 112.
EDSCHMID Kasimir (1890) 69.
EESTEREN Cornelis van (1897) 115.
EGGELING Viking (1880-1925) 132.
EHRENFELS Christian von (1859-1932) 97, 98.
EIFFEL Gustave (1832-1923) 11, 25, 199.
EINSTEIN Albert (1879-1955) 17, 74, 75, 97/99, 113, 182, 189.
EISENSTEIN Sergei (1898-1948) 15, 84.
EISNER Lotte H. 56.
ELIADE Mircea 15, 56, 58.
ELIOT T. S. (1888-1965) 137.
ELIZABETH of Austria (1837-1898) 15.
ELUARD Paul (1895-1952) 84, 115, 146, 148, 170, 182, 183.
ENDELL August (1871-1925) 45.
ENESCO Georges (1881-1955) 17.
ENSOR James (1860-1949) 13, 14, 16, 56.
EPSTEIN Jacob (1880-1959) 69.
ERNST Max (1891) 115, 116, 148, 151, 157, 160, 163, 182, 212.
ESTÈVE Maurice (1904) 205.

FARMAN Henri (1874-1958) 137.
FAULKNER William (1897-1962) 10, 170, 183.
FAURE Elie (1873-1937) 137, 169.
FAUTRIER Jean (1898-1964) 42, 133, 205.
FEBVRE Lucien (1878-1956) 135.
FINSTERLIN Hermann 190.
FISCHINGER Oskar 132.
FLAUBERT Gustave (1821-1880) 134.
FLEISCHER 99.
FOCILLON Henri (1881-1943) 12, 96.
FORD Henry (1863-1947) 82.
FORT Paul (1872-1960) 113.
FOUQUET Jean (c. 1425-c. 1480) 77.
FOUILHOUX 194.
FOURASTIÉ Jean (1907) 24, 135.
FRAENKEL Theodore (1896) 148.
FRANCASTEL Pierre (1900) 42, 113, 171, 206.
FRANCIS Sam (1923) 42.
FREUD Sigmund (1856-1939) 10, 16, 46, 74, 145, 182, 212.
FRIEDMANN Georges (1902) 94, 135.
FROMENTIN Eugène (1820-1876) 205.
FULLER Richard Buckminster (1895) 190, 191, 195.

GABO Naum (1890) 99, 116, 183.
GALLÉ Emile (1846-1904) 25.
GANCE Abel (1889) 99.
GARAMOND Claude (1481-1551) 84.
GARGALLO Pablo (1881-1934) 83, 84.
GARNIER Paul 94.
GARNIER Tony (1869-1948) 42, 47, 51, 190, 197.
GAUDI Antoni (1852-1926) 25, 37, 38, 42, 146, 148.

GAUDIER-BRZESKA Henri (1891-1915) 131.
GAUGUIN Paul (1848-1903) 15, 75, 77.
GEBSER Jean (1905) 206.
GÉRICAULT Théodore (1791-1824) 98.
GIACOMETTI Alberto (1901) 123, 127, 162.
GIBBS Josiah Willard (1839-1903) 16, 133.
GIDE André (1869-1951) 9, 10, 14, 183, 184.
GIEDION Siegfried 137, 171, 195.
GILBRETH Frank B. (1868-1924) 98, 99, 110.
GIOTTO (c. 1265-1337) 17, 73, 87.
GIORGIONE (1476/77-1510) 83.
GOEMANS Camille 147.
GOLDMANN Lucien 63.
GONCOURT Edmond de (1822-1896) 12.
GONZALEZ Julio (1876-1942) 72, 74, 84, 138, 143.
GORKY Arshile (1905-1948) 205, 207, 210.
GOURMONT Remy de (1858-1915) 24.
GRAVE Jean 15.
GRIFFITH D. W. (1875-1948) 99.
GRIS Juan (1887-1927) 42, 87, 92, 116, 137, 170.
GROMAIRE Marcel (1892) 137.
GROPIUS Walter (1883) 25, 49, 137, 146, 190, 195.
GROSZ George (1893-1959) 57, 58, 62, 69, 94, 148.
GRUBER Francis (1912-1948) 69.
GUIMARD Hector (1867-1942) 25, 42.
GUTIERREZ SOLANA José (1886-1945) 57, 69.
GUYS Constantin (1802-1892) 98.

HAGEN Friedrich 183.
HANKAR Paul (1859-1901) 42, 45.
HANLEY 72.
HARRISON Wallace Kirkman (1895) 194.
HASEK Jaroslav (1882-1923) 183.
HAUSMANN Raoul (1886) 116, 148, 162.
HECKEL Erich (1883-1944) 94.
HEIDEGGER Martin (1889) 10, 56, 58, 115.
HEISENBERG Werner (1901) 83, 133.
HEMINGWAY Ernest (1898-1961) 183.
HENNEBIQUE François (1842-1921) 199.
HERTZ Gustav (1887) 16.
HILBERSEIMER Ludwig (1885) 195.
HILDEBRAND Adolf von (1847-1921) 76.
HÖCH Hannah (1889) 148, 162.
HODLER Ferdinand (1853-1918) 42.
HOFFMANN Josef (1870-1956) 35, 37, 39, 42.
HOFMEISTER 194.
HÖGER Fritz (1877-1949) 67, 69.
HONEGGER Arthur (1892-1955) 94, 99, 137.
HOOD Raymond (1881-1934) 194.
HORTA Victor (1861-1947) 25, 42, 45.
HUIDOBRO Vicente (1889) 132.
HÜLSENBECK Richard (1892) 148, 165.
HUSSERL Edmund (1859-1938) 10, 17, 132, 145.
HUSZAR Vilmos (1885) 169.
HUXLEY Aldous (1894-1963) 138.
HUYGHE René (1906) 136.
HUYSMANS J. K. (1848-1907) 25, 183.

ICTINOS 11.
IHERING Herbert 69.
INFELD Leopold (1898) 74.

INGRES Jean-Dominique (1780-1867) 10, 131, 134.
INHELDER B. 74.
IONESCO Eugène (1911) 148.

JACOB Max (1876-1944) 17, 132, 170.
JAKOBSON Roman 83, 118.
JAMES Henry (1843-1916) 75.
JANCO Marcel (1895) 148, 165.
JARRY Alfred (1873-1907) 13, 94, 159, 183.
JEANNERET, see LE CORBUSIER.
JESPERS Oscar (1887) 69.
JONES Ernest 212.
JOOSS Kurt 69.
JOYCE James (1882-1941) 72, 83, 84, 133, 148, 170, 182, 183.
JUNG Carl Gustav (1875-1961) 74, 145.
JUNG Franz 148.

KAFKA Franz (1883-1924) 11, 56, 57, 170, 183.
KAHNWEILER Daniel-Henry (1884) 14, 131.
KAKABADZE David (c. 1890) 137.
KANDINSKY Wassily (1866-1944) 14, 56, 74, 99, 115/118, 123, 124, 131, 137, 146, 169, 170, 172, 180, 183, 205, 206.
KANT Immanuel (1724-1804) 82.
KATZ David (1884-1953) 72, 75.
KEMENY Zoltan (1907-1965) 148.
KEPES György 170.
KIERKEGAARD Sören (1813-1855) 13, 58.
KIESLER Frederick J. (1896) 137, 190.
KIRCHNER Ernst Ludwig (1880-1938) 55, 58, 59, 65, 69, 85, 94.
KLEE Paul (1879-1940) 17, 71, 74, 83, 84, 99, 115/118, 123, 131, 137, 151, 153, 169/172, 175, 182, 183, 205/207.
KÖHLER Wolfgang (1887) 72.
KOHTZ Otto (1880-1956) 190.
KOKOSCHKA Oskar (1886) 57, 65, 69.
KRAUS Karl 46.
KROPOTKIN Peter (1842-1921) 15.
KUBICKI 116.
KUBIN Alfred (1877-1959) 57, 146.
KUPKA Frank (1871-1954) 98, 169/171.

Lac (Lamartine) 182.
LA FONT DE SAINT-YENNE 145.
LA FRESNAYE Roger de (1885-1925) 42.
LANG Fritz (1890) 69.
LARIONOV Michael (1881) 99, 169.
LAURENS Henri (1885-1954) 74, 93, 116.
LAUTRÉAMONT (1846-1870), cf. DUCASSE 11, 14, 183.
LEBESGUE Henri (1875-1941) 133.
LECK Bart van der (1876) 131, 169.
LE CORBUSIER (1887-1965) 36, 37, 42, 43, 46, 49, 50, 84, 97, 137, 146, 169, 182, 184, 190, 192, 195, 206.
LEDOUX Claude-Nicolas (1736-1806) 11, 51, 146.
LEFEBVRE Henri (1900) 44.
LÉGER Fernand (1881-1955) 42, 94, 96, 99, 101, 105, 115, 116, 132, 137, 138, 141, 169, 171, 184, 212.
LÉGLISE Paul 113.
LENI Paul (1885-1929) 69.
LEONARDO DA VINCI (1452-1519) 25, 73, 117, 146, 197.
LEONIDOV J. J. 190.
LESSING Gotthold Ephraim (1729-1781) 99.
LÉVI-STRAUSS Claude (1908) 72, 84, 119.
LÉVY-BRUHL Lucien (1857-1939) 85.

LINDER Max (1883-1925) 15.
LIPCHITZ Jacques (1891) 74, 91, 116, 212.
LIPPOLD Richard (1915) 83.
LISSAJOUS Jules (1822-1880) 98.
LISSITZKY El (1890-1941) 131, 169, 172, 179, 190.
LOMBROSO Gina (†1944) 94.
LOOS Adolf (1870-1933) 37, 42, 44, 46, 48, 172, 190.
LUCKHARDT Hans (1890-1954) and Wassili (1889) 190.
LUGNÉ-POE Aurélien-Marie (1869-1940) 14, 113.
LUKACS Georg (1885) 10.
LUMIÈRE Louis (1864-1948) 27.
LUPASCO Stéphane 25, 83, 148.

MACKINTOSH Charles Rennie (1868-1928) 37, 40, 42, 206.
MCKINLEY William (1843-1901) 15.
MACKMURDO Arthur H. (1851-1942) 25.
MACMURRAY 194.
MAETERLINCK Maurice (1862-1949) 146.
MAGRITTE René (1898) 151, 154.
MAHLER Gustav (1860-1911) 57.
MAILLART Robert (1872-1940) 42, 199, 201.
MALEVICH Kasimir (1878-1935) 75, 101, 104, 116, 122, 123, 137, 169/172, 190, 195.
MALLARMÉ Stéphane (1842-1898) 113, 131, 133, 170, 182.
MALLET-STEVENS Robert (1886-1945) 190.
MAN RAY (1890) 132, 148, 160, 164, 170.
MANDROU Robert 10.
MANN Thomas (1875-1955) 183.
MARC Franz (1880-1916) 99, 205, 206.
MARCHI Virgilio 190.
MAREY Jules-Etienne (1830-1904) 98, 99, 108, 109.
MARIN John (1870-1954) 99.
MARINETTI Filippo Tommaso (1876-1944) 94/96, 161, 197.
MARTIN DU GARD Roger (1881-1958) 15.
MARTINET André 117.
MARX Karl (1818-1883) 41, 82, 146.
MASEREEL Frans (1889) 69.
MASSON André (1896) 133, 205, 207, 209, 212.
MATHIEU Georges (1921) 72, 133.
MATISSE Henri (1869-1954) 14, 17, 73/75, 77, 78, 83, 85, 115, 116, 172, 182, 187.
MATTA ECHAURREN Roberto Sebastiano (1912) 10, 69, 83, 148, 205, 212.
MAXWELL James Clerk (1831-1879) 16, 75.
MEHRING Walter (1896) 148.
MÉLIÈS Georges (1861-1938) 13, 95, 99, 148.
MENDEL Gregor (1822-1884) 74.
MENDELSOHN Erich (1887-1953) 37, 57, 69, 190, 193.
MERLEAU-PONTY Maurice (1908-1961) 9, 24, 74, 95, 96, 145, 169, 170, 172, 206, 207.
MEUNIER Henri (1873-1922) 30.
MEYER Adolf (1881-1929) 49.
MICHAUX Henri (1899) 146, 148, 206.
MICHELANGELO (1475-1564) 182.
MICHELET Jules (1798-1874) 134.
MIES VAN DER ROHE Ludwig (1886) 42, 84, 137, 146, 182, 183, 190, 192, 195.
MILTON May 15, 28, 32, 33.

MINKOWSKI Hermann (1864-1909) 97, 182.
Missa Solemnis (Beethoven) 182.
MIRÓ Joan (1893) 115, 118, 123, 125, 146, 205, 207, 212.
MOHOLY-NAGY Laszlo (1895-1946) 99, 108, 112, 113, 116, 132, 133, 170, 172, 177, 183.
MOLES Abraham 71, 72.
MONDRIAN Piet (1872-1944) 42, 75, 84, 137, 169/172, 182, 184, 212.
MONET Claude (1840-1926) 11, 134.
MONTESQUIEU (1689-1755) 134.
MOORE Henry (1898) 37, 74, 151, 156.
MORAVIA Alberto (1907) 183.
MORIN Edgar 148.
MORRIS Charles 15.
MORRIS William (1834-1896) 25.
MOULOD Noël 131, 171, 172.
MOUNIER Emmanuel (1905-1950) 94, 134.
MUCHA Alphonse (1860-1939) 15, 30.
MUMFORD Lewis (1895) 55, 96, 137.
MUNARI Bruno 113.
MUNCH Edvard (1863-1944) 13, 18, 19, 42, 55, 56, 58.
MUSIL Robert (1880-1942) 55, 148, 182, 184.
MUTHESIUS Hermann (1861-1927) 35, 36.
MUYBRIDGE Eadweard (1830-1904) 98.
MYERS F. W. H. (1843-1901) 145.

NERVI Pier Luigi (1891) 11, 42.
NEUTRA Richard Joseph (1892) 42, 190.
NICHOLSON Ben (1894) 118.
NIETZSCHE Friedrich (1844-1900) 15, 41, 145.
NOLDE Emil (1867-1956) 57, 58, 60, 69, 77.

OBUCHOW Nicholas 132.
OLBRICH Josef Maria (1867-1908) 35, 45.
OROZCO José Clemente (1883-1949) 69.
OZENFANT Amédée (1886) 169.

PACIOLI Luca 116, 117.
PANSAERS Clément 148.
PASCAL Blaise (1623-1662) 10.
PAULHAN Jean (1884) 147.
PAVLOV Ivan Petrovitch (1849-1936) 118.
PECHSTEIN Max (1881-1955) 57, 85.
PÉGUY Charles (1873-1914) 74.
PÉLERIN VIATOR Jean (1435/40-1524) 117.
PENFIELD Edward (1866-1925) 16.
PÉRET Benjamin (1899-1959) 148, 183.
PERMEKE Constant (1886-1952) 69.
PERRET Auguste (1874-1954) 42, 44, 47, 84, 190, 199, 200.
PEVSNER Antoine (1884-1962) 99, 116, 172, 181, 182, 184.
PIAGET Jean (1896) 74.
PICABIA Francis (1879-1953) 101, 104, 132, 148, 151, 161, 165.
PICASSO Pablo (1881) 10, 11, 15, 16, 18, 21, 23, 37, 42, 67, 68, 72, 74, 75, 85, 83/87, 89, 90, 99, 115, 116, 119, 120, 131, 132, 137, 147, 169, 170, 172, 182/184, 186, 205, 206, 212.
PIERO DELLA FRANCESCA (1410/20-1492) 43.
PIRANESI (1720-1778) 146, 195.
PISCATOR Erwin (1893) 57.
PLANCK Max (1858-1947) 17, 74, 75, 182, 189.

PLANTIN Christophe (c. 1515-1589) 132.
PLEKHANOV G. V. (1857-1918) 116.
POE Edgar Allan (1809-1849) 131.
POELZIG Hans (1869-1936) 57, 66, 69.
POINCARÉ Jules Henri (1854-1912) 74.
POLLOCK Jackson (1912-1956) 97, 133, 183, 212, 213.
PONENTE Nello 10.
PONGE Francis (1899) 206.
POPOVA Lyubov Sergeievna (1889-1924) 172, 176.
PORTINARI Candido (1903) 69.
POUND Ezra (1885) 131.
POUSSIN Nicolas (1594-1665) 73, 182.
PROKOFIEV Sergei (1891-1953) 137.
PROUST Marcel (1871-1922) 9, 10, 206.
PUVIS DE CHAVANNES Pierre (1824-1898) 42.

QUENEAU Raymond (1903) 72, 147, 148, 182, 183.

RACINE Jean (1639-1699) 182.
RAGGHIANTI Carlo Ludovico 113.
RAPHAEL Max 85.
RAUSCHENBERG Robert (1925) 42.
RAYMOND Marcel (1897) 83, 183.
RAYNAL Maurice (1884-1954) 10.
READ Sir Herbert 42, 43.
REDON Odilon (1840-1916) 17.
REINHARD 194.
REINHARDT Max (1873-1943) 57, 69.
REMBRANDT (1606-1669) 13, 205.
RENAN Ernest (1823-1892) 12, 26.
RENOIR Pierre-Auguste (1841-1919) 11, 12.
REVERDY Pierre (1889-1960) 133, 170, 183.
RIBEMONT-DESSAIGNES Georges (1884) 148, 183.
RICHTER Hans (1888) 110, 115, 132, 148, 165.
RIEGL Alois (1858-1905) 76.
RIEMANN Bernhard (1826-1866) 17, 74.
RIEMERSCHMID Richard (1868-1957) 35, 45.
RIETVELD Gerrit (1888-1964) 190, 199, 202.
RIGADIN 15.
RIGAUD Jacques (1899-1929) 148.
RILKE Rainer Maria (1875-1926) 17, 56, 95, 148, 206.
RIMBAUD Arthur (1854-1891) 73.
RIVIÈRE Jacques (1886-1925) 160.
RODIN Auguste (1840-1917) 12.
ROLLAND Romain (1866-1944) 15, 74, 165.
ROMAINS Jules (1885) 74, 75, 118.
ROTHKO Mark (1903) 42.
ROUAULT Georges (1871-1958) 69, 77, 79.
ROUSSEAU the Douanier, Henri (1844-1910) 17, 148.
ROUSSEL Raymond (1877-1933) 75.
ROYÈRE Jean 75.
RUANO Eoly Benito 11.
RUBENS Peter Paul (1577-1640) 134.
RUSKIN John (1819-1900) 25, 26, 36, 44, 94.
RUSSELL Morgan (1886-1953) 98.
RUSSOLO Luigi (1885-1947) 95, 99, 132.
RUTHERFORD Lord (1871-1937) 74.
RUTTMANN Walter (1887-1941) 132.
RYSSELBERGHE, see VAN RYSSELBERGHE.

SAINT-SIMON (1760-1825) 25, 197.
SANT'ELIA Antonio (1888-1916) 57, 97, 146, 190, 195, 197/199.
SARTRE Jean-Paul (1905) 75, 87.
SATIE Erik (1866-1925) 83, 94, 132, 160.
SCHAROUN Hans (1893) 190.
SCHELLING Friedrich (1775-1854) 74.
SCHLEMMER Oskar (1888-1943) 42, 109, 110, 113, 137.
SCHLOEZER Boris de 72.
SCHMARSOW 76.
SCHMIDT-ROTTLUFF Karl (1884) 94.
SCHNEIDER René 10.
SCHÖNBERG Arnold (1874-1951) 14, 57, 69, 72, 83, 84, 148, 182, 183.
SCHÖFFER Nicolas (1912) 72.
SCHOPENHAUER Arthur (1788-1860) 44.
SCHUMACHER 35.
SCHWITTERS Kurt (1887-1948) 116, 118, 132, 144, 148, 163.
SCRIABIN Alexander (1872-1915) 57, 132.
SÉRUSIER Paul (1865-1927) 13.
SERVAES Albert (1883) 69.
SERVRANCKX Victor (1897) 137.
SEURAT Georges (1859-1891) 10, 37, 42, 43, 46.
SEVERINI Gino (1883) 95, 101, 102.
SHANNON C. E. 159.
SHELLEY Percy Bysshe (1792-1822) 11.
SIQUEIROS, David ALFARO (1898) 69.
SOFFICI Ardengo (1879) 116.
SOUPAULT Philippe (1897) 170.
SOURIAU Paul (1852-1925) 44.
SOUTINE Chaim (1894-1943) 58, 61, 69.
SPENGLER Oswald (1880-1936) 16.
SPINOZA Baruch (1632-1677) 13.
STADLER Ernst (1883-1914) 69.
STAM Mart (1899) 195.
STAROBINSKI Jean (1920) 182.
STEICHEN Edward (1879) 170.
STEIN Gertrude (1874-1946) 183.
STEINBECK John (1902) 183.
STEINLEN Théophile Alexandre (1859-1923) 15, 31.
STRAMM August (1874-1915) 69, 148.
STRAVINSKY Igor (1882) 14, 83, 115.
STRINDBERG August (1849-1912) 15, 133.

SULLIVAN Louis (1856-1924) 42, 44, 45.
SULLIVAN Pat 99.
SURVAGE Léopold (1879) 132.
SUTHERLAND Graham (1903) 69.

TAINE Hippolyte (1828-1893) 12, 134.
TANG KWEI 207.
TANGUY Yves (1900-1955) 151, 155.
TATLIN Vladimir (1885-1956) 84, 131, 132, 190, 191.
TÄUBER Sophie (1889-1943) 148, 165.
TAUT Bruno (1880-1938) 146, 190.
TAUT Max (1884) 146, 190.
TAYLOR Frederick Winslow (1856-1915) 82, 98.
TCHELITCHEW 205.
Thinker (Rodin) 83.
TIFFANY Louis Comfort (1848-1933) 25.
TOBEY Mark (1890) 183, 207, 208.
TOLSTOY Leo (1828-1910) 11, 26, 36.
TOULOUSE-LAUTREC Henri de (1864-1901) 13/15, 18, 22, 28, 32, 33, 42, 98.
TOYNBEE Arnold J. (1889) 16.
TRAKL Georg (1887-1914) 55, 69.
TURNER J.M.W. (1775-1851) 134.
TZARA Tristan (1896) 148, 165.

UCCELLO Paolo (c. 1396-1475) 77, 98.
Ulysses (Joyce, 1922) 72, 84, 182.
UNAMUNO Miguel de (1864-1936) 16.

VALENSI Henri (1883) 132.
VALÉRY Paul (1871-1945) 9, 10, 75, 131, 145, 165.
VAN DE VELDE Henry (1863-1957) 25, 26, 35, 36, 42/46, 190.
VAN DER VLUGT Llendert C. (1896-1936) 190, 193,194.
VAN DOESBURG Theo (1883-1931) 75, 115, 169, 171/173, 195.
VAN EYCK Jan (c. 1390-1441) 77.
VAN GOGH Vincent (1853-1890) 13, 17, 37, 58, 75, 77, 83, 116.
VAN RYSSELBERGHE Theo (1862-1926) 16, 30.
VANTONGERLOO Georges (1886) 190.
VARESE Edgar (1885) 83.

VASARI Giorgio (1511-1574) 98.
VEDOVA Emilio (1919) 69.
VEIDT Conrad (1893-1943) 65.
VERHAEREN Emile (1855-1916) 74, 94.
VIDAL DE LA BLACHE Paul (1845-1918) 135.
VILDRAC Charles (1882) 74.
VILLON Jacques (1875-1963) 14, 16, 29, 131, 178.
VIOLLET-LE-DUC Eugène (1814-1879) 44, 45.
VLAMINCK Maurice (1876-1958) 75, 77, 85.
VOISIN Gabriel (1880) 137.
VOLLARD Ambroise (1867-1939) 14.
VOYSEY Charles F. A. (1857-1941) 42, 45.
VUILLARD Edouard (1868-1940) 13, 16.

WAGNER Otto (1841-1918) 42, 44/46, 49, 197.
WAGNER Richard (1813-1883) 131.
WALDEN Herwarth (1878) 14.
WATSON John B. (1878-1958) 72, 118.
WATT James (1736-1819) 182.
WEBERN Anton von (1883-1945) 57, 69, 84.
WEISMANN August (1834-1914) 74.
WELLS H. G. (1866-1946) 133.
WERFEL Franz (1890-1945) 56, 69.
WERTHEIMER Max (1880-1943) 72.
WESNIN Alexander (1883-1933) 190.
WHITMAN Walt (1819-1892) 74, 94.
WIENE Robert (1881-1938) 65, 69.
WIENER Norbert (1894) 72, 133, 159.
WILDE Oscar (1854-1900) 25.
WILFRED Thomas 132.
WIRTH Léon 135.
WÖLFFLIN Heinrich (1864-1945) 76.
WOLS (1913-1951) 205/207, 211.
WORRINGER Wilhelm (1881) 17, 25, 56.
WRIGHT Frank Lloyd (1869-1959) 11, 37, 42, 48, 51, 148, 190, 193, 199, 203.
WRIGHT Stanton Macdonald (1890) 98.

ZADKINE Ossip (1890) 57, 69, 212.
ZOLA Emile (1840-1902) 12.

LIST OF ILLUSTRATIONS

ARP Jean (1887). Big Head, Little Body, 1923. Colored Wood. (26×23½″) Jean Arp Collection, Meudon, near Paris . . 150

BEHRENS Peter (1868-1940). Hall of the Administrative Buildings of the Farbwerke, Höchst-Frankfurt, 1920-1925 . . 67

BISTOLFI Leonardo (1859-1933). Poster for the First International Exhibition of Modern Decorative Art, Turin, 1902. Color Lithograph. (47¼×63″) Wittamer Collection, Brussels 31

BOCCIONI Umberto (1882-1916). Unique Form of Continuity in Space, 1913. Bronze. (Height 45¼″) Civica Galleria d'Arte Moderna, Milan 103

— Drawing after "States of Mind: Those Who Stay," 1912. (12¾×16¾″) Collection of Mr and Mrs Herbert M. Rothschild, New York 109

BONNARD Pierre (1867-1947). The Ice Rink, 1898. (39¼×29½″) Professor Hans R. Hahnloser Collection, Bern . . . 20

— Poster for "La Revue Blanche," 1894. Four-color Lithograph. (30×23¼″) Kunstgewerbemuseum, Zurich . . 30

BRANCUSI Constantin (1876-1957). Mademoiselle Pogany, 1919. Marble. Collection Mr and Mrs Lee A. Ault, New York 126

BRAQUE Georges (1882-1963). L'Estaque, 1907. (31⅜×27¾″) Collection Colonel Samuel A. Berger, New York . . 80

— Landscape, 1908. (31⅞×25½″) Kunstmuseum, Basel 88

— Violette de Parme, 1914. (18⅞×25¼″) Sir Edward Hulton Collection, London 120

— Washstand in front of a Window, 1942. (51¼×38¼″) Louvre, Paris 188

BRETON André (1896). Poem-Object, 1941. Assemblage: carved wood bust of man, wood and metal lantern, photograph in metal frame, toy boxing gloves, mounted on wood board and black paper with inscription painted in gouache and oil. (18×21″) Museum of Modern Art, New York 163

BRINKMANN Johannes Andreas (1902-1949) and Llendert C. van der VLUGT (1896-1936). The Van Nelle Tobacco Factory, Rotterdam, 1930 193-194

CALDER Alexander (1898). Hanging Mobile in Motion, 1936. Aluminum and Steel Wire. (Length 28″) Mrs Mary Callery Collection, Paris 111

CARRÀ Carlo (1881). Interventionist Manifestation, 1914. Collage on Cardboard. (15⅛×11¾″) Dr Gianni Mattioli Collection, Milan 121

CHAGALL Marc (1887). The Poet, 1911. (77½×57½″) Philadelphia Museum of Art 152

CHÉRET Jules (1836-1932). Poster for the Palais de Glace, Champs-Elysées, Paris, 1894. Color Lithograph. (96½×34¼″) Kunstgewerbemuseum, Zurich 31

CHERNIKOV Iakov (1887-1951). Constructivist Research Project, about 1930. Drawing 191

CHIRICO Giorgio de (1888). Hector and Andromache, 1917. (35⅜×23½″) Dr Gianni Mattioli Collection, Milan . . 139

DALI Salvador (1904). Night and Day of the Body, 1936. Gouache. (11¾×15¾″) Urvater Collection, Brussels . . . 154

DELAUNAY Robert (1885-1941). The Eiffel Tower, 1910. (79¾×54⅜″) Solomon R. Guggenheim Museum, New York 106

DERAIN André (1880-1954). L'Estaque, Three Trees, 1906. (39⅜×31⅞″) Collection of Ayala and Sam Zacks, Toronto 81

DOESBURG Theo van (1883-1931). Composition in Black and White, 1918. (29¼×21½″) Kunstmuseum, Basel (on loan from the Emanuel Hoffmann Foundation) 173

DUCHAMP Marcel (1887). Nude descending a Staircase, No. 2, 1912. (58×35″) Philadelphia Museum of Art 100

— Rotoreliefs, Optical Disks, 1935. Cover of "Minotaure," No. 6, Winter 1935 110

— The Bride stripped bare by her Bachelors, Even (The Large Glass), 1915-1923. (115×64″) Philadelphia Museum of Art 142

— Ready Made (Bicycle Wheel, Metal and Wood), Third Version, 1951. (Height 52″) Sidney Janis Gallery, New York 161

DUCHAMP-VILLON Raymond (1876-1918). Horse, 1914. Bronze. (Height 39⅜″) Musée National d'Art Moderne, Paris 140

EDGERTON Harold E. (1903). Swirls and Eddies of a Tennis Stroke, 1939. Stroboscopic Photograph. Massachusetts Institute of Technology, Cambridge, Mass. 111-112

— Splash of a Drop of Milk falling into a Saucer of Milk, 1936. Stroboscopic Photograph. Massachusetts Institute of Technology, Cambridge, Mass. 112

ERNST Max (1891). Surrealism and Painting, 1942. (76¾×91¾″) Collection William N. Copley, New York 157

— The Preparation of Bone Glue, 1921. Collage. Museum of Modern Art, New York 163

FULLER Richard Buckminster (1895). Design for a Tower Garage, 1927 191

GARNIER Tony (1869-1948). Project for an Industrial City: Four Views of Dwelling-Houses, 1902-1904. From "Une Cité industrielle," Editions Charles Massin, Paris, 1917, p. 112 47-48

GAUDI Antoni (1852-1926). Entrance of Güell Park, Barcelona, 1900-1914 38

GIACOMETTI Alberto (1901). Head, 1932. Marble. (Height 15″) Stedelijk Museum, Amsterdam 127
— Objects Mute and Mobile. Collage from the Magazine "Le Surréalisme au service de la Révolution," No. 3, Paris, December 1931. (Double page, 10⅞×7½″) 162

GONZALEZ Julio (1876-1942). Woman combing her Hair, 1937. Wrought Iron. (Height 84″) Roberta Gonzalez Collection, Paris 143

GORKY Arshile (1905-1948). The Unattainable, 1945. (41⅛×29¼″) Baltimore Museum of Art 210

GRIS Juan (1887-1927). Smoker, 1913. (28⅞×21½″) Collection Mr and Mrs. Armand P. Bartos, New York . . . 92

GROPIUS Walter (1883) and Adolf MEYER (1881-1929). Fagus Works at Alfeld an der Leine, Germany, 1911-1914 . 49

GROSZ George (1893-1959). The Funeral (Homage to the Poet Oskar Panizza), 1917-1918. (55⅛×43¼″) Staatsgalerie, Stuttgart 62

HAUSMANN Raoul (1886). Photomontage, 1920 162

HÖCH Hannah (1889). Photomontage, 1920 162

HOFFMANN Josef (1870-1956). The Palais Stoclet, Brussels, 1906-1911 39

HÖGER Fritz (1877-1949). The Chile House, Hamburg, 1922-1923 67

KANDINSKY Wassily (1866-1944). Points in an Arc, 1927. (26×19¼″) Private Collection 124
— Floating, 1927. (18×21¼″) Marlborough-Gerson Gallery Inc., New York 180

KIRCHNER Ernst Ludwig (1880-1938). The Street, 1913. (47½×35⅞″) Museum of Modern Art, New York 59
— Title Page of the Catalogue of the "Die Brücke" Exhibition, 1912. Woodcut. (6×2¼″) Staatsgalerie, Stuttgart . . 65

KLEE Paul (1879-1940). A Girl's Adventure, 1922. Watercolor. (17¼×12⅜″) Tate Gallery, London 153
— Color Scale (Grey Dominant), 1930. Pastel and Size on Paper mounted on Cardboard. (15¾×11⅞″) Paul Klee Foundation, Bern 175

KOKOSCHKA Oskar (1886). Murder, about 1908. Illustration for "Hoffnung der Frauen." Pen and Ink Drawing. (9¾×9⅜″) Staatsgalerie, Stuttgart 65

LAURENS Henri (1885-1954). Wood Construction, 1919. (15×10⅜″) Maurice Raynal Collection, Paris 93

LE CORBUSIER (1887-1965), Charles-Edouard Jeanneret, called. Villa Savoye at Poissy, near Paris, 1928-1930 . . . 49-50
— Villa Savoye at Poissy, near Paris, 1928-1930. First floor with ramp leading to upper terraces 50
— Study for a Contemporary City of Three Million Inhabitants, with Through Traffic Lanes, 1922 192
— The Ministry of Education at Rio de Janeiro, 1937-1943. Associated architects: Lucio Costa, Carlos Leao, Jorge Moreira, Oscar Niemeyer, Alfonso Reidy, Ernani Vasconcelos 204

LÉGER Fernand (1881-1955). Woman in Blue (second state), 1912. (76½×51¼″) Kunstmuseum, Basel 105
— The Motor, 1918. (53⅛×46½″) René Gaffé Collection, Cagnes (Alpes-Maritimes) 141

LIPCHITZ Jacques (1891). Standing Woman, 1918-1919. Stone. (Height 38⅜″) Kunstmuseum, Basel 91

LISSITZKY El (1890-1941). Proun 99, 1924. (50¾×39″) Yale University Art Gallery, New Haven, Conn. 179

LOOS Adolf (1870-1933). Steiner House, Vienna, 1910 48

MACKINTOSH Charles Rennie (1868-1928). Main Entrance of the Glasgow School of Art, 1898-1909 40

MAGRITTE René (1898). Pink Bells, Sky in Tatters, 1930. (28¾×39⅜″) Urvater Collection, Brussels 154

MAILLART Robert (1872-1940). Bridge over the River Thur at Felsegg, near St Gall (Switzerland), 1933 201

MALEVICH Kasimir (1878-1935). Woman with Water Pails: Dynamic Arrangement, 1912. (31⅝×31⅝″) Museum of Modern Art, New York 104
— An Englishman in Moscow, 1914. (34⅝×22⅜″) Stedelijk Museum, Amsterdam 122

MAN RAY (1890). Rayograph, 1923. (9½×7″) Museum of Modern Art, New York 164

MAREY Jules-Etienne (1830-1904). Study of a Man Walking. From the Magazine "La Nature" of September 29, 1883 109

MARINETTI Filippo Tommaso (1876-1944). Letter from a Pretty Girl to an Old-fashioned Gentleman. From "Les mots en liberté futuriste," Edizioni futuriste di "poesia", Milan, 1919 161

MASSON André (1896). Tangle, 1941. (16⅛×13″) André Masson Collection, Paris 209

MATISSE Henri (1869-1954). Gipsy, 1906. (21⅝×18⅛″) Musée de l'Annonciade, Saint-Tropez 78
— The Dream, 1940. (31⅞×25½″) Private Collection 187

MENDELSOHN Erich (1887-1953). The Schocken Department Store, Chemnitz, 1928 193

MEUNIER Henri (1873-1922). Design for the Poster "Cartes postales artistiques," 1898. Oil on Cardboard. (24⅜×36¼″) Wittamer Collection, Brussels 30

MEYER Adolf (1881-1929) and Walter GROPIUS (1883). The Fagus Works at Alfeld an der Leine, Germany, 1911-1914 49

MIES VAN DER ROHE Ludwig (1886). Model of a Glass Skyscraper with a Metal Skeleton, 1920 192
— Project for an Office Building with a Concrete Skeleton, 1922 192

MIRÓ Joan (1893). Dutch Interior I, 1928. (36⅛×28¾″) Museum of Modern Art, New York 125

MOHOLY-NAGY Laszlo (1895-1946). Space Modulator. Detroit Institute of Arts 112
— A. 11, 1924. (45⅝×53¾″) Solomon R. Guggenheim Museum, New York 177

MONDRIAN Piet (1872-1944). Composition in Yellow, Red, Blue and Black, 1921. (23⅜×23⅜″) Gemeentemuseum, The Hague 174

MOORE Henry (1898). The Helmet, 1939-1940. Bronze. (Height 12″) Mrs Irina Moore Collection, Much Hadham, Herts 156

MUCHA Alphonse (1860-1939). Poster for Job Cigarette Paper, 1898. Lithograph. (59⅛×39⅜″) Schweizerische Landesbibliothek, Bern 30

MUNCH Edvard (1863-1944). The Cry, 1893. (35¾×28¾″) National Gallery, Oslo 19

NEW YORK, Rockefeller Center, 1931-1939. Executed by three architectural firms: Reinhard and Hofmeister; Corbett, Harrison and MacMurray; Hood and Fouilhoux 194

NOLDE Emil (1867-1956). Candle Dancers, 1912. (39½×34″) Nolde Museum, Seebüll, near Niebüll (Schleswig-Holstein) 60

PERRET Auguste (1874-1954). Apartment Building at 25bis, Avenue Franklin, Paris, 1902 47
— Nave of the Church of Notre-Dame at Le Raincy, near Paris, 1922 200

PEVSNER Antoine (1884-1962). Developable Surface Construction, 1938. Copper. (25⅛×20″) Private Collection, Basel 181

PICABIA Francis (1879-1953). Dances at the Spring, 1912. (47⅝×47⅝″) Philadelphia Museum of Art 104
— Title Page of the Magazine "Dada," 4-5, Zurich, May 15, 1919. (10¾×7″) 161

PICASSO Pablo (1881). Diners, 1901. (18½×24½″) Rhode Island School of Design, Providence, R. I. 21
— Tumblers, 1905. (35⅜×28″) Staatsgalerie, Stuttgart 23
— Guernica, 1937. (11 ft 6 in.×25 ft 8 in.) Owned by the Artist (on loan to the Museum of Modern Art, New York) 67-68
— Guernica Postscriptum, Weeping Woman, October 28, 1937. (16¼×10¾″) Fogg Art Museum, Harvard University, Cambridge, Mass. 68
— Les Demoiselles d'Avignon, 1907. (8 ft×7 ft 8 in.) Museum of Modern Art, New York 86
— Accordionist (Pierrot), 1911. (51¼×35¼″) Solomon R. Guggenheim Museum, New York 89
— Man with a Pipe, 1915. (51¼×35¼″) Art Institute of Chicago 90
— Papier Collé, 1913. (18⅞×25⅛″) Moderna Museet, Stockholm 120
— Woman asleep in a Red Armchair, 1932. (51¼×38″) Mr and Mrs Victor W. Ganz Collection, New York 186

POELZIG Hans (1869-1936). Grosses Schauspielhaus, Berlin, 1919 (destroyed) 66

POLLOCK Jackson (1912-1956). Totem Lesson III, 1945. (70⅛×62″) Lee Krasner Pollock Collection, Courtesy of Marlborough-Gerson Gallery Inc., New York 213

POPOVA Lyubov Sergeievna (1889-1924). Architectonic Painting, 1917. (31½×38⅝″) Museum of Modern Art, New York 176

RICHTER Hans (1888). Film Study, 1926. Hans Richter Collection 110

RIETVELD Gerrit (1888-1964). The Villa Schröder, Utrecht, 1924 202

RIO DE JANEIRO, Ministry of Education, 1937-1943. Architects: Le Corbusier, Lucio Costa, Carlos Leao, Jorge Moreira, Oscar Niemeyer, Alfonso Reidy, and Ernani Vasconcelos 204

ROUAULT Georges (1871-1958). Head of a Clown, about 1908. (23⅝×18½″) Dumbarton Oaks Collection, Washington, D.C. 79

RYSSELBERGHE Theo van (1862-1926). Poster for the Fourth Annual "Salon de la Libre Esthétique," Brussels, 1897. Color Lithograph. (39⅜×30¾″) Wittamer Collection, Brussels 30

SANT'ELIA Antonio (1888-1916). Project for "The New City," 1914. Watercolor. (12×8¼″) Margherita G. Sarfatti Collection, Rome 198

SCHLEMMER Oskar (1888-1943). Dance of Sticks and Dance of Circles, 1927. Experimental Theater of the Bauhaus 109-110

SCHWITTERS Kurt (1887-1948). Construction for Noble Lady, 1919. (40½×33″) Los Angeles County Museum of Art 144
— Merz Construction (Hanover), begun in 1924 (destroyed in the Second World War) 163

SEVERINI Gino (1883). Blue Dancer, 1912. (24×18″) Dr Gianni Mattioli Collection, Milan 102

SOUTINE Chaïm (1894-1943). Woman in Red, 1922. (35×21″) Dr and Mrs Harry Bakwin Collection, New York . . 61

STEINLEN Théophile (1859-1923). Poster for "Mothu et Doria, Scènes Impressionnistes," about 1894. Color Lithograph. (51½×36¾″) Kunstgewerbemuseum, Zurich 31

TANGUY Yves (1900-1955). A Thousand Times, 1933. (25½×19⅝″) Urvater Collection, Brussels 155

TATLIN Vladimir (1885-1956). Project for a Monument to the Third International, Moscow, 1920 191

TOBEY Mark (1890). Broadway, 1935. Tempera on Masonite Board. (26×19¼″) Metropolitan Museum of Art, New York 208

TOULOUSE-LAUTREC Henri de (1864-1901). Messaline, 1900-1901. (36⅝×26¾″) E. G. Bührle Foundation, Zurich 22
— Poster for May Milton, 1895. Four-color Lithograph. (30⅞×23½″) Musée Toulouse-Lautrec, Albi 32

VILLON Jacques (1875-1963). Bar Scene, 1899. Lithograph. (51⅛×37⅜″) Bibliothèque des Arts Décoratifs, Paris . . 29
— Space, 1932. (45¾×35″) Galerie Louis Carré, Paris 178
VLUGT Llendert van der (1896-1936) and Johannes Andreas BRINKMANN (1902-1949). The Van Nelle Tobacco Factory,
    Rotterdam, 1929-1930 193-194
WAGNER Otto (1841-1918). Main Hall of the Vienna Postal Savings Bank, 1904-1906 49
WIENE Robert (1881-1938). Scene from the Film "The Cabinet of Dr Caligari," with the Actor Conrad Veit, 1919. Museum
    of Modern Art, New York 65-66
WOLS (1913-1951). Le Bateau ivre, about 1945. (36¼×28¾″) Kunsthaus, Zurich 211
WRIGHT Frank Lloyd (1869-1959). Martin House, Oakpark, Buffalo, N.Y., 1904 48
— Car Park of the Johnson Wax Company, Racine, Wisconsin, 1939 193
— Kaufman House, "Falling Water," at Bear Run, Pa., 1936 203

PRINTED ON THE PRESSES OF
EDITIONS D'ART ALBERT SKIRA
15 SEPTEMBER 1965

COLOR PLATES ENGRAVED BY

ACTUAL, BIENNE

(pages 19, 38, 39, 40, 59, 60, 78, 79, 80, 81, 86, 104 top and bottom, 105, 106, 121, 122, 124, 125, 142, 143, 150, 154 top and bottom, 156, 174, 176, 177, 178, 179, 180, 186, 187, 188, 190, 204, 208, 209, 213),

LUX, LA CHAUX-DE-FONDS

(pages 20, 21, 22, 23, 61, 62, 88, 89, 90, 91, 92, 93, 100, 102, 103, 120 top and bottom, 126, 127, 139, 140, 141, 144, 152, 153, 155, 157, 173, 175, 181, 200, 201, 202, 203, 210, 211), and

ABEREGG, STEINER & CO., BERN
(dustjacket).

BLACK AND WHITE PLATES BY IMPRIMERIES RÉUNIES S.A., LAUSANNE.

PHOTOGRAPHS BY

Alpenland, Vienna (page 49 upper left), Maurice Babey, Basel (pages 38, 47-48, 88, 91, 93, 141, 143, 150, 155, 173, 178, 181, 187, 201, 210, 211), Carlo Bevilacqua, Milan (pages 102, 103, 121, 139), Henry B. Beville, Alexandria, Va. (pages 79, 81, 100, 104 bottom, 142, 152, 186), Paul Bijtebier, Uccle-Brussels (page 154 top and bottom), Bildarchiv Foto, Marburg (page 66), Joachim Blauel, Munich (page 124), Lee Boltin, New York (pages 61, 80, 92, 104 top, 157, 179, 208), Chevojon, Paris (page 47), Geoffrey Clements Inc., New York (pages 106, 161 upper left), Harold E. Edgerton, Cambridge, Mass. (pages 111-112 and 112 bottom), Michael Fedison, Greensburg, Pa. (page 203), Lux Feininger (pages 109-110), John R. Freeman & Co. Ltd., London (page 153), A. Frequin, The Hague (page 202), Marcel Gautherot, Rio de Janeiro (page 204), Kurt Gerlach, Vienna (page 48 upper right), Graphic-Photo, Paris (pages 140, 200), Lucien Hervé, Paris (pages 49-50 top and 50 bottom), Martin Hesse, Bern (pages 20, 22), Hans Hinz, Basel (pages 105, 175), Louis Loose, Brussels (pages 30 upper right and lower left, 31 lower right, 39), Herbert Matter, New York (page 111 top), Heinz Müller, Stuttgart (page 65 upper left), Van Ojen, The Hague (pages 193-194 top), La Photothèque, Paris (pages 78, 188, 209), Oscar Savio, Rome (page 190), John D. Schiff, New York (page 109 lower left), John Swain & Son Ltd., Glasgow (page 40), Thomas Airviews, New York (page 194 bottom), USIS (page 48 bottom and page 193 bottom), O. Vaering, Oslo (page 19), Zoltán Wegner, London (page 120 bottom), and the photographic services of the following museums and libraries: Albi, Musée Toulouse-Lautrec (page 32), Amsterdam, Stedelijk Museum (pages 122, 127), Bern, Schweizerische Landesbibliothek (page 30 lower right), Cambridge, Mass., Fogg Art Museum, Harvard University (page 68 upper right), Chicago, Art Institute (page 90), Detroit, Institute of Arts (page 112 top), Hamburg, Staatliche Landesbildstelle (page 67 upper right), Hanover, Landesgalerie (page 163 lower right), The Hague, Gemeentemuseum (page 174), Los Angeles, County Museum of Art (page 144), New York, Museum of Modern Art (pages 59, 65-66, 67-68 bottom, 86, 125, 163 lower left, 164, 176), New York, Solomon R. Guggenheim Museum (pages 89, 177), Paris, Musée des Arts décoratifs (page 29), Providence, Rhode Island School of Design (page 21), Stockholm, Nationalmuseum (page 120 top), Stuttgart, Staatsgalerie (pages 23, 62, 65 lower left), Zurich, Kunstgewerbemuseum (pages 30 upper left, 31 left, 31 upper right). Other photographs by courtesy of Farbwerke A.G., Höchst-Frankfurt (page 67 upper left), Mrs Irina Moore, Much Hadham, Herts (page 156), Nolde Stiftung, Seebüll (page 60), Hans Richter, Southbury, Conn. (page 110 bottom), Marlborough-Gerson Gallery Inc., New York (pages 180, 213) and Staempfli Gallery, New York (page 126).

PRINTED IN SWITZERLAND

DATE DUE

J Higgs		Indef.	

GAYLORD   PRINTED IN U.S.A.